IQ
PUZZLES

TEST YOUR MENTAL AGILITY TO THE LIMIT WITH...

IQ PUZZLES

Capella

This edition published in 2007 by Arcturus Publishing Limited
26/27 Bickels Yard, 151–153 Bermondsey Street,
London SE1 3HA

Copyright © 2007 Arcturus Publishing Limited
Puzzles copyright © 2007 Puzzle Press Ltd

ISBN-13: 978-1-84193-628-4
ISBN-10: 1-84193-628-6

Printed in Malaysia

INTRODUCTION

Thinking can be fun, as this book proves. Within these pages you will find more than 580 puzzles offering a mixture of challenges at different levels of difficulty to test your mental agility.

The puzzles range from those concerning location – where to place dominoes, for example – through mathematics to logical and perceptual puzzles. None of the puzzles requires specific knowledge of a subject, beyond a basic grasp of maths. What you will need to solve them is logical thinking allied to concentration.

The six sections of the book are not graded by difficulty, although if taken in isolation some puzzles in Section 6 might seem more difficult than those in Section 1. If you start with Section 1 and work your way progressively through the book, you should find that you are able to solve puzzles in the later sections in the same time, or less, than puzzles in the earlier sections as your mind becomes attuned to thinking logically.

With some puzzles taking minutes to solve and others providing tougher competition, you will never know what to expect and so never be bored.

The solutions to all the puzzles can be found at the back of the book.

1

A standard set of 28 dominoes has been laid out as shown. Can you draw in the edges of them all? The check-box is provided as an aid and the domino already placed will help.

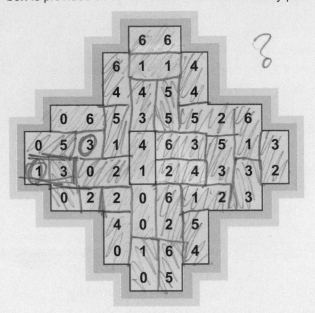

0-0	0-1	0-2	0-3	0-4	0-5	0-6
✓	✓		✓	✓	✓	✓

1-1	1-2	1-3	1-4	1-5	1-6	2-2
✓	✓		✓	✓	✓	✓

2-3	2-4	2-5	2-6	3-3	3-4	3-5
✓	✓	✓	✓	✓	✓	✓

3-6	4-4	4-5	4-6	5-5	5-6	6-6
✓	✓	✓	✓	✓	✓	✓

2

Given that scales A and B balance perfectly, how many spades are needed to balance scale C?

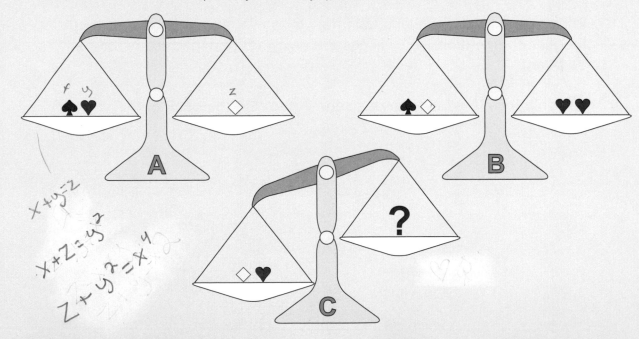

3

Every row and column in this grid originally contained one heart, one club, one diamond, one spade and two blank squares, although not necessarily in that order.

Every symbol with a black arrow refers to the first of the four symbols encountered when travelling in the direction of the arrow. Every symbol with a white arrow refers to the second of the four symbols encountered in the direction of the arrow.

Can you complete the original grid?

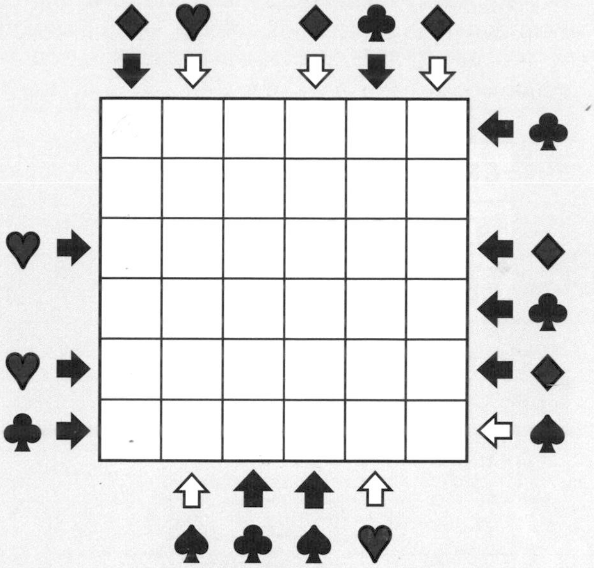

4

The blank squares below should be filled with whole numbers between 1 and 30 inclusive, any of which may occur more than once, or not at all.

The numbers in every horizontal row add up to the totals on the right, as do the two long diagonal lines; whilst those in every vertical column add up to the totals along the bottom.

							116
				17	17		88
8	13	11	8		24	6	71
22	5	21		23	18	28	133
16	22	19	11		23		112
2		4	21	14			99
	23	29	6	25			117
24	2	30	16	2		30	115
100	96	129	80	88	131	111	133

5

Draw in the missing hands on the final clock.

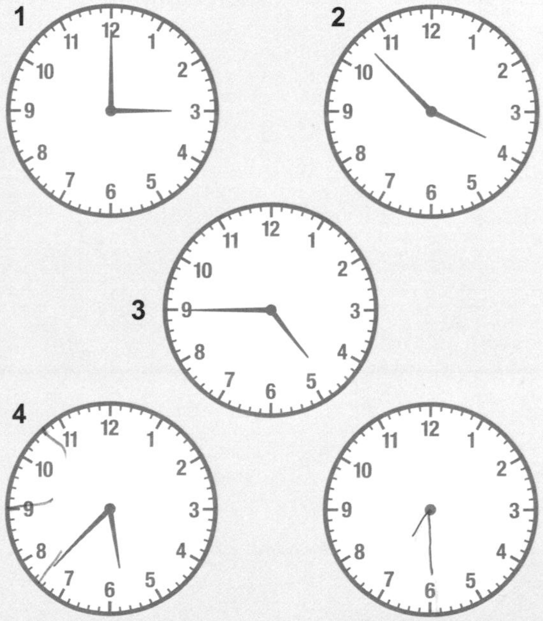

Can you place the hexagons into the grid, so that where any hexagon touches another along a straight line, the number in both triangles is the same? No rotation of any hexagon is allowed!

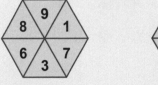

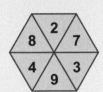

Twelve L-shapes like the ones here need to be inserted in the grid and each L has one hole in it.

There are three pieces of each of the four kinds shown here and any piece may be turned or flipped over before being put in the grid. No pieces of the same kind touch, even at a corner.

The pieces fit together so well that you cannot see any spaces between them; only the holes show.

Can you tell where the Ls are?

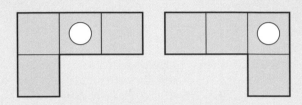
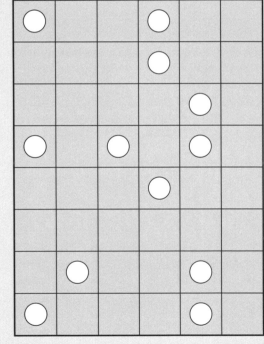
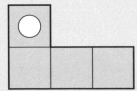
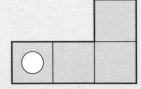

In this puzzle, an amateur coin collector has been out with his metal detector, searching for booty. He didn't have time to dig up all the coins he found, so has made a grid map, showing their locations, in the hope that if he loses the map, at least no-one else will understand it…

Those squares containing numbers are empty, but where a number appears in a square, it indicates how many coins are located in the squares (up to a maximum of eight) surrounding the numbered one, touching it at any corner or side. There is only one coin in any individual square.

Place a circle into every square containing a coin.

1				3				
	2					1	0	
	2		3		3	2		
	1	3		4	4		1	
2	2							
	3			5	4			
3			2	2		3		0
2		1		4			1	
		2			2			

The grid should be filled with numbers from 1 to 6, so that each number appears just once in every row and column. The clues refer to the digit totals in the squares, eg A 1 2 3 = 6 means that the numbers in squares A1, A2 and A3 add up to 6.

1 C D E 2 = 11

2 C D 3 = 9

3 E F 4 = 7

4 A B 5 = 10

5 C D 6 = 3

6 A 1 2 = 5

7 B 2 3 4 = 7

8 C 4 5 = 4

9 D 4 5 = 6

10 E 5 6 = 7

11 F 5 6 = 8

	A	B	C	D	E	F
1	z 5					
2	z 5	y 7	x 11	x 11	x 11	
3		y 7	0 9	0 9		
4		y 7	3-1 4	H 241 6 51	7	7
5	10	10	3-1 4	H 24 6 51	7	8
6			Δ 1-2	Δ 1-2	7	8

Each of the small squares in the grid below contains either A, B or C. Every row and column has exactly two of each letter. Can you tell the letter in each square?

Across

1 The Bs are in adjacent squares.
2 The Bs are in adjacent squares.
3 The Cs are in adjacent squares.
4 The Bs are in adjacent squares.
5 The Cs are further right than the Bs.
6 The As are further right than the Bs.

Down

1 The As are in adjacent squares.
2 The As are both between the Cs.
3 No two adjacent squares contain the same letter.
4 No two adjacent squares contain the same letter.
5 No two adjacent squares contain the same letter.
6 The Bs are lower than the As.

	1	2	3	4	5	6
1	C	C	B	B	A	A
2		A		B	A	A
3		A	C	C	B	B
4		C			B	B
5					C	C
6	B	C	B	A	A	C

11

The object of this puzzle is to trace a single path from the top left corner to the bottom right corner of the grid, travelling through all of the cells in either a horizontal, vertical or diagonal direction.

Every cell must be entered once only and your path should take you through the numbers in the sequence 1-2-3-4-5-6-1-2-3-4-5-6, etc.

Can you find the way?

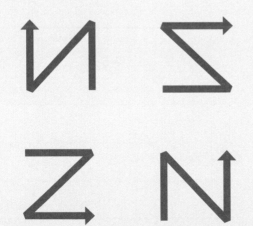

1	5	6	1	1	3
2	4	2	6	2	4
3	3	4	5	1	5
4	5	3	2	2	6
1	6	4	1	4	3
2	3	5	6	5	6

数 独

KAMIKAZE

Niveau 1

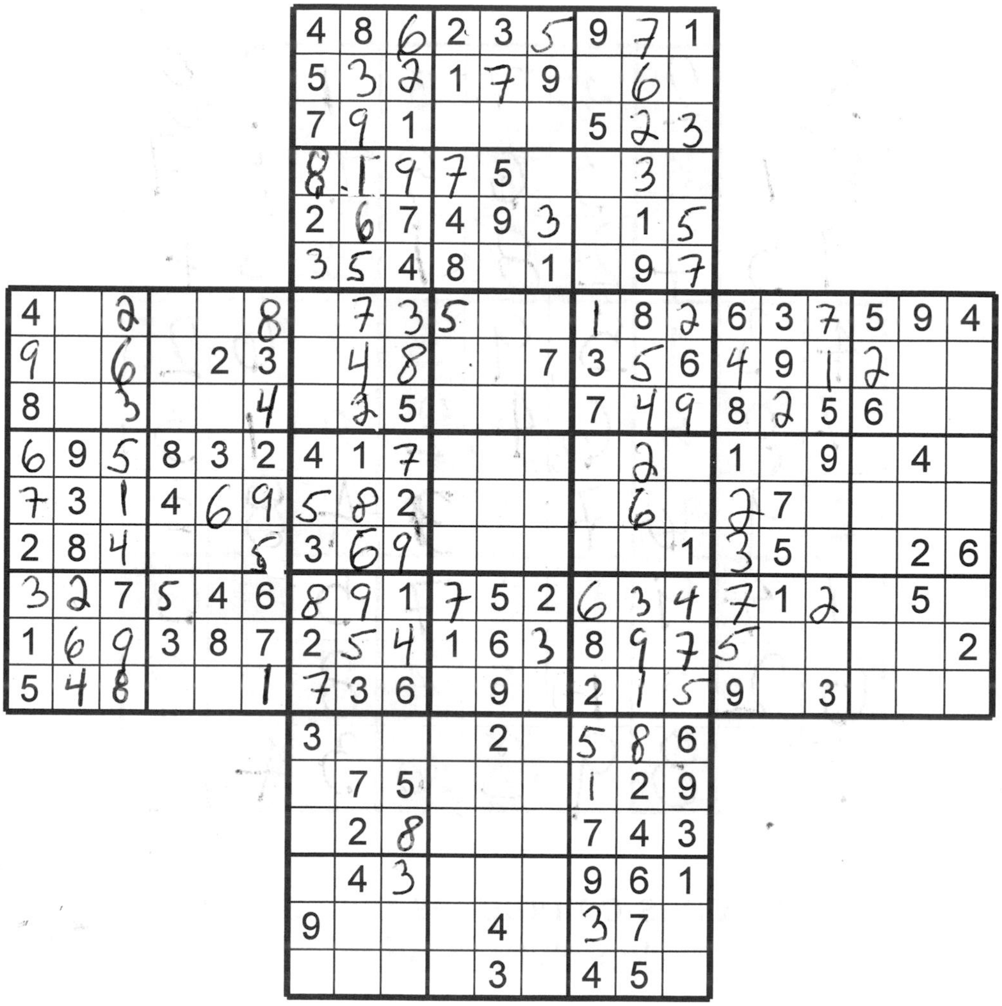

ready been filled in. A
hat row or column.

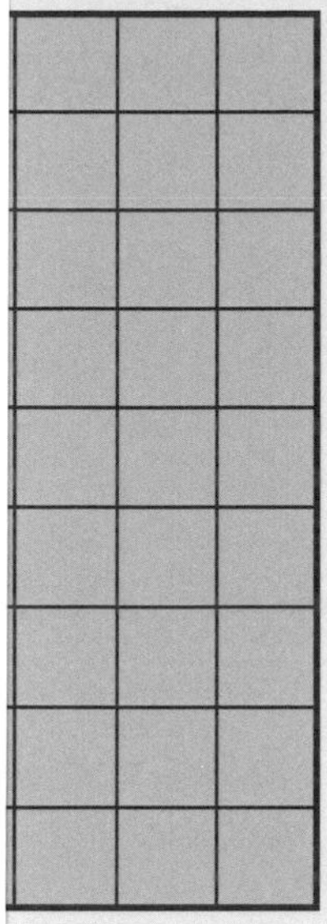

			3
			2
			4
			1
			1
			1
			1
			3
			4

3	1	4

lthough two or more

SCORE

✓✓
✓✓✗
✗
✗
✗✗✗
✓✓✓✓

13

14

Draw a single continuous loop, by connecting the dots. No line may cross the path of another.

The figure inside each set of any four surrounding dots indicates the total number of surrounding lines.

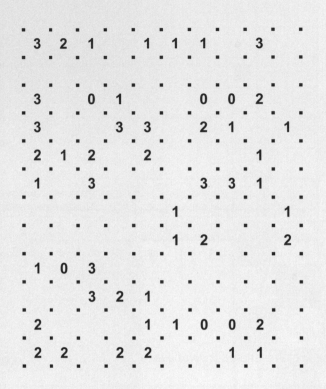

15

Each horizontal row and vertical column should contain different shapes and different numbers.

Every square will contain one number and one shape and no combination may be repeated anywhere else in the puzzle.

1   2   3   4   5

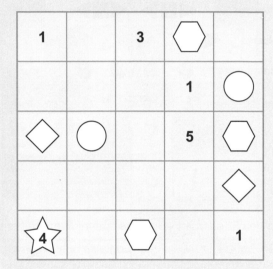

16

Given that the letters are valued 1-26 according to their places in the alphabet, can you crack the mystery code to reveal the missing letter?

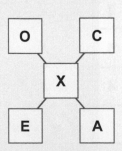

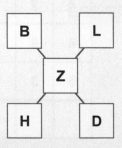

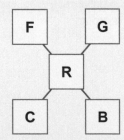

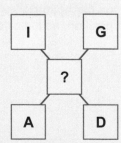

12

A set of dominoes is to be placed in four rows as shown below. The numbers indicate which values are shown on all the dominoes in each column and the relevant half of the domino in every row. Find out where each domino is placed by carefully comparing rows and columns to determine the possible positions of certain dominoes: for instance, if any column contains only one 6, then the domino 6/6 isn't in that column.

A set of dominoes consists of:

0/0, 0/1, 0/2, 0/3, 0/4, 0/5, 0/6, 1/1, 1/2, 1/3, 1/4, 1/5, 1/6, 2/2,

2/3, 2/4, 2/5, 2/6, 3/3, 3/4, 3/5, 3/6, 4/4, 4/5, 4/6, 5/5, 5/6, 6/6.

	0, 2, 2, 4, 4, 4, 5, 5.	0, 1, 2, 2, 2, 3, 3, 6.	3, 4, 5, 5, 6, 6, 6, 6.	1, 1, 1, 3, 3, 3, 5, 6.	0, 0, 2, 2, 2, 5, 5, 5.	0, 1, 1, 3, 4, 4, 4, 4.	0, 0, 0, 1, 1, 3, 6, 6.
0, 4, 4, 5, 6, 6, 6.							
0, 2, 2, 3, 3, 4, 5.							
2, 2, 4, 5, 5, 5, 6.							
0, 0, 1, 1, 2, 3, 6.							
1, 1, 1, 3, 4, 5, 5.							
0, 0, 0, 0, 1, 3, 6.							
1, 1, 2, 3, 4, 4, 6.							
2, 2, 3, 3, 4, 5, 6.							

Place the eight tiles into the puzzle grid so that all adjacent numbers on each tile match up. Tiles may be rotated through 360 degrees, but none may be flipped over.

2	2
4	3

1	4
1	3

3	2
4	2

2	3
4	3

3	4
1	1

4	3
2	4

3	2
4	1

1	1
3	3

3	1				
2	2				

Place all twelve of the pieces into the grid. Any may be rotated or flipped over, but none may touch another, not even diagonally. The numbers outside the grid refer to the number of consecutive black squares; and each block is separated from the others by at least one white square. For instance, '3 2' could refer to a row with none, one or more white squares, then three black squares, then at least one white square, then two more black squares, followed by any number of white squares.

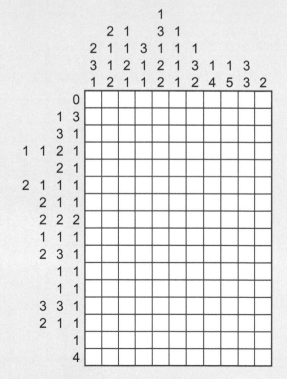

In the diagram below, which letter should replace the question mark?

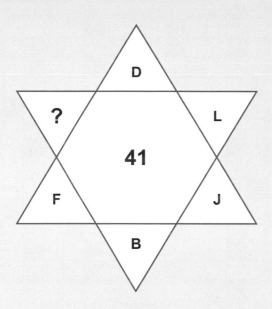

In the square below, change the positions of six numbers, one per horizontal row, vertical column and long diagonal line of six smaller squares, in such a way that the numbers in each row, column and long diagonal line total exactly 150. Any number may appear more than once in a row, column or line.

32	12	18	25	31	36
39	25	23	14	32	24
36	23	25	19	13	25
16	36	25	31	19	28
13	27	25	29	23	24
18	18	25	34	39	18

22

Every brick in this pyramid contains a number which is the sum of the two numbers below it, so that F=A+B, etc. Just work out the missing numbers!

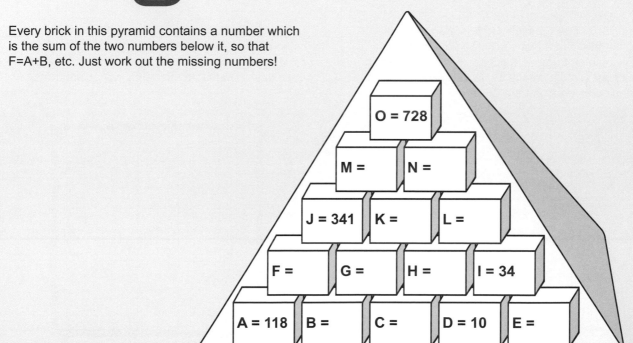

With the starter already given, can you fit all of the remaining listed numbers into this grid? Take care, this puzzle may not be as easy as it looks!

11	273	758	5378	78906
15	357	909	5638	91435
30	366	1594	6285	172855
37	388	2367	6308	292630
60	426	2723	6613	345679
64	493	2853	7646	365489
66	614	4277	8038	627583
70	620	4326	8467	636430
72 ✓	625	4638	8610	678340
80	628	4784	9102	763890
216	677	5105	62349	787739
247	738	5218	73980	936735

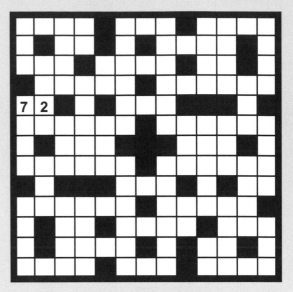

The chart gives directions to a hidden treasure behind the centre black square in the grid. Move the indicated number of spaces north, south, east and west (eg 4N means move four squares north) stopping at every square once only to arrive there. At which square should you start?

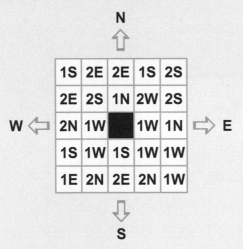

Fill the grid so that every horizontal row and vertical column contains the numbers 1-5. The 'greater than' or 'less than' signs indicate where a number is larger or smaller than that in the neighbouring square.

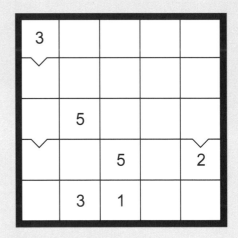

Each of the eight segments of the spider's web should be filled with a different number from 1 to 8, in such a way that every ring also contains a different number from 1 to 8.

The segments run from the outside of the spider's web to the centre, and the rings run all the way around.

Some numbers are already in place. Can you fill in the rest?

S E C T I O N

1

Every oval shape in this diagram contains a different letter of the alphabet from A to K inclusive. Use the clues to determine their locations. Reference in the clues to 'due' means in any location along the same horizontal or vertical line.

1 The A is further north than the B and further west than the C.

2 The D is due west of the E, which is due south of the J (which is further north than the C).

3 The F is next to and west of the G, which is due south of (but not next to) the H.

4 The I is next to and south of the E, which is further west than the K (which is not next to the B).

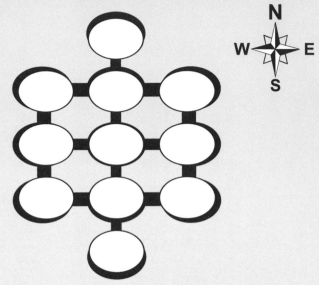

28

Fill the three empty circles with the symbols +, − and x in some order, to make a sum which totals the number in the centre. Each symbol must be used once and calculations are made in the direction of travel.

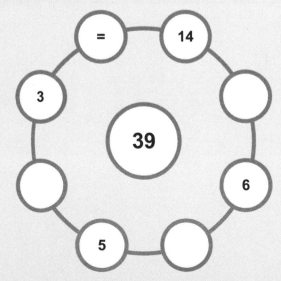

29

The numbers at the top and on the left side show the quantity of single-digit numbers (1-9) used in that row and column. The numbers at the bottom and on the right show the sum of the digits. A number may appear more than once in a row or column, but no numbers are in squares that touch, even at a corner.

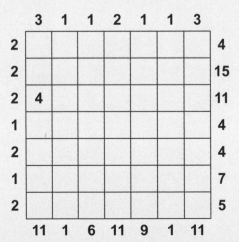

	3	1	1	2	1	1	3	
2								4
2								15
2	4							11
1								4
2								4
1								7
2								5
	11	1	6	11	9	1	11	

Using the numbers below, complete these six equations (three reading across and three reading downwards). Every number is used once.

	1		2		3		5
		6		7		9	

	−		×		=	20
+		×		+		
	×		+	4	=	31
×		+		−		
8	−		+		=	2
=		=		=		
72		25		8		

In the grid below, which number should replace the question mark?

28	32	16	15	20	44	7
38	41	3	2	6	45	27
34	32	1	65	1	17	12
32	1	2	4	13	55	55
8	45	3	56	10	19	21
23	4	12	42	21	14	46
3	52	?	42	32	3	8

When the box below is folded to form a cube, just one of the five options (A, B, C, D or E) can be produced. Which?

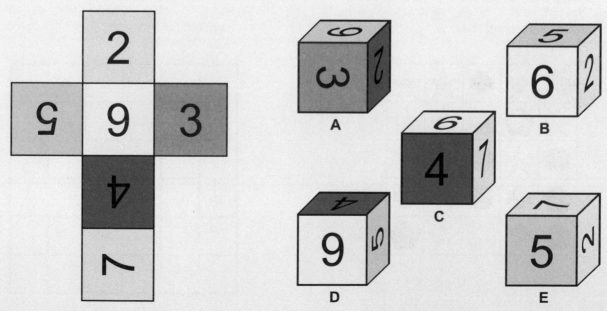

33

In this puzzle, an amateur coin collector has been out with his metal detector, searching for booty. He didn't have time to dig up all the coins he found, so has made a grid map, showing their locations, in the hope that if he loses the map, at least no-one else will understand it…

Those squares containing numbers are empty, but where a number appears in a square, it indicates how many coins are located in the squares (up to a maximum of eight) surrounding the numbered one, touching it at any corner or side. There is only one coin in any individual square.

Place a circle into every square containing a coin.

						1			
1			1				1	1	0
		1	2			1	1		1
3			2		1				
	4								
	4		2		0			2	
	3			1				2	
		2				1			1
2		5			3				2
1				4			4		

34

Each symbol stands for a different number. In order to reach the correct total at the end of each row and column, what is the value of the circle, cross, pentagon, square and star?

					= 28
					= 31
					= 22
					= 15
					= 26
= 26	= 20	= 25	= 25	= 26	

35

Every row and column of this grid should contain one each of the letters A, B, C, D, E and F. Each of the six shapes (marked by thicker lines) should also contain one each of the letters A, B, C, D, E and F. Can you complete the grid?

			C	B	A
	E				D
		F			

A standard set of 28 dominoes has been laid out as shown. Can you draw in the edges of them all? The check-box is provided as an aid and the domino already placed will help.

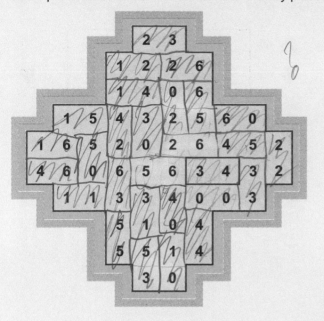

0-0	0-1	0-2	0-3	0-4	0-5	0-6
✓	✓	✓	✓	✓	✓	✓

1-1	1-2	1-3	1-4	1-5	1-6	2-2
✓	✓	✓	✓	✓	✓	✓

2-3	2-4	2-5	2-6	3-3	3-4	3-5
✓	✓	✓	✓	✓	✓	✓

3-6	4-4	4-5	4-6	5-5	5-6	6-6
✓	✓	✓	✓	✓	✓	✓

Each of the small squares in the grid below contains either A, B or C. Every row and column has exactly two of each letter. Can you tell the letter in each square?

Across

1 The Cs are further right than the As.
2 The As are in adjacent squares.
3 Each B is next to and right of an A.
4 Each B is next to and right of a C.
5 No two adjacent squares contain the same letter.
6 The Bs are in adjacent squares.

Down

1 The Bs are in adjacent squares.
2 Each C is directly next to and below an A.
3 The Cs are both between the Bs.
4 The Cs are both between the Bs.
5 The Bs are lower than the Cs.
6 The Bs are in adjacent squares.

38

Every row and column in this grid originally contained one heart, one club, one diamond, one spade and two blank squares, although not necessarily in that order.

Every symbol with a black arrow refers to the first of the four symbols encountered when travelling in the direction of the arrow. Every symbol with a white arrow refers to the second of the four symbols encountered in the direction of the arrow.

Can you complete the original grid?

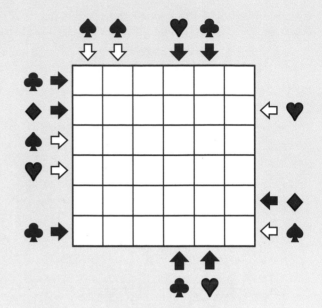

39

The blank squares below should be filled with whole numbers between 1 and 30 inclusive, any of which may occur more than once, or not at all.

The numbers in every horizontal row add up to the totals on the right, as do the two long diagonal lines; whilst those in every vertical column add up to the totals along the bottom.

							123
		3		23	24		128
11	29				1		118
1		10	24	10		22	94
25	4	24	12	18		18	113
22	20	27		17	9	30	151
	16		1	15	5	13	85
30		11	18	15	28	7	131
118	**119**	**117**	**111**	**123**	**85**	**147**	**98**

40

A   is to   B

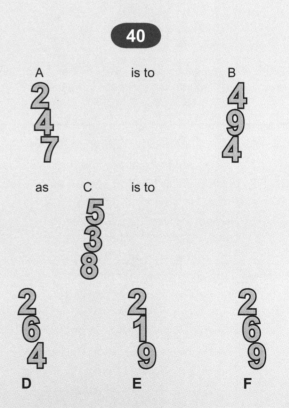

as   C   is to

D   E   F

22

Can you place the hexagons into the grid, so that where any hexagon touches another along a straight line, the number in both triangles is the same? No rotation of any hexagon is allowed!

Twelve L-shapes like the ones here need to be inserted in the grid and each L has one hole in it.

There are three pieces of each of the four kinds shown here and any piece may be turned or flipped over before being put in the grid. No pieces of the same kind touch, even at a corner.

The pieces fit together so well that you cannot see any spaces between them; only the holes show.

Can you tell where the Ls are?

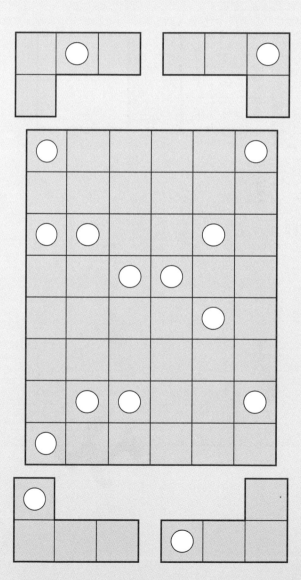

Which of the four lettered alternatives (A, B, C or D) fits most logically into the empty square?

4	6	9
3	5	7
4	6	8

4	9	6
3	7	5
4	8	6

9	4	6
5	7	3
8	4	6

A

9	6	4
5	7	3
6	8	4

B

6	4	9
5	3	7
6	4	8

?

6	9	4
7	5	3
8	4	6

C

6	9	4
5	7	3
6	8	4

D

Which four pieces can be fitted together to form an exact copy of this shape?

A

B

C

D

E

F

G

H

I

J

S E C T I O N

1

Can you place the vessels into the diagram? Some parts of vessels or sea squares have already been filled in. A number to the right or below a row or column refers to the number of occupied squares in that row or column.

Any vessel may be positioned horizontally or vertically, but no part of a vessel touches part of any other vessel, either horizontally, vertically or diagonally.

Empty Area of Sea: ≈

Aircraft Carrier: ◀■■▶

Battleships: ◀■▶   ◀■▶

Cruisers: ◀▶   ◀▶   ◀▶

Submarines: ● ● ● ●

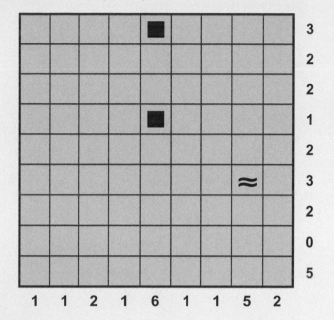

3
2
2
1
2
3
2
0
5

1 1 2 1 6 1 1 5 2

Can you fill each square in the bottom line with the correct digit?

Every square in the solution contains only one digit from each of the lettered lines above, although two or more squares in the solution may contain the same digit.

At the end of every row is a score, which shows:

a the number of digits placed in the correct finishing position on the bottom line, as indicated by a tick; and

b the number of digits which appear on the bottom line, but in a different position, as indicated by a cross.

SCORE

4	6	6	5	✗
6	4	2	7	✗
0	3	4	4	✓✓✓
0	3	0	0	✓
0	5	7	1	✗
				✓✓✓✓

The grid should be filled with numbers from 1 to 6, so that each number appears just once in every row and column. The clues refer to the digit totals in the squares, eg A 1 2 3 = 6 means that the numbers in squares A1, A2 and A3 add up to 6.

1 A B 3 = 11

2 C D 4 = 9

3 D E F 5 = 6

4 C D 6 = 10

5 A 5 6 = 8

6 B 5 6 = 5

7 C 1 2 = 3

8 D 1 2 3 = 11

9 E 2 3 = 10

10 F 1 2 = 10

11 A B 1 = 4

	A	B	C	D	E	F
1						
2						
3						
4						
5						
6						

The object of this puzzle is to trace a single path from the top left corner to the bottom right corner of the grid, travelling through all of the cells in either a horizontal, vertical or diagonal direction.

Every cell must be entered once only and your path should take you through the numbers in the sequence 1-2-3-4-5-6-1-2-3-4-5-6, etc.

Can you find the way?

1	6	1	2	4	5
2	5	4	3	3	6
3	4	5	6	2	1
5	4	4	1	3	2
6	3	5	3	4	5
1	2	6	1	2	6

49

Draw a single continuous loop, by connecting the dots. No line may cross the path of another.

The figure inside each set of any four surrounding dots indicates the total number of surrounding lines.

```
2  1     1           1  2
                1  2
   1  3           1  3        2
   1     2  1  1           0  2
3  0  1  2              1
3     1  3  2  1  3  2        2
   1                    0  1
   1  3              3  1     1
1           0           2  1
         1  3
2  0              0  1
2     1              1  2  1
```

50

Each horizontal row and vertical column should contain different shapes and different numbers.

Every square will contain one number and one shape and no combination may be repeated anywhere else in the puzzle.

1   2   3   4   5

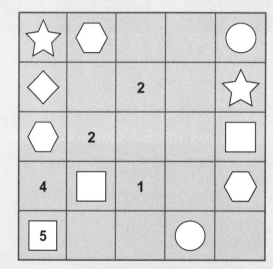

51

Given that the letters are valued 1-26 according to their places in the alphabet, can you crack the mystery code to reveal the missing letter?

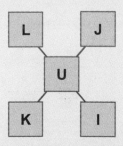

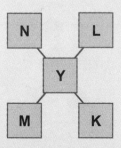

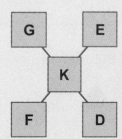

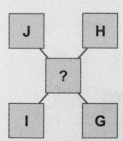

52

Which is the odd one out?

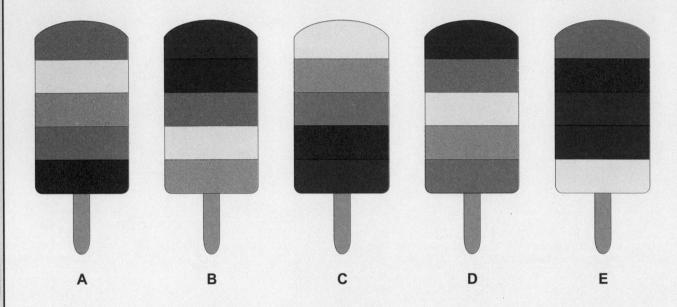

A   B   C   D   E

53

Which of the alternatives (A, B, C or D) comes next in this sequence?

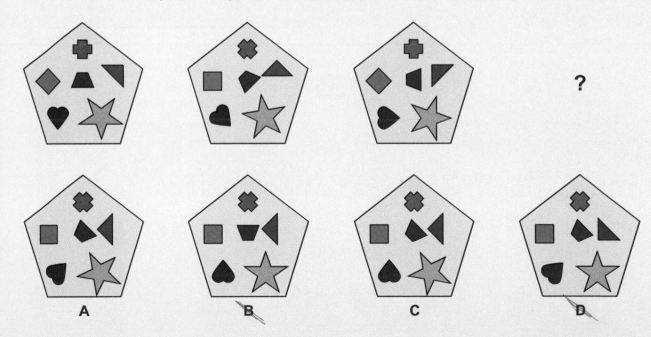

A   B   C   D

Place the eight tiles into the puzzle grid so that all adjacent numbers on each tile match up. Tiles may be rotated through 360 degrees, but none may be flipped over.

Place all twelve of the pieces into the grid. Any may be rotated or flipped over, but none may touch another, not even diagonally. The numbers outside the grid refer to the number of consecutive black squares; and each block is separated from the others by at least one white square. For instance, '3 2' could refer to a row with none, one or more white squares, then three black squares, then at least one white square, then two more black squares, followed by any number of white squares.

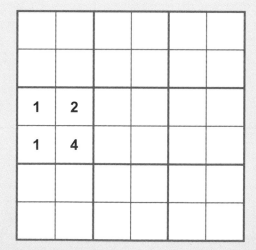

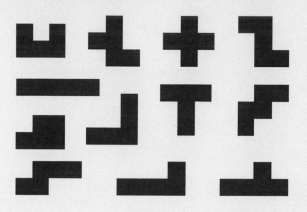

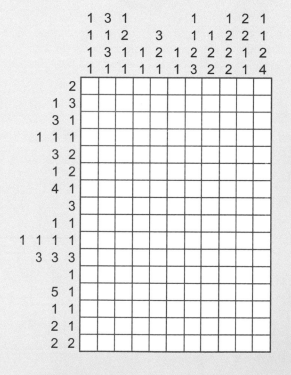

56

In the diagram below, which number should replace the question mark?

57

In the square below, change the positions of six numbers, one per horizontal row, vertical column and long diagonal line of six smaller squares, in such a way that the numbers in each row, column and long diagonal line total exactly 162. Any number may appear more than once in a row, column or line.

21	10	33	19	37	21
23	27	23	34	27	19
23	45	27	41	12	18
36	32	27	17	10	31
27	27	43	28	27	30
23	12	29	27	28	58

58

Every brick in this pyramid contains a number which is the sum of the two numbers below it, so that F=A+B, etc. Just work out the missing numbers!

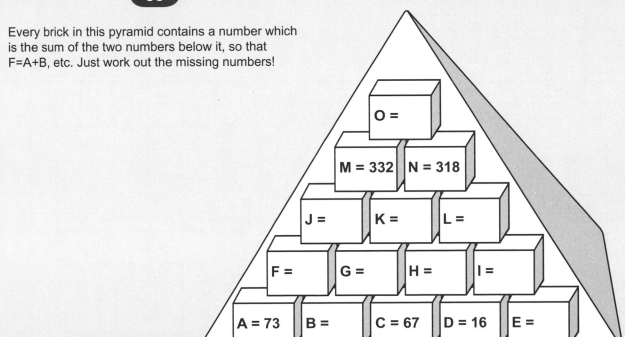

With the starter already given, can you fit all of the remaining listed numbers into this grid? Take care, this puzzle may not be as easy as it looks!

10	159	581	5338	75120
20	167	627	6189	75475
29	195	653	7463	85781
49	255	704	8319	85901
57	301	751	12307	180372
61	305	754	13697	186988
75	315	783	37406	346058
80	416	859	45424	450678
111	434	890	50013	573862
122	453	901	56731	714511
128	510	4155	59109	741001
143 ✓	570	4162	60070	783820

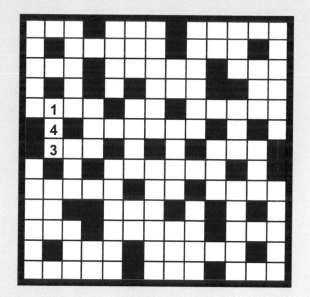

The chart gives directions to a hidden treasure behind the centre black square in the grid. Move the indicated number of spaces north, south, east and west (eg 4N means move four squares north) stopping at every square once only to arrive there. At which square should you start?

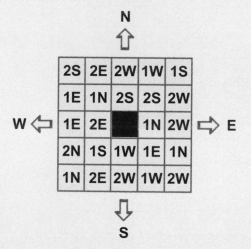

Fill the grid so that every horizontal row and vertical column contains the numbers 1-5. The 'greater than' or 'less than' signs indicate where a number is larger or smaller than that in the neighbouring square.

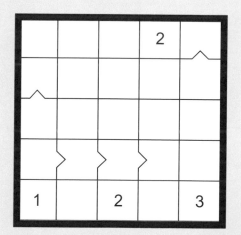

Each of the eight segments of the spider's web should be filled with a different number from 1 to 8, in such a way that every ring also contains a different number from 1 to 8.

The segments run from the outside of the spider's web to the centre, and the rings run all the way around.

Some numbers are already in place. Can you fill in the rest?

Every oval shape in this diagram contains a different letter of the alphabet from A to K inclusive. Use the clues to determine their locations. Reference in the clues to 'due' means in any location along the same horizontal or vertical line.

1 The A is next to and north of the I, which is next to and east of the B.

2 The C is next to and south of the D, which is due south of (but not next to) the I.

3 The D is next to and west of the E, which is next to and south of the K.

4 The G is next to and east of the H, which is next to and north of the J.

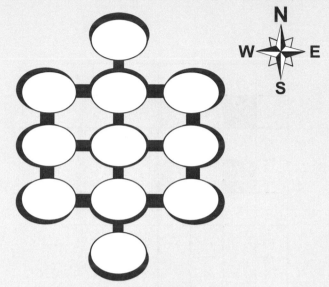

64

Fill the three empty circles with the symbols +, − and x in some order, to make a sum which totals the number in the centre. Each symbol must be used once and calculations are made in the direction of travel.

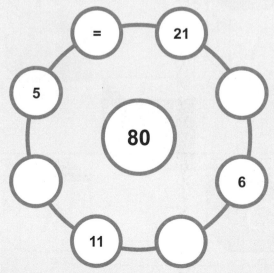

65

The numbers at the top and on the left side show the quantity of single-digit numbers (1-9) used in that row and column. The numbers at the bottom and on the right side show the sum of the digits. A number may appear more than once in a row or column, but no numbers are in squares that touch, even at a corner.

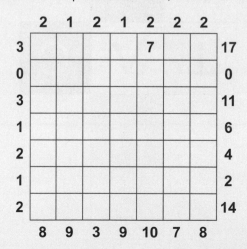

2	1	2	1	2	2	2	
3					7			17
0								0
3								11
1								6
2								4
1								2
2								14
8	9	3	9	10	7	8	

66

Using the numbers below, complete these six equations (three reading across and three reading downwards). Every number is used once.

	1	2	3	4
	6	8	9	

	+		−		=	7
x		x		−		
7	−		x		=	18
−		−		+		
	x	5	−		=	2
=		=		=		
26		4		11		

67

In the grid below, which number should replace the question mark?

5	61	1	22	52	32	2
16	32	34	45	33	34	12
41	4	14	41	1	46	4
43	73	?	9	5	59	54
53	83	35	58	42	3	95
67	6	43	45	35	52	88
42	8	77	47	99	41	12

68

When the box below is folded to form a cube, just one of the five options (A, B, C, D or E) can be produced. Which?

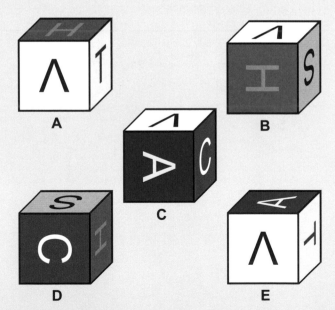

69

In this puzzle, an amateur coin collector has been out with his metal detector, searching for booty. He didn't have time to dig up all the coins he found, so has made a grid map, showing their locations, in the hope that if he loses the map, at least no-one else will understand it…

Those squares containing numbers are empty, but where a number appears in a square, it indicates how many coins are located in the squares (up to a maximum of eight) surrounding the numbered one, touching it at any corner or side. There is only one coin in any individual square.

Place a circle into every square containing a coin.

	0				1		2	3	
			3	3					
	2				2		1		1
			3						1
0		2					2		
		1			1	1			3
0				4				4	
					3				
2	2						4	3	
			2		1			1	

70

Every row and column of this grid should contain one each of the letters A, B, C, D, E and F. Each of the six shapes (marked by thicker lines) should also contain one each of the letters A, B, C, D, E and F. Can you complete the grid?

	D		C	B	A
	F	E			

71

Each symbol stands for a different number. In order to reach the correct total at the end of each row and column, what is the value of the circle, cross, pentagon, square and star?

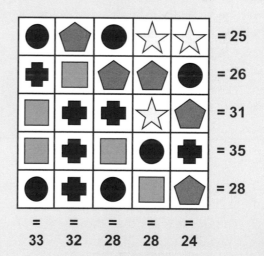

●	⬠	●	☆	☆	= 25
✚	■	⬠	⬠	●	= 26
■	✚	✚	☆	⬠	= 31
■	✚	■	●	✚	= 35
●	✚	●	■	⬠	= 28
= 33	= 32	= 28	= 28	= 24	

A standard set of 28 dominoes has been laid out as shown. Can you draw in the edges of them all? The checkbox is provided as an aid and the domino already placed will help.

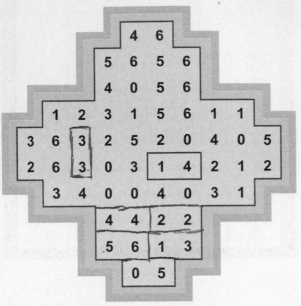

0-0	0-1	0-2	0-3	0-4	0-5	0-6
					✓	

1-1	1-2	1-3	1-4	1-5	1-6	2-2
		✓	✓			✓

2-3	2-4	2-5	2-6	3-3	3-4	3-5
				✓		

3-6	4-4	4-5	4-6	5-5	5-6	6-6
	✓				✓	

73

Each of the small squares in the grid below contains either A, B or C. Every row and column has exactly two of each letter. Can you tell the letter in each square?

Across

1 The As are next to and right of the Cs.
2 The As are in adjacent squares.
3 The Bs are both between the As.
4 The As are both between the Cs.
5 The As are both between the Bs.
6 The As are in adjacent squares.

Down

1 The Cs are in adjacent squares.
2 Each A is directly next to and below a B.
3 No two adjacent squares contain the same letter.
4 No two adjacent squares contain the same letter.
5 The Bs are lower than the Cs.
6 The Bs are lower than the As.

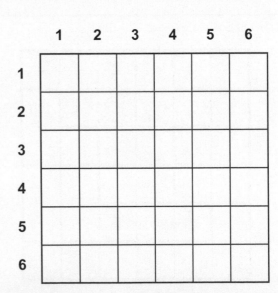

Every row and column in this grid originally contained one heart, one club, one diamond, one spade and two blank squares, although not necessarily in that order.

Every symbol with a black arrow refers to the first of the four symbols encountered when travelling in the direction of the arrow. Every symbol with a white arrow refers to the second of the four symbols encountered in the direction of the arrow.

Can you complete the original grid?

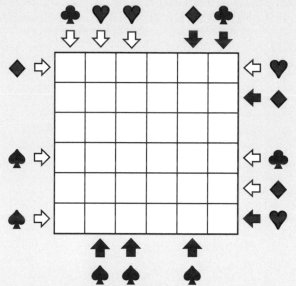

The blank squares below should be filled with whole numbers between 1 and 30 inclusive, any of which may occur more than once, or not at all.

The numbers in every horizontal row add up to the totals on the right, as do the two long diagonal lines; whilst those in every vertical column add up to the totals along the bottom.

							110
28	13		13	19		21	124
22	13		2	24	3	27	118
	2	17	10		2		84
7		15	5	6		12	83
29	25		5		5	4	99
7	21	5	11		2	24	90
27	30	10		13	13		115
138	132	90	52	118	63	120	98

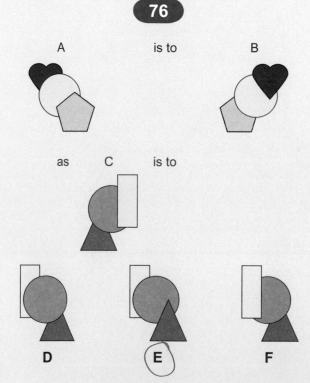

A   is to   B

as   C   is to

D   E   F

77

Can you place the hexagons into the grid, so that where any hexagon touches another along a straight line, the number in both triangles is the same? No rotation of any hexagon is allowed!

78

Twelve L-shapes like the ones here need to be inserted in the grid and each L has one hole in it.

There are three pieces of each of the four kinds shown here and any piece may be turned or flipped over before being put in the grid. No pieces of the same kind touch, even at a corner.

The pieces fit together so well that you cannot see any spaces between them; only the holes show.

Can you tell where the Ls are?

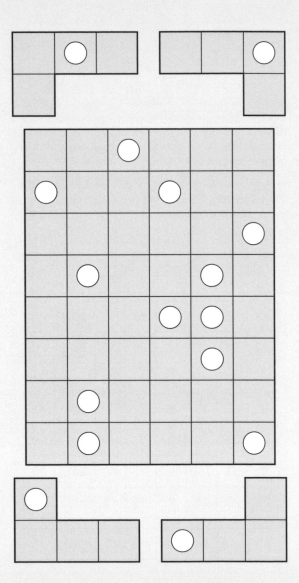

Given that scales A and B balance perfectly, how many diamonds are needed to balance scale C?

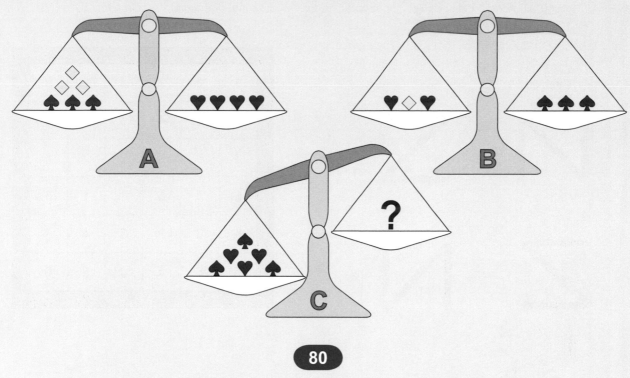

Which of the four lettered alternatives (A, B, C or D) fits most logically into the empty square?

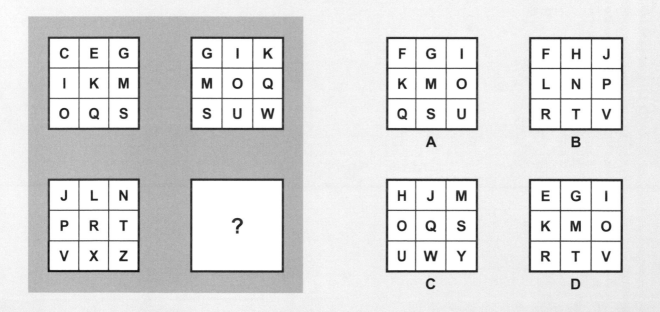

The object of this puzzle is to trace a single path from the top left corner to the bottom right corner of the grid, travelling through all of the cells in either a horizontal, vertical or diagonal direction.

Every cell must be entered once only and your path should take you through the numbers in the sequence 1-2-3-4-5-6-1-2-3-4-5-6, etc.

Can you find the way?

1	2	3	4	5	6
2	1	4	3	1	3
3	6	5	2	2	4
5	4	6	1	1	5
4	3	2	3	4	6
5	6	1	2	5	6

The grid should be filled with numbers from 1 to 6, so that each number appears just once in every row and column. The clues refer to the digit totals in the squares, eg A 1 2 3 = 6 means that the numbers in squares A1, A2 and A3 add up to 6.

1 D E 6 = 3

2 A 2 3 = 6

3 B 2 3 = 10

4 C 3 4 = 9

5 D 3 4 = 6

6 E 4 5 = 9

7 F 4 5 = 11

8 C D E 1 = 12

9 C D E 2 = 11

10 E F 3 = 5

11 A B 4 = 4

	A	B	C	D	E	F
1						
2						
3						
4						
5						
6						

S E C T I O N 1

Can you fill each square in the bottom line with the correct digit?

Every square in the solution contains only one digit from each of the lettered lines above, although two or more squares in the solution may contain the same digit.

At the end of every row is a score, which shows:

a the number of digits placed in the correct finishing position on the bottom line, as indicated by a tick; and

b the number of digits which appear on the bottom line, but in a different position, as indicated by a cross.

SCORE

4	5	4	7	✗
6	5	7	2	✔ ✗
0	4	5	2	✔ ✔
1	1	5	5	✔ ✗
3	1	0	5	✗
				✔ ✔ ✔ ✔

Can you place the vessels into the diagram? Some parts of vessels or sea squares have already been filled in. A number to the right or below a row or column refers to the number of occupied squares in that row or column.

Any vessel may be positioned horizontally or vertically, but no part of a vessel touches part of any other vessel, either horizontally, vertically or diagonally.

Empty Area of Sea:

Aircraft Carrier:

Battleships:

Cruisers:

Submarines:

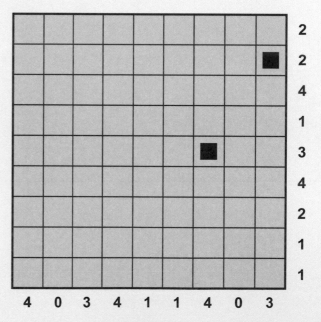

2
2
4
1
3
4
2
1
1

4 0 3 4 1 1 4 0 3

Draw a single continuous loop, by connecting the dots. No line may cross the path of another

The figure inside each set of any four surrounding dots indicates the total number of surrounding lines.

```
2 1     1     1     1
        1     1     2     3
    0       2           2 2 3
1     0 1 2     3
        3           3 2 1 1
3       2           1 1
                1           1
        3               3 2
2           1     0 1 2 3
    1 2       2           3
    2                 1 0
1 1 2 2 2 1         2 2
```

Each horizontal row and vertical column should contain different shapes and different numbers.

Every square will contain one number and one shape and no combination may be repeated anywhere else in the puzzle.

1   2   3   4   5

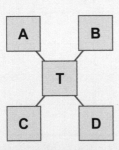 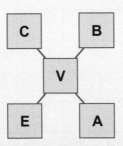 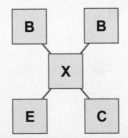 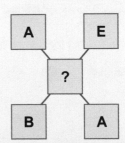

Given that the letters are valued 1-26 according to their places in the alphabet, can you crack the mystery code to reveal the missing letter?

```
A       B       C       B       B       B       A       E
    T               V               X               ?
C       D       E       A       E       C       B       A
```

A set of dominoes is to be placed in four rows as shown below. The numbers indicate which values are shown on all the dominoes in each column and the relevant half of the domino in every row. Find out where each domino is placed by carefully comparing rows and columns to determine the possible positions of certain dominoes: for instance, if any column contains only one 6, then the domino 6/6 isn't in that column.

A set of dominoes consists of:

0/0, 0/1, 0/2, 0/3, 0/4, 0/5, 0/6, 1/1, 1/2, 1/3, 1/4, 1/5, 1/6, 2/2,

2/3, 2/4, 2/5, 2/6, 3/3, 3/4, 3/5, 3/6, 4/4, 4/5, 4/6, 5/5, 5/6, 6/6.

1, 1, 1, 2, 2, 2, 4, 5.	0, 0, 0, 4, 5, 5, 5, 6.	0, 3, 3, 4, 4, 4, 6, 6.	0, 1, 1, 1, 2, 3, 5, 6.	0, 1, 1, 2, 2, 2, 4, 6.	0, 3, 3, 3, 3, 4, 5, 6.	0, 2, 3, 4, 5, 5, 6, 6.

2, 3, 3, 3 3, 5, 6.

1, 1, 2, 5, 5, 6, 6.

0, 1, 2, 4, 4, 5, 6.

0, 0, 1, 2, 2, 4, 4.

0, 0, 0, 2, 3, 5, 6.

0, 2, 2, 3, 3, 4, 5.

0, 1, 4, 4, 4, 5, 6.

1, 1, 1, 3, 5, 6, 6.

89

Place the eight tiles into the puzzle grid so that all adjacent numbers on each tile match up. Tiles may be rotated through 360 degrees, but none may be flipped over.

3	4
2	3

1	2
4	2

4	3
1	4

3	1
4	1

4	1
1	3

1	3
2	2

1	2
2	3

2	2
4	4

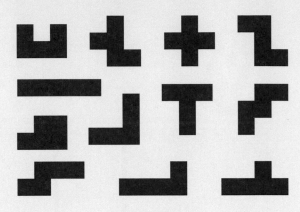

90

Place all twelve of the pieces into the grid. Any may be rotated or flipped over, but none may touch another, not even diagonally. The numbers outside the grid refer to the number of consecutive black squares; and each block is separated from the others by at least one white square. For instance, '3 2' could refer to a row with none, one or more white squares, then three black squares, then at least one white square, then two more black squares, followed by any number of white squares.

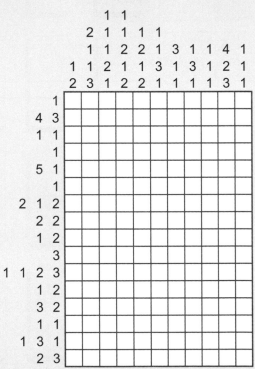

91

In the diagram below, which number should replace the question mark?

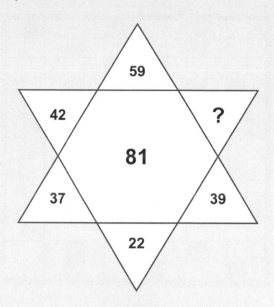

59

42

?

81

37

39

22

92

In the square below, change the positions of six numbers, one per horizontal row, vertical column and long diagonal line of six smaller squares, in such a way that the numbers in each row, column and long diagonal line total exactly 146. Any number may appear more than once in a row, column or line.

29	12	16	35	43	21
31	24	28	11	26	28
23	27	9	30	19	23
22	34	26	18	24	28
18	28	29	32	18	23
25	16	23	22	22	33

93

Every brick in this pyramid contains a number which is the sum of the two numbers below it, so that F=A+B, etc. Just work out the missing numbers!

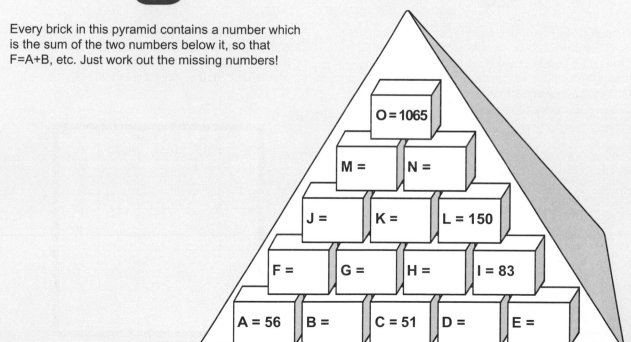

O = 1065

M =   N =

J =   K =   L = 150

F =   G =   H =   I = 83

A = 56   B =   C = 51   D =   E =

With the starter already given, can you fit all of the remaining listed numbers into this grid? Take care, this puzzle may not be as easy as it looks!

12	376	880	56050	90003
20	412	943	60909	90323
22	439	1089	61883	91070
32	500	1111	62005	91830
41	517	5018	63658	92020
61	542	7323	64825	93099
92 ✓	618	9560	70026	94889
96	750	9780	73010	96030
138	791	15090	75260	102040
147	802	20060	79090	401893
310	872	32060	82087	620183
328	874	53971	84216	700482

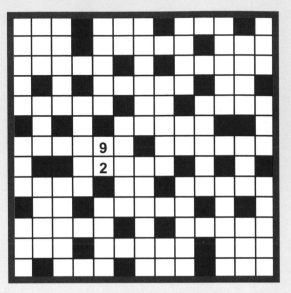

The chart gives directions to a hidden treasure behind the centre black square in the grid. Move the indicated number of spaces north, south, east and west (eg 4N means move four squares north) stopping at every square once only to arrive there. At which square should you start?

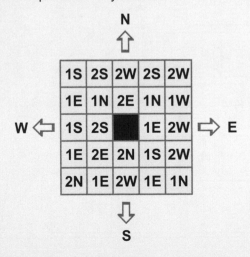

Fill the grid so that every horizontal row and vertical column contains the numbers 1-5. The 'greater than' or 'less than' signs indicate where a number is larger or smaller than that in the neighbouring square.

Each of the eight segments of the spider's web should be filled with a different number from 1 to 8, in such a way that every ring also contains a different number from 1 to 8.

The segments run from the outside of the spider's web to the centre, and the rings run all the way around.

Some numbers are already in place. Can you fill in the rest?

A standard set of 28 dominoes has been laid out as shown. Can you draw in the edges of them all? The check-box is provided as an aid and the domino already placed will help.

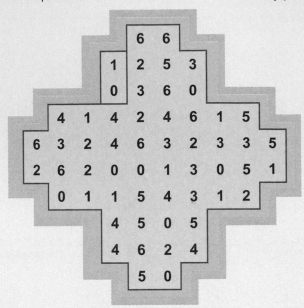

0-0	0-1	0-2	0-3	0-4	0-5	0-6
	✔					

1-1	1-2	1-3	1-4	1-5	1-6	2-2

2-3	2-4	2-5	2-6	3-3	3-4	3-5

3-6	4-4	4-5	4-6	5-5	5-6	6-6

2

Given that scales A and B balance perfectly, how many diamonds are needed to balance scale C?

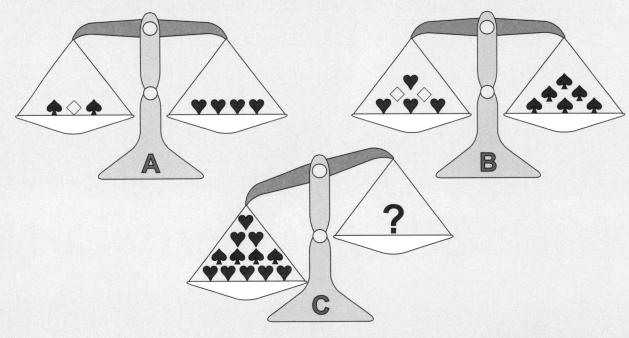

Every row and column in this grid originally contained one heart, one club, one diamond, one spade and two blank squares, although not necessarily in that order.

Every symbol with a black arrow refers to the first of the four symbols encountered when travelling in the direction of the arrow. Every symbol with a white arrow refers to the second of the four symbols encountered in the direction of the arrow.

Can you complete the original grid?

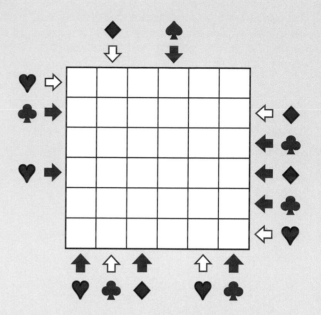

4

The blank squares below should be filled with whole numbers between 1 and 30 inclusive, any of which may occur more than once, or not at all.

The numbers in every horizontal row add up to the totals on the right, as do the two long diagonal lines; whilst those in every vertical column add up to the totals along the bottom.

							109
	14	21	7			14	81
	4			9	28	8	133
21	22	4		26		13	113
20	7	9			29		137
6		12		12	27	4	84
8	1		16	21	20	24	118
6	15	15		17	18	8	90
107	**67**	**113**	**111**	**107**	**150**	**101**	**86**

5

Draw in the missing hands on the final clock.

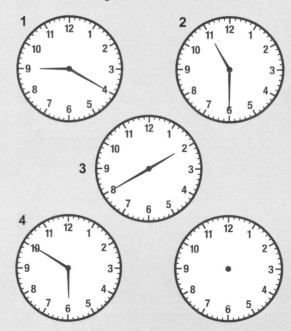

Can you place the hexagons into the grid, so that where any hexagon touches another along a straight line, the number in both triangles is the same? No rotation of any hexagon is allowed!

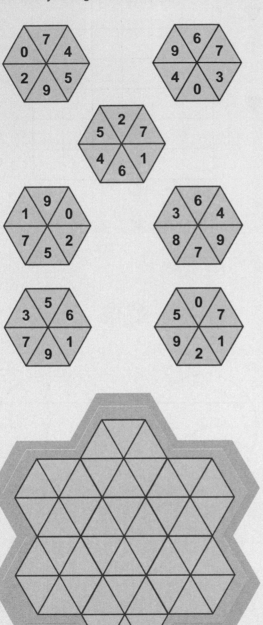

Twelve L-shapes like the ones here need to be inserted in the grid and each L has one hole in it.

There are three pieces of each of the four kinds shown here and any piece may be turned or flipped over before being put in the grid. No pieces of the same kind touch, even at a corner.

The pieces fit together so well that you cannot see any spaces between them; only the holes show.

Can you tell where the Ls are?

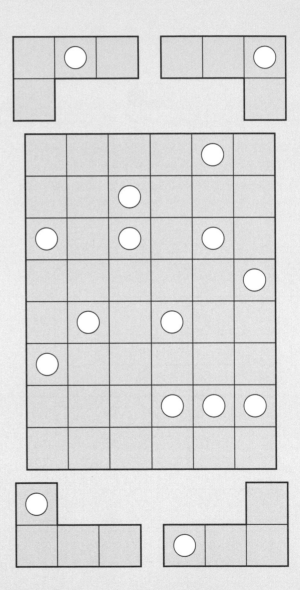

In this puzzle, an amateur coin collector has been out with his metal detector, searching for booty. He didn't have time to dig up all the coins he found, so has made a grid map, showing their locations, in the hope that if he loses the map, at least no-one else will understand it…

Those squares containing numbers are empty, but where a number appears in a square, it indicates how many coins are located in the squares (up to a maximum of eight) surrounding the numbered one, touching it at any corner or side. There is only one coin in any individual square.

Place a circle into every square containing a coin.

		2				1			
2		3		2					1
		2	0		2		1		1
		4				2			2
4			3					1	
4				5		1			
	3							0	
0		1	1			1	2		1
			1		1				

The grid should be filled with numbers from 1 to 6, so that each number appears just once in every row and column. The clues refer to the digit totals in the squares, eg A 1 2 3 = 6 means that the numbers in squares A1, A2 and A3 add up to 6.

1 B 2 3 = 7

2 C 3 4 = 5

3 D 3 4 = 9

4 E 1 2 = 9

5 F 4 5 = 6

6 A B 1 = 6

7 C D 2 = 5

8 E F 3 = 4

9 A B 4 = 3

10 C D E 5 = 10

11 A B C 6 = 9

	A	B	C	D	E	F
1						
2						
3						
4						
5						
6						

10

Each of the small squares in the grid below contains either A, B or C. Every row and column has exactly two of each letter. Can you tell the letter in each square?

Across

1 The Bs are further right than the Cs.
2 The Cs are next to and right of the As.
3 The Bs are further right than the As.
4 No two adjacent squares contain the same letter.
5 The As are further right than the Cs.
6 The As are further right than the Bs.

Down

1 The Bs are lower than the As.
2 The As are in adjacent squares.
3 The Bs are in adjacent squares.
4 Each C is directly next to and below an A.
5 Each B is directly next to and below a C.
6 The As are lower than the Bs.

	1	2	3	4	5	6
1						
2						
3						
4						
5						
6						

11

The object of this puzzle is to trace a single path from the top left corner to the bottom right corner of the grid, travelling through all of the cells in either a horizontal, vertical or diagonal direction.

Every cell must be entered once only and your path should take you through the numbers in the sequence 1-2-3-4-1-2-3-4, etc.

Can you find the way?

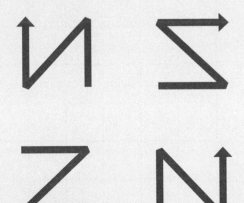

1	1	2	1	2	1	2	3
2	3	4	3	4	3	4	4
1	4	1	3	2	1	1	2
2	3	2	4	4	3	2	3
4	3	1	2	3	4	1	4
1	2	3	4	4	1	3	1
4	3	1	2	2	1	2	2
1	2	3	4	3	4	3	4

52

Can you place the vessels into the diagram? Some parts of vessels or sea squares have already been filled in. A number to the right or below a row or column refers to the number of occupied squares in that row or column.

Any vessel may be positioned horizontally or vertically, but no part of a vessel touches part of any other vessel, either horizontally, vertically or diagonally.

Empty Area of Sea:

Aircraft Carrier:

Battleships:

Cruisers:

Submarines:

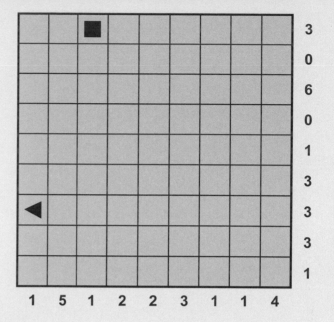

Can you fill each square in the bottom line with the correct digit?

Every square in the solution contains only one digit from each of the lettered lines above, although two or more squares in the solution may contain the same digit.

At the end of every row is a score, which shows:

a the number of digits placed in the correct finishing position on the bottom line, as indicated by a tick; and

b the number of digits which appear on the bottom line, but in a different position, as indicated by a cross.

				SCORE
0	0	1	1	✓ ✗
0	3	7	3	✗
1	6	6	0	✗ ✗
3	2	5	0	✗
5	4	2	0	✓ ✗
				✓ ✓ ✓ ✓

SECTION 2

53

14

Draw a single continuous loop, by connecting the dots. No line may cross the path of another.

The figure inside each set of any four surrounding dots indicates the total number of surrounding lines.

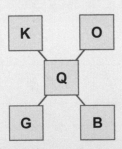
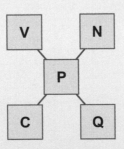

15

Each horizontal row and vertical column should contain different shapes and different numbers.

Every square will contain one number and one shape and no combination may be repeated anywhere else in the puzzle.

1   2   3   4   5

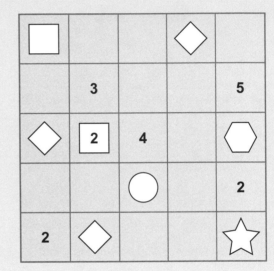

16

Given that the letters are valued 1-26 according to their places in the alphabet, can you crack the mystery code to reveal the missing letter?

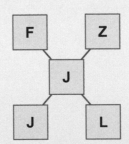
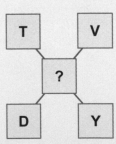

A set of dominoes is to be placed in four rows as shown below. The numbers indicate which values are shown on all the dominoes in each column and the relevant half of the domino in every row. Find out where each domino is placed by carefully comparing rows and columns to determine the possible positions of certain dominoes: for instance, if any column contains only one 6, then the domino 6/6 isn't in that column.

A set of dominoes consists of:

0/0, 0/1, 0/2, 0/3, 0/4, 0/5, 0/6, 1/1, 1/2, 1/3, 1/4, 1/5, 1/6, 2/2,

2/3, 2/4, 2/5, 2/6, 3/3, 3/4, 3/5, 3/6, 4/4, 4/5, 4/6, 5/5, 5/6, 6/6.

?	2, 2, 2, 4, 4, 4, 6, 6,	0, 1, 2, 2, 2, 3, 5, 6.	1, 1, 1, 1, 1, 2, 3, 5.	0, 0, 3, 3, 4, 6, 6, 6.	1, 3, 3, 4, 4, 4, 5, 5.	0, 0, 0, 0, 2, 4, 5, 5.	0, 1, 3, 3, 5, 5, 6, 6.
0, 0, 1, 2, 2, 5, 6.							
2, 2, 3, 3, 5, 5, 5.							
0, 1, 1, 2, 2, 4, 4.							
0, 1, 3, 4, 4, 6, 6.							
0, 1, 4, 6, 6, 6, 6.							
0, 0, 1, 1, 2, 5, 6.							
1, 2, 3, 3, 4, 4, 5.							
0, 3, 3, 3, 4, 5, 5.							

Place the eight tiles into the puzzle grid so that all adjacent numbers on each tile match up. Tiles may be rotated through 360 degrees, but none may be flipped over.

4	3
1	2

1	3
4	4

1	2
1	4

1	2
4	2

4	1
3	4

3	1
4	4

1	2
1	1

1	3
4	1

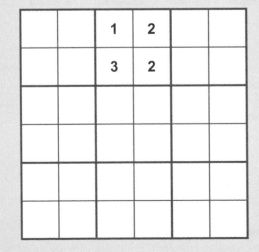

Place all twelve of the pieces into the grid. Any may be rotated or flipped over, but none may touch another, not even diagonally. The numbers outside the grid refer to the number of consecutive black squares; and each block is separated from the others by at least one white square. For instance, '3 2' could refer to a row with none, one or more white squares, then three black squares, then at least one white square, then two more black squares, followed by any number of white squares.

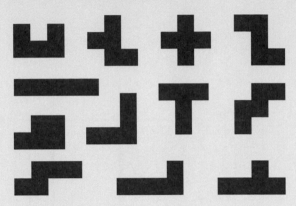

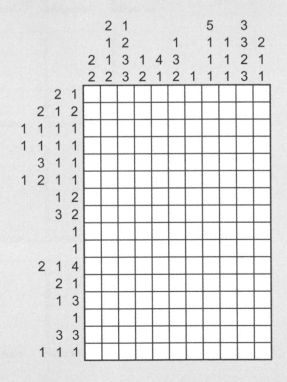

20

In the diagram below, which letter should replace the question mark?

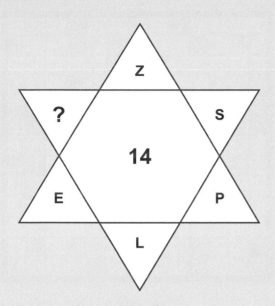

21

In the square below, change the positions of six numbers, one per horizontal row, vertical column and long diagonal line of six smaller squares, in such a way that the numbers in each row, column and long diagonal line total exactly 173. Any number may appear more than once in a row, column or line.

58	15	19	26	31	12
29	37	28	25	33	30
14	35	28	43	19	29
48	39	33	8	24	33
21	32	34	30	19	36
15	24	28	36	35	32

22

Every brick in this pyramid contains a number which is the sum of the two numbers below it, so that F=A+B, etc. Just work out the missing numbers!

O =

M = 640   N = 469

J =   K =   L =

F =   G = 154   H =   I = 95

A =   B = 127   C =   D =   E =

With the starter already given, can you fit all of the remaining listed numbers into this grid? Take care, this puzzle may not be as easy as it looks!

50	384	762	7631	46757
51	409	816	7638 ✓	54218
53	419	844	7640	65985
62	452	849	8614	74883
68	500	865	8648	75931
70	535	970	8934	78593
116	564	1963	18903	86389
156	582	4265	30911	94266
289	636	4574	32154	178549
303	658	6038	33043	634955
326	675	6448	34918	753884
347	694	6539	39124	863442

The chart gives directions to a hidden treasure behind the centre black square in the grid. Move the indicated number of spaces north, south, east and west (eg 4N means move four squares north) stopping at every square once only to arrive there. At which square should you start?

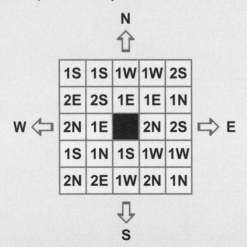

Fill the grid so that every horizontal row and vertical column contains the numbers 1-5. The 'greater than' or 'less than' signs indicate where a number is larger or smaller than that in the neighbouring square.

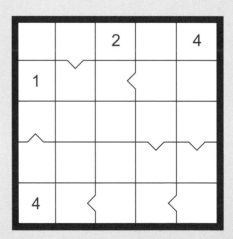

58

Each of the eight segments of the spider's web should be filled with a different number from 1 to 8, in such a way that every ring also contains a different number from 1 to 8.

The segments run from the outside of the spider's web to the centre, and the rings run all the way around.

Some numbers are already in place. Can you fill in the rest?

S
E
C
T
I
O
N

2

Every oval shape in this diagram contains a different letter of the alphabet from A to K inclusive. Use the clues to determine their locations. Reference in the clues to 'due' means in any location along the same horizontal or vertical line.

1 The A is next to and east of the B, which is further south than the E.

2 The C is further north than the G, but further south than the H (which is further south than the F).

3 The D is next to and east of the J, which is next to and south of the F.

4 The E is next to and east of the I, which is next to and north of the K.

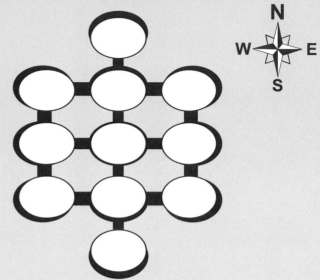

28

Fill the three empty circles with the symbols +, – and x in some order, to make a sum which totals the number in the centre. Each symbol must be used once and calculations are made in the direction of travel.

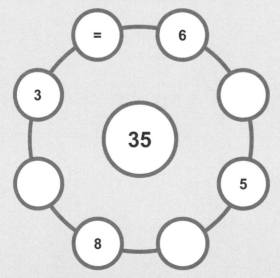

29

The numbers at the top and on the left side show the quantity of single-digit numbers (1-9) used in that row and column. The numbers at the bottom and on the right side show the sum of the digits. A number may appear more than once in a row or column, but no numbers are in squares that touch, even at a corner.

	3	0	2	2	2	0	3	
2								7
2								14
2			2					8
1								2
2								12
1								3
2								16
	20	0	6	16	9	0	11	

Using the numbers below, complete these six equations (three reading across and three reading downwards). Every number is used once.

In the grid below, which number should replace the question mark?

2		3		4		5
	6		7		9	

	x		–		=	22
–		+		+		
	x		+	1	=	15
x		x		–		
8	–		x		=	8
=		=		=		
56		60		2		

38	3	16	15	32	37	34
12	31	28	39	27	25	13
19	40	25	25	25	24	17
15	40	47	7	24	27	15
21	?	21	35	29	10	29
26	19	16	32	10	25	47
44	12	22	22	28	27	20

When the box below is folded to form a cube, just one of the five options (A, B, C, D or E) can be produced. Which?

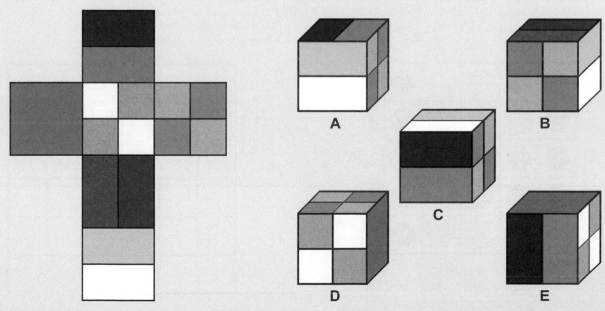

A

B

C

D

E

33

In this puzzle, an amateur coin collector has been out with his metal detector, searching for booty. He didn't have time to dig up all the coins he found, so has made a grid map, showing their locations, in the hope that if he loses the map, at least no-one else will understand it…

Those squares containing numbers are empty, but where a number appears in a square, it indicates how many coins are located in the squares (up to a maximum of eight) surrounding the numbered one, touching it at any corner or side. There is only one coin in any individual square.

Place a circle into every square containing a coin.

				2	3			1	
	4	3					2		2
				2	4		2	2	
2		2					1		
	0	1		1					
			2					1	
	2	1				1	2		
					5	4			
	1		1					4	
				1	3			3	1

34

Each symbol stands for a different number. In order to reach the correct total at the end of each row and column, what is the value of the circle, cross, pentagon, square and star?

✚	●	■	☆	✚	= 28
●	⬟	☆	■	●	= 33
●	✚	●	■	⬟	= 30
✚	●	✚	☆	✚	= 22
☆	☆	■	■	✚	= 33
=	=	=	=	=	
26	27	34	39	20	

35

Every row and column of this grid should contain one each of the letters A, B, C, D, E and F. Each of the six shapes (marked by thicker lines) should also contain one each of the letters A, B, C, D, E and F. Can you complete the grid?

		D	C	B	A
	E				
				F	

A standard set of 28 dominoes has been laid out as shown. Can you draw in the edges of them all? The check-box is provided as an aid and the domino already placed will help.

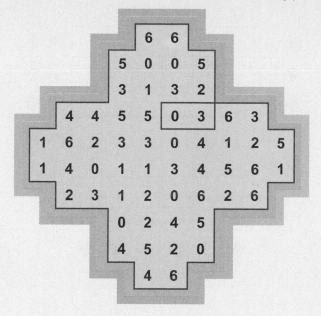

0-0	0-1	0-2	0-3	0-4	0-5	0-6
			✔			

1-1	1-2	1-3	1-4	1-5	1-6	2-2

2-3	2-4	2-5	2-6	3-3	3-4	3-5

3-6	4-4	4-5	4-6	5-5	5-6	6-6

Each of the small squares in the grid below contains either A, B or C. Every row and column has exactly two of each letter. Can you tell the letter in each square?

Across

1 The Cs are both between the As.
2 The As are in adjacent squares.
3 The Bs are in adjacent squares.
4 No two adjacent squares contain the same letter.
5 The As are both between the Cs.
6 The Cs are further right than the Bs.

Down

1 No two adjacent squares contain the same letter.
2 The Bs are both between the Cs.
3 Each B is directly next to and below an A.
4 The Cs are lower than the As.
5 The Cs are both between the Bs.
6 The As are in adjacent squares.

	1	2	3	4	5	6
1						
2						
3						
4						
5						
6						

Every row and column in this grid originally contained one heart, one club, one diamond, one spade and two blank squares, although not necessarily in that order.

Every symbol with a black arrow refers to the first of the four symbols encountered when travelling in the direction of the arrow. Every symbol with a white arrow refers to the second of the four symbols encountered in the direction of the arrow.

Can you complete the original grid?

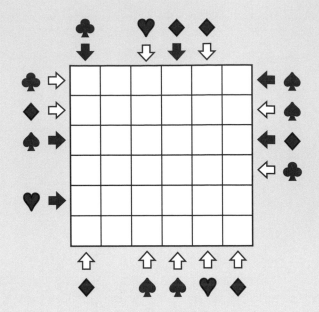

39

The blank squares below should be filled with whole numbers between 1 and 30 inclusive, any of which may occur more than once, or not at all.

The numbers in every horizontal row add up to the totals on the right, as do the two long diagonal lines; whilst those in every vertical column add up to the totals along the bottom.

							141
	25	29	1	3			98
16	5			15		15	94
	6		23	9	2	10	88
	12	20	24		1	19	90
30		11	25	24	4	15	117
	26	25	20	12	15	26	132
28			30	21	12	13	126
132	94	117	137	87	54	124	102

40

A   is to   B

as   C   is to

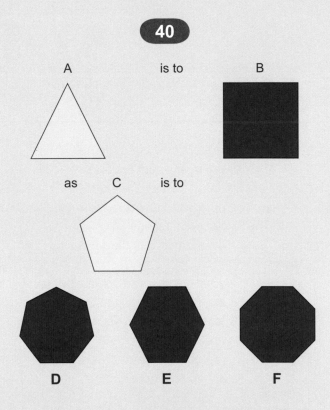

D   E   F

Can you place the hexagons into the grid, so that where any hexagon touches another along a straight line, the number in both triangles is the same? No rotation of any hexagon is allowed!

Twelve L-shapes like the ones here need to be inserted in the grid and each L has one hole in it.

There are three pieces of each of the four kinds shown here and any piece may be turned or flipped over before being put in the grid. No pieces of the same kind touch, even at a corner.

The pieces fit together so well that you cannot see any spaces between them; only the holes show.

Can you tell where the Ls are?

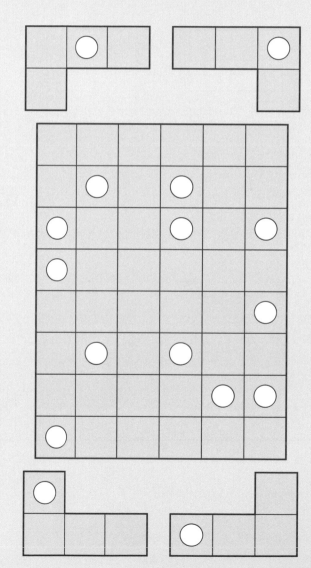

Which of the four lettered alternatives (A, B, C or D) fits most logically into the empty square?

17	6	15
4	3	9
22	8	12

12	17	6
3	9	15
4	22	8

8	12	17
9	15	6
3	4	22

?

4	22	8
6	17	12
15	9	3

A

4	22	8
6	17	12
15	3	9

B

3	4	22
17	12	8
6	15	9

C

22	8	12
15	6	17
9	3	4

D

44

Which four pieces can be fitted together to form an exact copy of this shape?

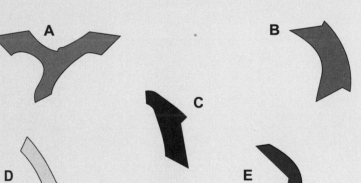

A

B

C

F

G

D

E

H

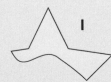
I

J

Can you place the vessels into the diagram? Some parts of vessels or sea squares have already been filled in. A number to the right or below a row or column refers to the number of occupied squares in that row or column.

Any vessel may be positioned horizontally or vertically, but no part of a vessel touches part of any other vessel, either horizontally, vertically or diagonally.

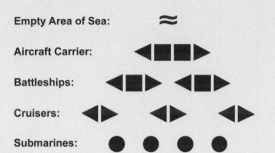

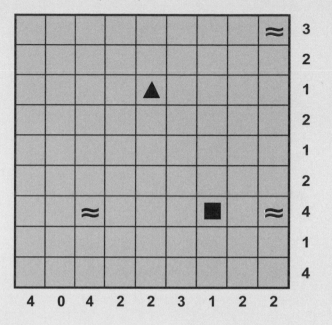

46

Can you fill each square in the bottom line with the correct digit?

Every square in the solution contains only one digit from each of the lettered lines above, although two or more squares in the solution may contain the same digit.

At the end of every row is a score, which shows:

a   the number of digits placed in the correct finishing position on the bottom line, as indicated by a tick; and

b   the number of digits which appear on the bottom line, but in a different position, as indicated by a cross.

SCORE

7	0	1	1	✓✓✓
7	2	4	1	✓✓
1	7	1	0	✓✗✗
5	1	4	3	✓
6	5	2	1	✓
				✓✓✓✓

S E C T I O N

2

The grid should be filled with numbers from 1 to 6, so that each number appears just once in every row and column. The clues refer to the digit totals in the squares, eg A 1 2 3 = 6 means that the numbers in squares A1, A2 and A3 add up to 6.

1 E 4 5 6 = 15

2 F 2 3 = 8

3 B C 1 = 7

4 A B 2 = 6

5 C D E 3 = 8

6 C D 4 = 3

7 A B 5 = 5

8 A B 6 = 9

9 A 3 4 = 11

10 B 3 4 = 6

11 C 5 6 = 6

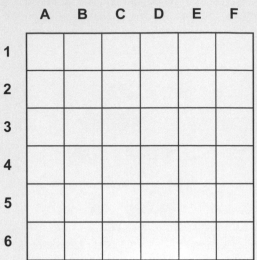

	A	B	C	D	E	F
1						
2						
3						
4						
5						
6						

48

The object of this puzzle is to trace a single path from the top left corner to the bottom right corner of the grid, travelling through all of the cells in either a horizontal, vertical or diagonal direction.

Every cell must be entered once only and your path should take you through the numbers in the sequence 1-2-3-4-1-2-3-4, etc.

Can you find the way?

1	2	3	4	3	1	2	4
4	3	1	2	1	4	3	1
1	2	4	3	2	1	3	2
3	2	1	3	3	4	3	4
1	4	4	2	2	4	2	1
2	2	3	4	1	2	3	4
3	1	4	1	2	1	2	1
4	1	2	3	3	4	3	4

49

Draw a single continuous loop, by connecting the dots. No line may cross the path of another.

The figure inside each set of any four surrounding dots indicates the total number of surrounding lines.

```
3       1   1   1

   3        0       1       3   0

3           3

      2     1           1

                  0         3   2

1   1     0           1       1

1   1         2   0           2

   0   1             1         2

            3               0

1           0   2   1   0     3

1               1       1             0

2       1       1           3
```

50

Each horizontal row and vertical column should contain different shapes and different numbers.

Every square will contain one number and one shape and no combination may be repeated anywhere else in the puzzle.

1   2   3   4   5

3	◯			
②	☆4		5	☐
	3			
	2	◯		
4	☐			◇

51

Given that the letters are valued 1-26 according to their places in the alphabet, can you crack the mystery code to reveal the missing letter?

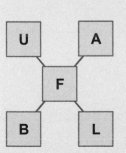

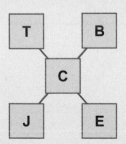

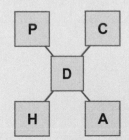

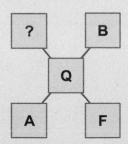

Which is the odd one out?

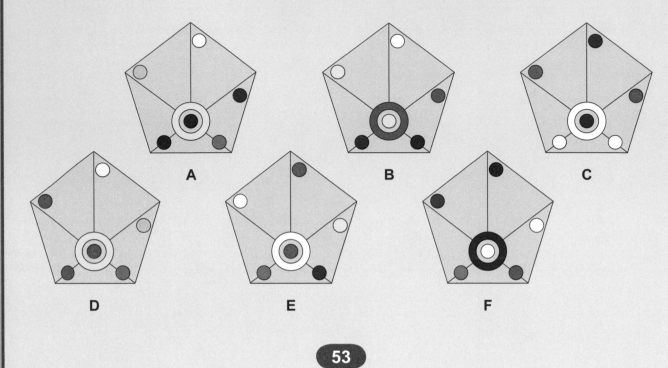

A   B   C

D   E   F

53

What comes next in this sequence?

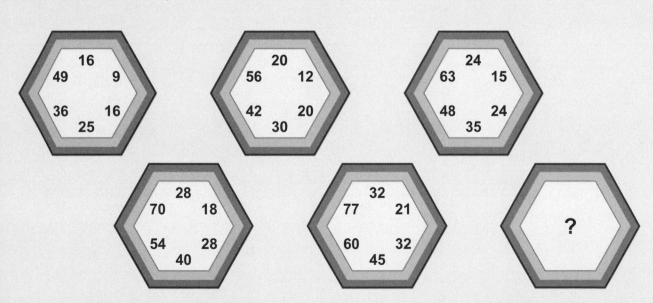

Place the eight tiles into the puzzle grid so that all adjacent numbers on each tile match up. Tiles may be rotated through 360 degrees, but none may be flipped over.

4	2
2	1

1	3
2	4

1	4
1	3

1	4
4	1

3	1
4	2

4	2
1	4

4	3
2	4

3	4
3	1

4	4				
1	1				

Place all twelve of the pieces into the grid. Any may be rotated or flipped over, but none may touch another, not even diagonally. The numbers outside the grid refer to the number of consecutive black squares; and each block is separated from the others by at least one white square. For instance, '3 2' could refer to a row with none, one or more white squares, then three black squares, then at least one white square, then two more black squares, followed by any number of white squares.

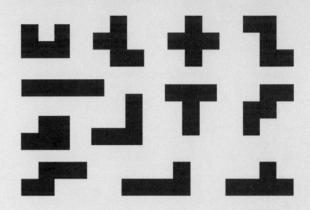

56

In the diagram below, which number should replace the question mark?

57

In the square below, change the positions of six numbers, one per horizontal row, vertical column and long diagonal line of six smaller squares, in such a way that the numbers in each row, column and long diagonal line total exactly 191. Any number may appear more than once in a row, column or line.

26	21	48	24	73	14
37	31	21	32	36	31
40	49	31	52	20	30
24	39	36	41	24	30
6	47	21	52	10	34
37	19	31	21	31	27

58

Every brick in this pyramid contains a number which is the sum of the two numbers below it, so that F=A+B, etc. Just work out the missing numbers!

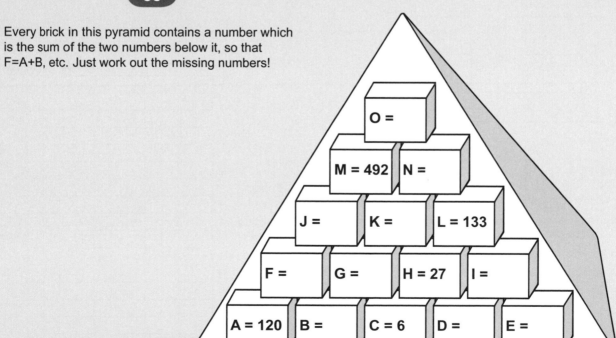

With the starter already given, can you fit all of the remaining listed numbers into this grid? Take care, this puzzle may not be as easy as it looks!

10	130	750	12259	71500
15	138 ✓	781	15406	80020
22	168	1389	19653	92649
30	189	2617	21034	93460
36	230	2730	24667	102400
38	417	2904	28416	507387
45	420	3009	39888	508098
50	436	3027	40422	528460
52	468	3109	42677	555606
85	483	3920	43520	673930
87	625	7928	46910	918035
99	670	8187	61093	945364

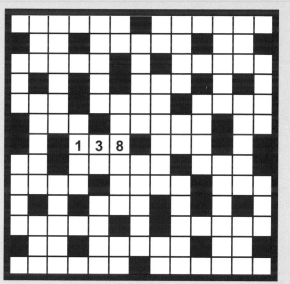

The chart gives directions to a hidden treasure behind the centre black square in the grid. Move the indicated number of spaces north, south, east and west (eg 4N means move four squares north) stopping at every square once only to arrive there. At which square should you start?

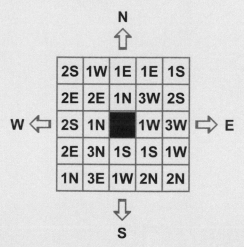

Fill the grid so that every horizontal row and vertical column contains the numbers 1-5. The 'greater than' or 'less than' signs indicate where a number is larger or smaller than that in the neighbouring square.

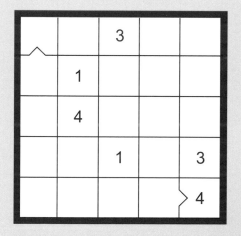

Each of the eight segments of the spider's web should be filled with a different number from 1 to 8, in such a way that every ring also contains a different number from 1 to 8.

The segments run from the outside of the spider's web to the centre, and the rings run all the way around.

Some numbers are already in place. Can you fill in the rest?

Every oval shape in this diagram contains a different letter of the alphabet from A to K inclusive. Use the clues to determine their locations. Reference in the clues to 'due' means in any location along the same horizontal or vertical line.

1 The A is next to and east of the E, which is due north of the B.

2 The C is next to and north of the J. The J is further west than the F and further north than the I.

3 The D is next to and west of the H (which is due north of the G).

4 The K is further south than the D, but further north than the E.

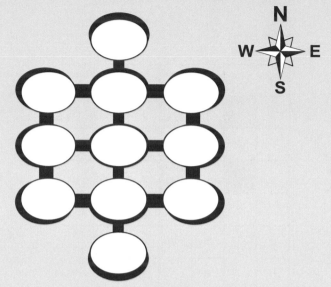

64

Fill the three empty circles with the symbols +, – and x in some order, to make a sum which totals the number in the centre. Each symbol must be used once and calculations are made in the direction of travel.

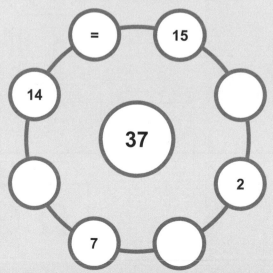

65

The numbers at the top and on the left side show the quantity of single-digit numbers (1-9) used in that row and column. The numbers at the bottom and on the right side show the sum of the digits. A number may appear more than once in a row or column, but no numbers are in squares that touch, even at a corner.

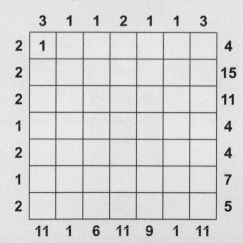

	3	1	1	2	1	1	3	
2	1							4
2								15
2								11
1								4
2								4
1								7
2								5
	11	1	6	11	9	1	11	

66

Using the numbers below, complete these six equations (three reading across and three reading downwards). Every number is used once.

	1		3		4		5
		6		7		8	

9	x		+		=	33
x	■	+	■	−		
	x		+	2	=	37
+	■	−	■	x		
	+		x		=	40
=		=		=		
46		6		32		

67

In the grid below, which number should replace the question mark?

32	33	31	34	30	35	29
15	16	14	17	13	18	12
7	8	6	9	5	10	4
78	79	77	80	76	81	75
28	29	27	30	26	31	25
46	47	45	48	44	?	43
4	5	3	6	2	7	1

68

When the box below is folded to form a cube, just one of the five options (A, B, C, D or E) can be produced. Which?

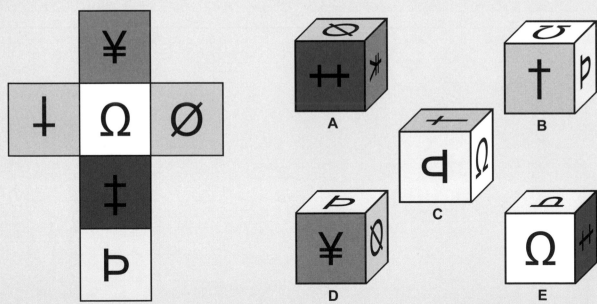

A

B

C

D

E

69

In this puzzle, an amateur coin collector has been out with his metal detector, searching for booty. He didn't have time to dig up all the coins he found, so has made a grid map, showing their locations, in the hope that if he loses the map, at least no-one else will understand it…

Those squares containing numbers are empty, but where a number appears in a square, it indicates how many coins are located in the squares (up to a maximum of eight) surrounding the numbered one, touching it at any corner or side. There is only one coin in any individual square.

Place a circle into every square containing a coin.

			1		3				0
	3						3	2	
		3	4					1	
1					1			2	1
1					0			3	
0	1	1				2			1
		1	1						
		3					2		
1	3			3		3		1	
		3			2				

70

Every row and column of this grid should contain one each of the letters A, B, C, D, E and F. Each of the six shapes (marked by thicker lines) should also contain one each of the letters A, B, C, D, E and F. Can you complete the grid?

	D		C	B	A
				E	
		F			

71

Each symbol stands for a different number. In order to reach the correct total at the end of each row and column, what is the value of the circle, cross, pentagon, square and star?

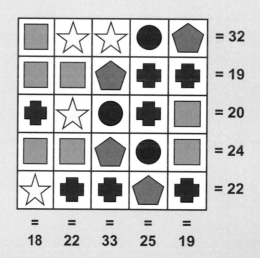

Row totals: = 32, = 19, = 20, = 24, = 22

Column totals: = 18, = 22, = 33, = 25, = 19

72

A standard set of 28 dominoes has been laid out as shown. Can you draw in the edges of them all? The checkbox is provided as an aid and the domino already placed will help.

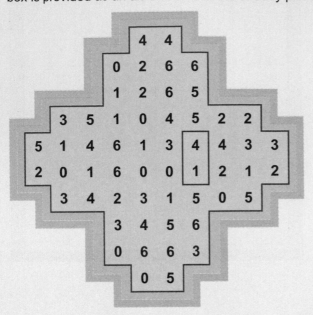

0-0	0-1	0-2	0-3	0-4	0-5	0-6

1-1	1-2	1-3	1-4	1-5	1-6	2-2
			✔			

2-3	2-4	2-5	2-6	3-3	3-4	3-5

3-6	4-4	4-5	4-6	5-5	5-6	6-6

73

Each of the small squares in the grid below contains either A, B or C. Every row and column has exactly two of each letter. Can you tell the letter in each square?

Across

1 The Cs are further right than the Bs.
2 No two adjacent squares contain the same letter.
3 The As are further right than the Cs.
4 The Cs are both between the As.
5 The Bs are further right than the As.
6 No two adjacent squares contain the same letter.

Down

1 Each B is directly next to and below a C.
2 The Bs are in adjacent squares.
3 The Cs are in adjacent squares.
4 The As are both between the Bs.
5 The Cs are in adjacent squares.
6 The Cs are lower than the Bs.

Every row and column in this grid originally contained one heart, one club, one diamond, one spade and two blank squares, although not necessarily in that order.

Every symbol with a black arrow refers to the first of the four symbols encountered when travelling in the direction of the arrow. Every symbol with a white arrow refers to the second of the four symbols encountered in the direction of the arrow.

Can you complete the original grid?

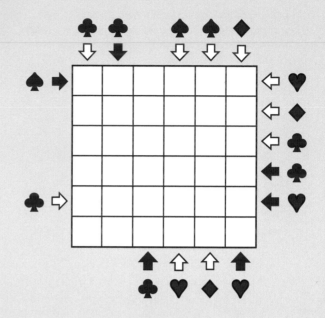

75

The blank squares below should be filled with whole numbers between 1 and 30 inclusive, any of which may occur more than once, or not at all.

The numbers in every horizontal row add up to the totals on the right, as do the two long diagonal lines; whilst those in every vertical column add up to the totals along the bottom.

							112
3		9	11	27	27	3	98
					17		142
	13		3	17	29	24	123
21		24	22	15		5	118
7	15			8	6	26	91
25	21	3		6	22	21	127
20		12	13	25	16	3	96
120	83	97	123	120	143	109	79

76

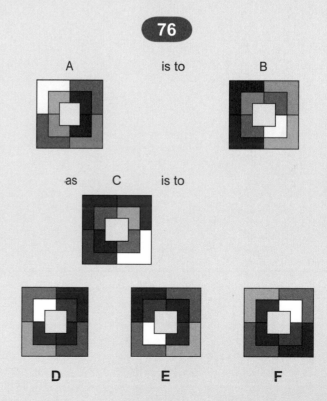

Can you place the hexagons into the grid, so that where any hexagon touches another along a straight line, the number in both triangles is the same? No rotation of any hexagon is allowed!

Twelve L-shapes like the ones here need to be inserted in the grid and each L has one hole in it.

There are three pieces of each of the four kinds shown here and any piece may be turned or flipped over before being put in the grid. No pieces of the same kind touch, even at a corner.

The pieces fit together so well that you cannot see any spaces between them; only the holes show.

Can you tell where the Ls are?

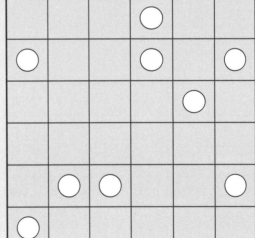

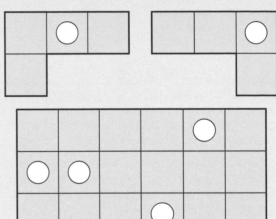

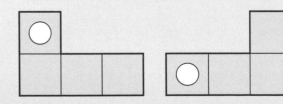

Given that scales A and B balance perfectly, how many spades are needed to balance scale C?

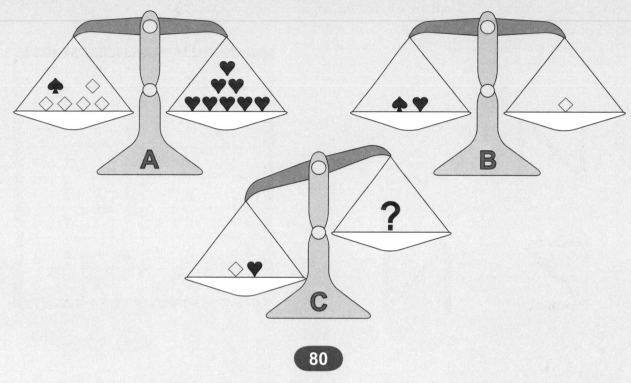

A   B   C

Which of the four lettered alternatives (A, B, C or D) fits most logically into the empty square?

6	7	9
12	16	21
27	34	42

15	16	18
21	25	30
36	43	51

12	13	15
18	22	27
33	40	48

A

11	12	14
17	19	23
29	35	43

B

10	11	13
16	20	25
31	38	46

?

11	12	13
15	18	22
27	33	40

C

12	13	15
18	23	28
34	41	49

D

The object of this puzzle is to trace a single path from the top left corner to the bottom right corner of the grid, travelling through all of the cells in either a horizontal, vertical or diagonal direction.

Every cell must be entered once only and your path should take you through the numbers in the sequence 1-2-3-4-1-2-3-4, etc.

Can you find the way?

1	2	3	2	1	2	4	1
1	4	1	4	3	4	3	2
2	3	2	2	1	4	2	3
3	3	1	3	1	3	1	4
4	2	4	4	3	2	2	3
1	2	1	4	1	1	1	4
4	3	4	3	2	4	2	3
1	2	3	4	1	2	3	4

The grid should be filled with numbers from 1 to 6, so that each number appears just once in every row and column. The clues refer to the digit totals in the squares, eg A 1 2 3 = 6 means that the numbers in squares A1, A2 and A3 add up to 6.

1 A 3 4 = 10

2 B 1 2 3 = 9

3 C 2 3 4 = 10

4 D 2 3 = 10

5 E 5 6 = 3

6 F 4 5 = 9

7 C D 1 = 9

8 E F 2 = 4

9 E F 3 = 7

10 D E 4 = 5

11 A B 5 = 8

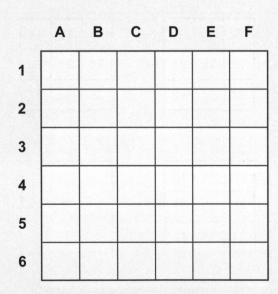

	A	B	C	D	E	F
1						
2						
3						
4						
5						
6						

Can you fill each square in the bottom line with the correct digit?

Every square in the solution contains only one digit from each of the lettered lines above, although two or more squares in the solution may contain the same digit.

At the end of every row is a score, which shows:

a the number of digits placed in the correct finishing position on the bottom line, as indicated by a tick; and

b the number of digits which appear on the bottom line, but in a different position, as indicated by a cross.

SCORE

1	2	5	2	✓
7	3	3	3	✗
5	4	6	2	✗
3	1	7	6	✗ ✗ ✗
3	0	4	7	✓
				✓ ✓ ✓ ✓

Can you place the vessels into the diagram? Some parts of vessels or sea squares have already been filled in. A number to the right or below a row or column refers to the number of occupied squares in that row or column.

Any vessel may be positioned horizontally or vertically, but no part of a vessel touches part of any other vessel, either horizontally, vertically or diagonally.

Empty Area of Sea: ≈

Aircraft Carrier: ◀■■▶

Battleships: ◀■▶ ◀■▶

Cruisers: ◀▶ ◀▶ ◀▶

Submarines: ● ● ● ●

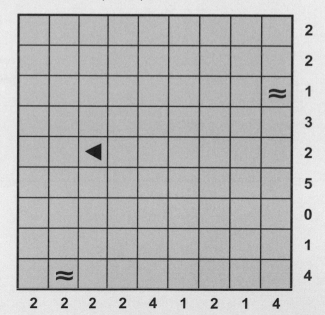

85

Draw a single continuous loop, by connecting the dots. No line may cross the path of another.

The figure inside each set of any four surrounding dots indicates the total number of surrounding lines.

```
3        1   1   2           3
1            0               3   1
2    1   1                   2
                  2   2
3        2               0   0   1
         1               2
2                3       1           1
    2                1           0   1
    2   2   1   3           3           2
    2   2   1           3               2
    2           0
        1       2       0       3       1
```

86

Each horizontal row and vertical column should contain different shapes and different numbers.

Every square will contain one number and one shape and no combination may be repeated anywhere else in the puzzle.

| 1 | 2 | 3 | 4 | 5 |

		1		
	1		◇5	
	5		2	
⬡	○			
5		2		4

87

Given that the letters are valued 1-26 according to their places in the alphabet, can you crack the mystery code to reveal the missing letter?

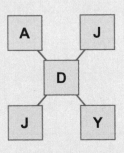

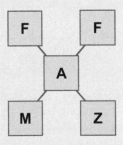

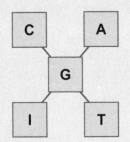

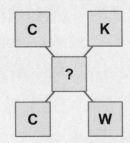

A set of dominoes is to be placed in four rows as shown below. The numbers indicate which values are shown on all the dominoes in each column and the relevant half of the domino in every row. Find out where each domino is placed by carefully comparing rows and columns to determine the possible positions of certain dominoes: for instance, if any column contains only one 6, then the domino 6/6 isn't in that column.

A set of dominoes consists of:

0/0, 0/1, 0/2, 0/3, 0/4, 0/5, 0/6, 1/1, 1/2, 1/3, 1/4, 1/5, 1/6, 2/2,

2/3, 2/4, 2/5, 2/6, 3/3, 3/4, 3/5, 3/6, 4/4, 4/5, 4/6, 5/5, 5/6, 6/6.

?	0, 1, 1, 3, 4, 5, 5, 5.	0, 2, 2, 2, 2, 3, 5, 6.	0, 0, 0, 1, 3, 3, 6, 6.	0, 1, 2, 2, 4, 4, 5, 6.	1, 2, 3, 3, 4, 4, 4, 6.	0, 0, 1, 4, 4, 5, 5, 5.	1, 1, 2, 3, 3, 6, 6, 6.
1, 1, 1, 2, 5, 5, 6.							
1, 2, 3, 3, 3, 6, 6.							
0, 0, 1, 5, 5, 5, 6.							
1, 1, 2, 4, 4, 6, 6.							
0, 0, 2, 3, 4, 5, 6.							
0, 0, 1, 2, 2, 4, 6.							
2, 3, 3, 3, 4, 4, 5.							
0, 0, 2, 3, 4, 4, 5.							

89

Place the eight tiles into the puzzle grid so that all adjacent numbers on each tile match up. Tiles may be rotated through 360 degrees, but none may be flipped over.

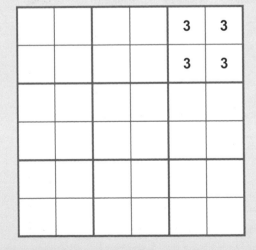

90

Place all twelve of the pieces into the grid. Any may be rotated or flipped over, but none may touch another, not even diagonally. The numbers outside the grid refer to the number of consecutive black squares; and each block is separated from the others by at least one white square. For instance, '3 2' could refer to a row with none, one or more white squares, then three black squares, then at least one white square, then two more black squares, followed by any number of white squares.

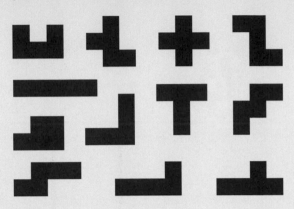

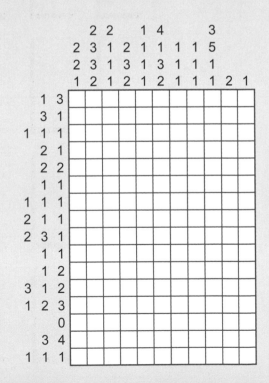

In the diagram below, which letter should replace the question mark?

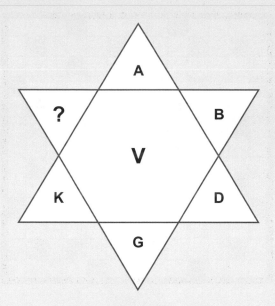

In the square below, change the positions of six numbers, one per horizontal row, vertical column and long diagonal line of six smaller squares, in such a way that the numbers in each row, column and long diagonal line total exactly 138. Any number may appear more than once in a row, column or line.

11	16	20	26	32	23
28	23	26	17	23	29
23	35	23	25	17	29
16	22	23	35	15	24
13	21	35	22	25	18
37	18	19	27	21	11

Every brick in this pyramid contains a number which is the sum of the two numbers below it, so that F=A+B, etc. Just work out the missing numbers!

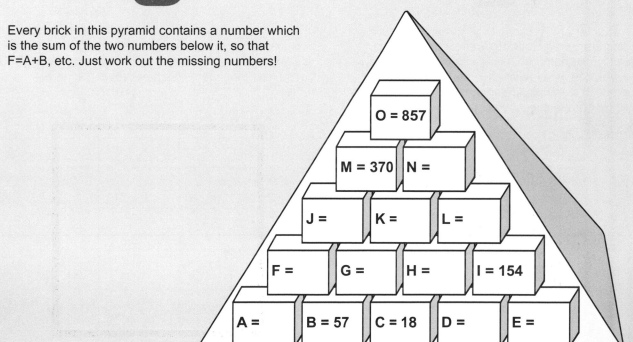

O = 857

M = 370   N =

J =   K =   L =

F =   G =   H =   I = 154

A =   B = 57   C = 18   D =   E =

With the starter already given, can you fit all of the remaining listed numbers into this grid? Take care, this puzzle may not be as easy as it looks!

18	146	512	1190	50187
19	157	530	1383	56975
21	160	548	3865	57730
26	216	607	4219	84120
28	321	639	5329	175737
48	327	741	5834	365373
59	340	799	6207	459770
60	377	846	7688	496570
63	419	876	8051	766598
81	433	920	8949	829770
90	471	960	19375	869666
92	499	980 ✓	43980	874333

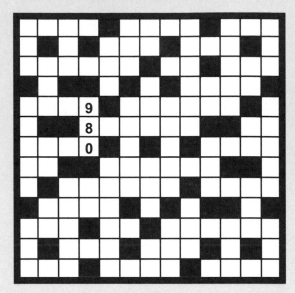

The chart gives directions to a hidden treasure behind the centre black square in the grid. Move the indicated number of spaces north, south, east and west (eg 4N means move four squares north) stopping at every square once only to arrive there. At which square should you start?

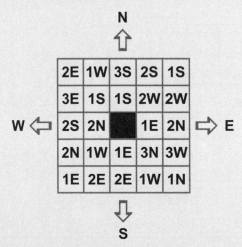

Fill the grid so that every horizontal row and vertical column contains the numbers 1-5. The 'greater than' or 'less than' signs indicate where a number is larger or smaller than that in the neighbouring square.

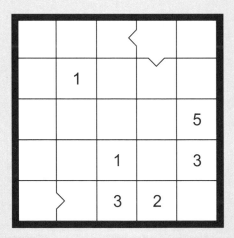

Each of the eight segments of the spider's web should be filled with a different number from 1 to 8, in such a way that every ring also contains a different number from 1 to 8.

The segments run from the outside of the spider's web to the centre, and the rings run all the way around.

Some numbers are already in place. Can you fill in the rest?

1

A standard set of 28 dominoes has been laid out as shown. Can you draw in the edges of them all? The check-box is provided as an aid and the domino already placed will help.

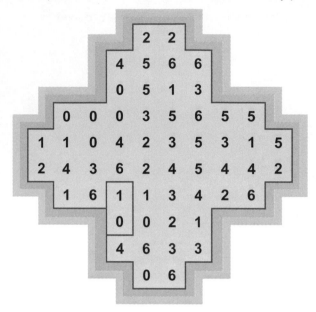

```
        2 2
      4 5 6 6
      0 5 1 3
  0 0 0 3 5 6 5 5
1 1 0 4 2 3 5 3 1 5
2 4 3 6 2 4 5 4 4 2
  1 6 1 1 3 4 2 6
      0 0 2 1
      4 6 3 3
        0 6
```

0-0	0-1	0-2	0-3	0-4	0-5	0-6
	✔					

1-1	1-2	1-3	1-4	1-5	1-6	2-2

2-3	2-4	2-5	2-6	3-3	3-4	3-5

3-6	4-4	4-5	4-6	5-5	5-6	6-6

2

Given that scales A and B balance perfectly, how many diamonds are needed to balance scale C?

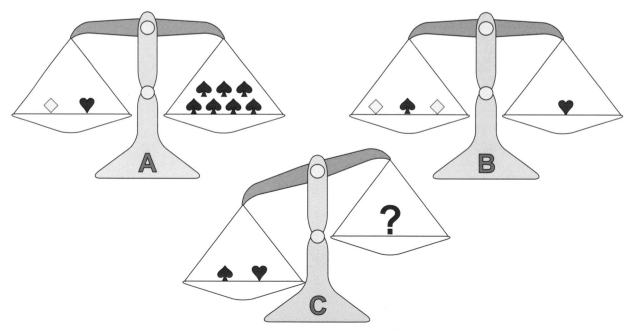

90

Every row and column in this grid originally contained one heart, one club, one diamond, one spade and two blank squares, although not necessarily in that order.

Every symbol with a black arrow refers to the first of the four symbols encountered when travelling in the direction of the arrow. Every symbol with a white arrow refers to the second of the four symbols encountered in the direction of the arrow.

Can you complete the original grid?

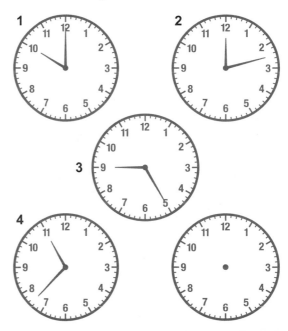

4

The blank squares below should be filled with whole numbers between 1 and 30 inclusive, any of which may occur more than once, or not at all.

The numbers in every horizontal row add up to the totals on the right, as do the two long diagonal lines; whilst those in every vertical column add up to the totals along the bottom.

5

Draw in the missing hands on the final clock.

							115
11	13	21	13	29		18	133
20	20			5	18	23	109
3		4	12	20	18		82
9	1	4		8			91
23		10	23		15	27	134
	6	17	21		19	2	99
	27	5	4	11	14		106
92	98	65	114	126	132	127	124

6

Can you place the hexagons into the grid, so that where any hexagon touches another along a straight line, the number in both triangles is the same? No rotation of any hexagon is allowed!

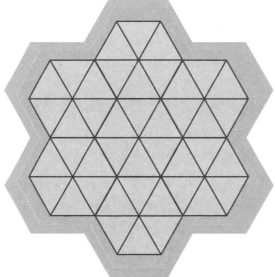

7

Twelve L-shapes like the ones here need to be inserted in the grid and each L has one hole in it.

There are three pieces of each of the four kinds shown here and any piece may be turned or flipped over before being put in the grid. No pieces of the same kind touch, even at a corner.

The pieces fit together so well that you cannot see any spaces between them; only the holes show.

Can you tell where the Ls are?

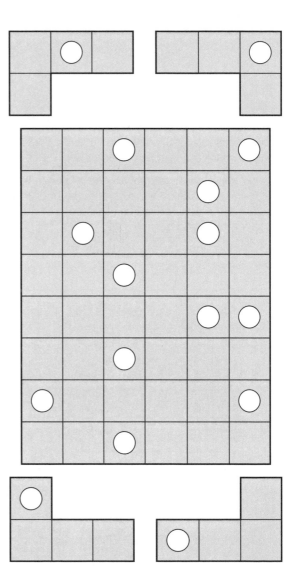

In this puzzle, an amateur coin collector has been out with his metal detector, searching for booty. He didn't have time to dig up all the coins he found, so has made a grid map, showing their locations, in the hope that if he loses the map, at least no-one else will understand it…

Those squares containing numbers are empty, but where a number appears in a square, it indicates how many coins are located in the squares (up to a maximum of eight) surrounding the numbered one, touching it at any corner or side. There is only one coin in any individual square.

Place a circle into every square containing a coin.

			1		3				
3		1				3			0
				1					
		4	2	0	1		2		0
					1		1	2	
3						2			1
1	1							4	
	2	3	2	2		4			
	2				3		4		

The grid should be filled with numbers from 1 to 6, so that each number appears just once in every row and column. The clues refer to the digit totals in the squares, eg A 1 2 3 = 6 means that the numbers in squares A1, A2 and A3 add up to 6.

1 B C D 6 = 13

2 A 2 3 = 8

3 B 1 2 = 7

4 C 2 3 = 7

5 D 3 4 5 = 6

6 E 5 6 = 6

7 F 5 6 = 8

8 D E 1 = 5

9 D E 2 = 9

10 E F 3 = 9

11 E F 4 = 8

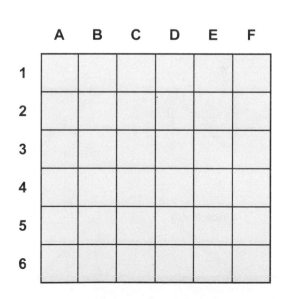

Each of the small squares in the grid below contains either A, B or C. Every row and column has exactly two of each letter. Can you tell the letter in each square?

Across

1 No two adjacent squares contain the same letter.
2 The Bs are both between the Cs.
3 The Bs are further right than the As.
4 No two adjacent squares contain the same letter.
5 The Cs are both between the Bs.
6 The As are both between the Cs.

Down

1 The Cs are in adjacent squares.
2 The Cs are lower than the As.
3 The As are in adjacent squares.
4 The Cs are both between the As.
5 Each B is directly next to and below a C.
6 Each A is directly next to and below a B.

	1	2	3	4	5	6
1						
2						
3						
4						
5						
6						

11

The object of this puzzle is to trace a single path from the top left corner to the bottom right corner of the grid, travelling through all of the cells in either a horizontal, vertical or diagonal direction.

Every cell must be entered once only and your path should take you through the numbers in the sequence 1-2-3-4-1-2-3-4, etc.

Can you find the way?

1	2	1	2	4	2	3	1
1	4	3	4	3	1	4	2
2	3	2	3	2	1	3	4
3	1	4	3	3	4	1	3
1	4	2	4	1	2	2	4
3	2	4	1	4	3	2	1
4	3	4	3	2	1	2	3
1	2	1	2	3	4	1	4

12

Can you place the vessels into the diagram? Some parts of vessels or sea squares have already been filled in. A number to the right or below a row or column refers to the number of occupied squares in that row or column.

Any vessel may be positioned horizontally or vertically, but no part of a vessel touches part of any other vessel, either horizontally, vertically or diagonally.

Empty Area of Sea: ≈

Aircraft Carrier: ◀■■■▶

Battleships: ◀■▶ ◀■■▶

Cruisers: ◀▶ ◀▶ ◀▶

Submarines: ● ● ● ●

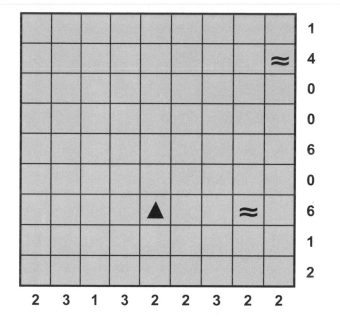

Grid row totals (top to bottom): 1, 4, 0, 0, 6, 0, 6, 1, 2

Grid column totals (left to right): 2, 3, 1, 3, 2, 2, 3, 2, 2

13

Can you fill each square in the bottom line with the correct digit?

Every square in the solution contains only one digit from each of the lettered lines above, although two or more squares in the solution may contain the same digit.

At the end of every row is a score, which shows:

  a the number of digits placed in the correct finishing position on the bottom line, as indicated by a tick; and

  b the number of digits which appear on the bottom line, but in a different position, as indicated by a cross.

				SCORE
5	1	0	5	✔✔
7	1	7	0	✔
4	7	5	2	✗✗✗
4	6	2	2	✗
3	3	1	2	✗
				✔✔✔✔

14

Draw a single continuous loop, by connecting the dots. No line may cross the path of another.

The figure inside each set of any four surrounding dots indicates the total number of surrounding lines.

```
    2  2  1  2
 2     2  2     1     0  2
          3
    1     3  2     0     0  2
 1              3        0
    1  0        0     3
    3  1        2  3  2  1  2
                      3  2
    2  2  2  2
             1  3        0  3
             2     0
 2  2     3     3  2  1     1
```

15

Each horizontal row and vertical column should contain different shapes and different numbers.

Every square will contain one number and one shape and no combination may be repeated anywhere else in the puzzle.

1   2   3   4   5

				1
⬡		◯	1	
	▢	2		⑤
		1	◯	4
②		☆		⬡3

16

Given that the letters are valued 1-26 according to their places in the alphabet, can you crack the mystery code to reveal the missing letter?

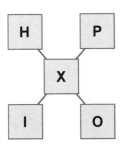

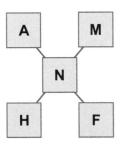

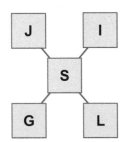

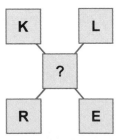

A set of dominoes is to be placed in four rows as shown below. The numbers indicate which values are shown on all the dominoes in each column and the relevant half of the domino in every row. Find out where each domino is placed by carefully comparing rows and columns to determine the possible positions of certain dominoes: for instance, if any column contains only one 6, then the domino 6/6 isn't in that column.

A set of dominoes consists of:

0/0, 0/1, 0/2, 0/3, 0/4, 0/5, 0/6, 1/1, 1/2, 1/3, 1/4, 1/5, 1/6, 2/2,

2/3, 2/4, 2/5, 2/6, 3/3, 3/4, 3/5, 3/6, 4/4, 4/5, 4/6, 5/5, 5/6, 6/6.

	2, 3, 4, 5, 5, 5, 5, 6.	1, 1, 1, 2, 3, 4, 4, 4.	0, 0, 1, 2, 3, 4, 4, 6.	1, 1, 3, 3, 3, 3, 5, 5.	2, 2, 2, 4, 5, 6, 6, 6.	0, 0, 0, 1, 2, 4, 6, 6.	0, 0, 0, 1, 2, 3, 5, 6.
1, 2, 2, 4, 4, 6, 6.							
1, 1, 1, 3, 3, 5, 5.							
0, 3, 3, 4, 4, 5, 5.							
0, 0, 0, 2, 3, 3, 6.							
0, 2, 2, 4, 5, 5, 6.							
0, 1, 2, 2, 5, 6, 6.							
0, 1, 1, 2, 3, 3, 4.							
0, 1, 4, 4, 5, 6, 6.							

18

Place the eight tiles into the puzzle grid so that all adjacent numbers on each tile match up. Tiles may be rotated through 360 degrees, but none may be flipped over.

4	1
3	1

3	2
4	2

3	4
3	4

3	1
2	2

1	2
2	3

3	1
2	1

4	3
3	2

2	2
3	3

1	4				
2	2				

19

Place all twelve of the pieces into the grid. Any may be rotated or flipped over, but none may touch another, not even diagonally. The numbers outside the grid refer to the number of consecutive black squares; and each block is separated from the others by at least one white square. For instance, '3 2' could refer to a row with none, one or more white squares, then three black squares, then at least one white square, then two more black squares, followed by any number of white squares.

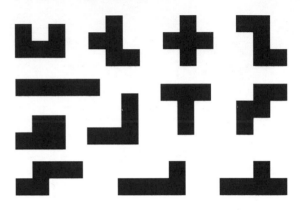

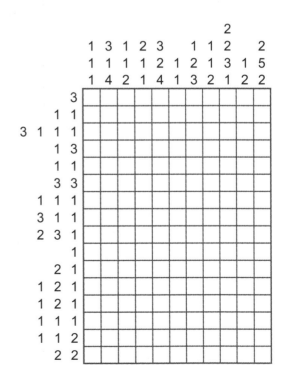

20

In the diagram below, which letter should replace the question mark?

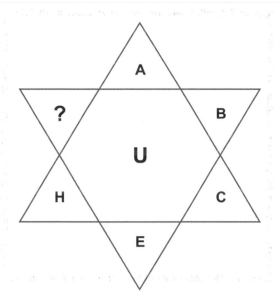

21

In the square below, change the positions of six numbers, one per horizontal row, vertical column and long diagonal line of six smaller squares, in such a way that the numbers in each row, column and long diagonal line total exactly 147. Any number may appear more than once in a row, column or line.

25	16	20	24	22	29
22	26	24	25	27	25
28	38	24	24	12	27
18	36	27	30	13	18
23	14	26	24	31	30
32	19	33	26	31	13

22

Every brick in this pyramid contains a number which is the sum of the two numbers below it, so that F=A+B, etc. Just work out the missing numbers!

O = 771

M =   N =

J = 275   K =   L =

F =   G =   H =   I = 142

A =   B =   C = 18   D = 46   E =

With the starter already given, can you fit all of the remaining listed numbers into this grid? Take care, this puzzle may not be as easy as it looks!

12	150	819	4248	82038
16	215	917	5327	94864
18	328 ✓	1346	5356	122956
26	347	1398	7145	170803
32	478	1442	7264	247794
36	535	1965	7404	251070
41	537	2279	7452	324785
45	541	2325	7626	363490
65	612	2378	8926	425655
84	710	3211	9482	454617
101	724	3619	30556	563117
116	750	3676	48692	818175

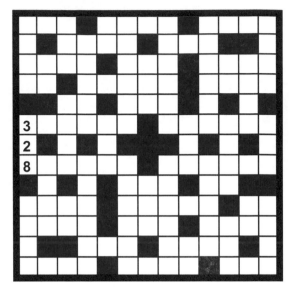

The chart gives directions to a hidden treasure behind the centre black square in the grid. Move the indicated number of spaces north, south, east and west (eg 4N means move four squares north) stopping at every square once only to arrive there. At which square should you start?

N

1E	3S	1S	1W	1W
1N	3E	2W	1S	1N
1S	3E	■	1W	2S
1S	1N	1E	2N	2W
2E	3N	1E	2W	1N

W ⇦   ⇨ E

S

Fill the grid so that every horizontal row and vertical column contains the numbers 1-5. The 'greater than' or 'less than' signs indicate where a number is larger or smaller than that in the neighbouring square.

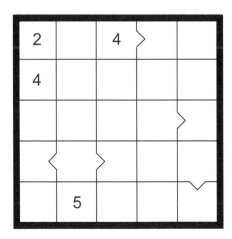

Each of the eight segments of the spider's web should be filled with a different number from 1 to 8, in such a way that every ring also contains a different number from 1 to 8.

The segments run from the outside of the spider's web to the centre, and the rings run all the way around.

Some numbers are already in place. Can you fill in the rest?

Every oval shape in this diagram contains a different letter of the alphabet from A to K inclusive. Use the clues to determine their locations. Reference in the clues to 'due' means in any location along the same horizontal or vertical line.

1   The A is next to and east of the G, which is due north of (but not next to) the F.

2   The B is due south of the E, which is due west of the G.

3   The D is due south of the I, which is next to and east of the K.

4   The H is next to the I, which is due west of the C, which is due north of the J.

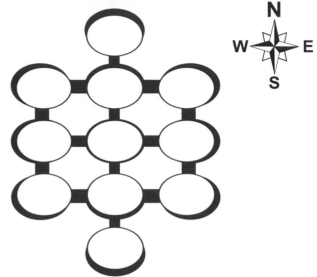

28

Fill the three empty circles with the symbols +, − and x in some order, to make a sum which totals the number in the centre. Each symbol must be used once and calculations are made in the direction of travel.

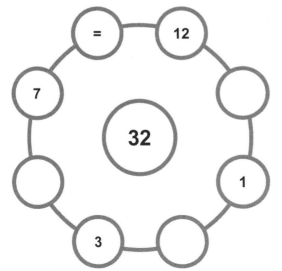

29

The numbers at the top and on the left side show the quantity of single-digit numbers (1-9) used in that row and column. The numbers at the bottom and on the right side show the sum of the digits. A number may appear more than once in a row or column, but no numbers are in squares that touch, even at a corner.

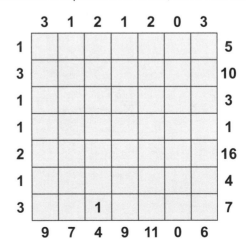

30

Using the numbers below, complete these six equations (three reading across and three reading downwards). Every number is used once.

	1		2		5	
6		7		8		9

	−		x	4	=	12
−	■	+	■	x		
	x		+		=	13
x	■	x	■	−		
	+	3	x		=	20
=		=		=		
56		33		30		

31

In the grid below, which number should replace the question mark?

19	13	42	77	26	38	16
15	9	38	73	22	34	12
11	5	34	69	18	30	8
7	1	30	65	14	26	4
12	6	35	70	19	31	9
17	11	40	75	24	36	14
22	16	45	80	?	41	19

32

When the box below is folded to form a cube, just one of the five options (A, B, C, D or E) can be produced. Which?

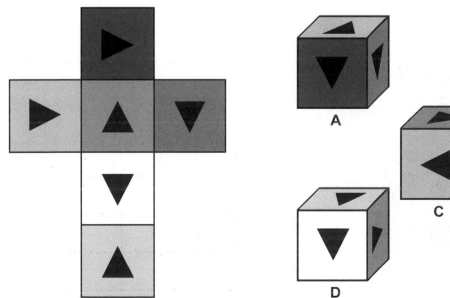

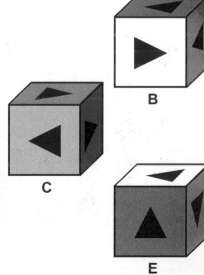

33

In this puzzle, an amateur coin collector has been out with his metal detector, searching for booty. He didn't have time to dig up all the coins he found, so has made a grid map, showing their locations, in the hope that if he loses the map, at least no-one else will understand it…

Those squares containing numbers are empty, but where a number appears in a square, it indicates how many coins are located in the squares (up to a maximum of eight) surrounding the numbered one, touching it at any corner or side. There is only one coin in any individual square.

Place a circle into every square containing a coin.

1				1		3	2		
	2				3				2
	0						2		
0		1			3	1	0		
		0				1		1	0
1		0			2				1
							3		
			2			4			3
2	2	4				3	2		
				4				1	

34

Each symbol stands for a different number. In order to reach the correct total at the end of each row and column, what is the value of the circle, cross, pentagon, square and star?

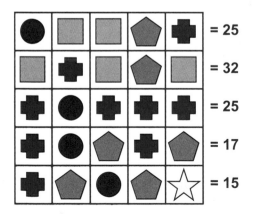

= 25
= 32
= 25
= 17
= 15

27   18   25   18   26

35

Every row and column of this grid should contain one each of the letters A, B, C, D, E and F. Each of the six shapes (marked by thicker lines) should also contain one each of the letters A, B, C, D, E and F. Can you complete the grid?

D			C	B	A
	F				E

36

A standard set of 28 dominoes has been laid out as shown. Can you draw in the edges of them all? The checkbox is provided as an aid and the domino already placed will help.

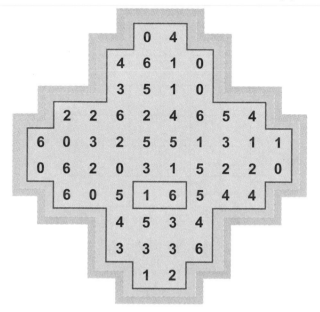

0-0	0-1	0-2	0-3	0-4	0-5	0-6

1-1	1-2	1-3	1-4	1-5	1-6	2-2
					✔	

2-3	2-4	2-5	2-6	3-3	3-4	3-5

3-6	4-4	4-5	4-6	5-5	5-6	6-6

37

Each of the small squares in the grid below contains either A, B or C. Every row and column has exactly two of each letter. Can you tell the letter in each square?

Across
1 No two adjacent squares contain the same letter.
2 The Cs are in adjacent squares.
3 The As are further right than the Bs.
4 The As are both between the Cs.
5 The Bs are further right than the As.
6 No two adjacent squares contain the same letter.

Down
1 Each B is directly next to and below an A.
2 The As are both between the Cs.
3 The As are lower than the Cs.
4 The As are both between the Bs.
5 The Cs are both between the Bs.
6 The Bs are both between the As.

Every row and column in this grid originally contained one heart, one club, one diamond, one spade and two blank squares, although not necessarily in that order.

Every symbol with a black arrow refers to the first of the four symbols encountered when travelling in the direction of the arrow. Every symbol with a white arrow refers to the second of the four symbols encountered in the direction of the arrow.

Can you complete the original grid?

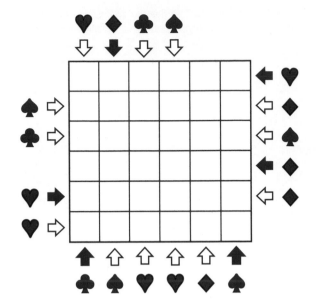

The blank squares below should be filled with whole numbers between 1 and 30 inclusive, any of which may occur more than once, or not at all.

The numbers in every horizontal row add up to the totals on the right, as do the two long diagonal lines; whilst those in every vertical column add up to the totals along the bottom.

							83
	26	5	8	12	16		111
24	5			14	2	10	89
	19	9	10	5	28	15	90
		13		15	27	19	103
	15	14	10	19		5	90
	14	3	21		23	2	84
18	30	20	6		17		110
114	110	86	72	83	127	85	89

A   is to   B

as   C   is to

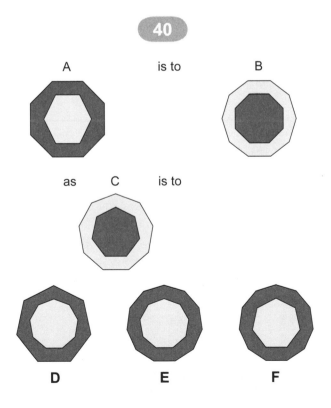

D   E   F

Can you place the hexagons into the grid, so that where any hexagon touches another along a straight line, the number in both triangles is the same? No rotation of any hexagon is allowed!

Twelve L-shapes like the ones here need to be inserted in the grid and each L has one hole in it.

There are three pieces of each of the four kinds shown here and any piece may be turned or flipped over before being put in the grid. No pieces of the same kind touch, even at a corner.

The pieces fit together so well that you cannot see any spaces between them; only the holes show.

Can you tell where the Ls are?

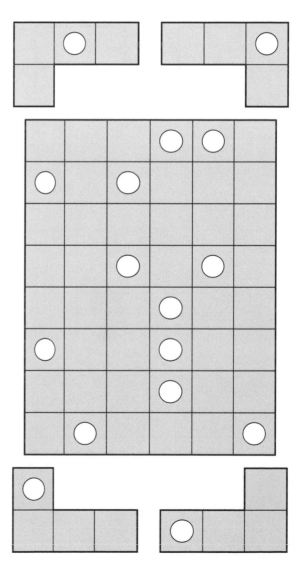

S E C T I O N 3

43

Which of the four lettered alternatives (A, B, C or D) fits most logically into the empty square?

29	11	16
12	2	12
19	40	13

12	5	26
10	32	13
15	17	24

17	16	37
18	10	19
20	14	3

?

9	28	16
14	7	12
42	16	10

A

9	28	16
14	7	12
42	15	10

B

9	29	16
13	7	12
41	15	10

C

9	29	16
12	7	13
41	16	10

D

44

Which four pieces can be fitted together to form an exact copy of this shape?

 **A**

B

C

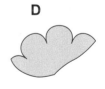 **D**

 E

 **F**

 G

 **H**

 **I**

 **J**

Can you place the vessels into the diagram? Some parts of vessels or sea squares have already been filled in. A number to the right or below a row or column refers to the number of occupied squares in that row or column.

Any vessel may be positioned horizontally or vertically, but no part of a vessel touches part of any other vessel, either horizontally, vertically or diagonally.

Empty Area of Sea: ≈

Aircraft Carrier: ◀■■▶

Battleships: ◀■▶ ◀■▶

Cruisers: ◀▶ ◀▶ ◀▶

Submarines: ● ● ● ●

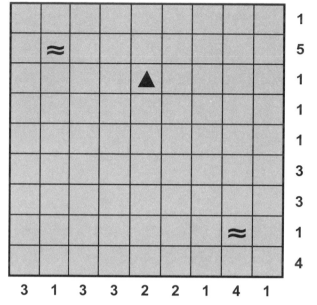

Can you fill each square in the bottom line with the correct digit?

Every square in the solution contains only one digit from each of the lettered lines above, although two or more squares in the solution may contain the same digit.

At the end of every row is a score, which shows:

  a the number of digits placed in the correct finishing position on the bottom line, as indicated by a tick; and

  b the number of digits which appear on the bottom line, but in a different position, as indicated by a cross.

				SCORE
2	1	2	4	✓ ✗ ✗
1	2	2	3	✓ ✗
5	6	1	6	✓ ✗
7	4	1	6	✓ ✗ ✗
0	7	1	6	✓ ✗
				✓✓✓✓

The grid should be filled with numbers from 1 to 6, so that each number appears just once in every row and column. The clues refer to the digit totals in the squares, eg A 1 2 3 = 6 means that the numbers in squares A1, A2 and A3 add up to 6.

1 B 5 6 = 7

2 C 2 3 = 8

3 D 1 2 = 3

4 E 3 4 5 = 13

5 F 4 5 6 = 6

6 B C 1 = 6

7 E F 2 = 5

8 A B 3 = 3

9 C D 4 = 7

10 C D 5 = 9

11 C D 6 = 7

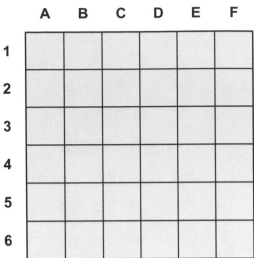

48

The object of this puzzle is to trace a single path from the top left corner to the bottom right corner of the grid, travelling through all of the cells in either a horizontal, vertical or diagonal direction.

Every cell must be entered once only and your path should take you through the numbers in the sequence 1-2-3-4-1-2-3-4, etc.

Can you find the way?

1	2	1	3	2	3	4	1
3	3	4	2	4	1	3	2
4	1	2	3	2	4	1	2
4	3	1	4	1	4	3	1
1	2	4	2	2	3	4	2
2	1	3	3	4	1	4	3
4	3	4	1	2	1	2	3
1	2	3	2	3	4	1	4

Draw a single continuous loop, by connecting the dots. No line may cross the path of another.

The figure inside each set of any four surrounding dots indicates the total number of surrounding lines.

Each horizontal row and vertical column should contain different shapes and different numbers.

Every square will contain one number and one shape and no combination may be repeated anywhere else in the puzzle.

1   2   3   4   5

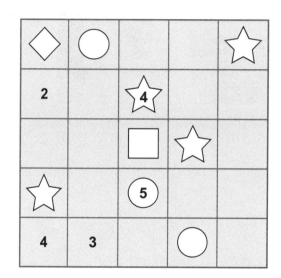

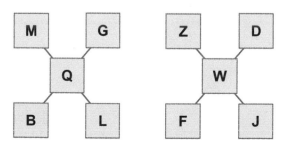

Given that the letters are valued 1-26 according to their places in the alphabet, can you crack the mystery code to reveal the missing letter?

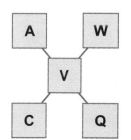

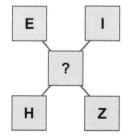

Which is the odd one out?

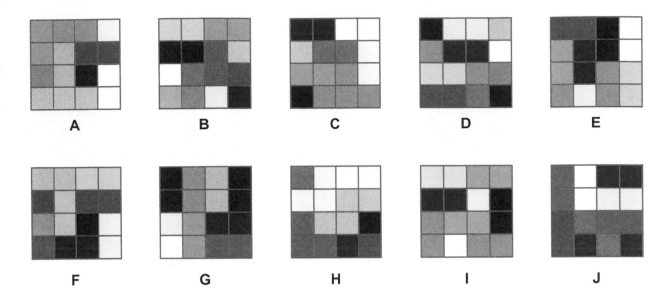

What number should be written on the unmarked yellow balloon?

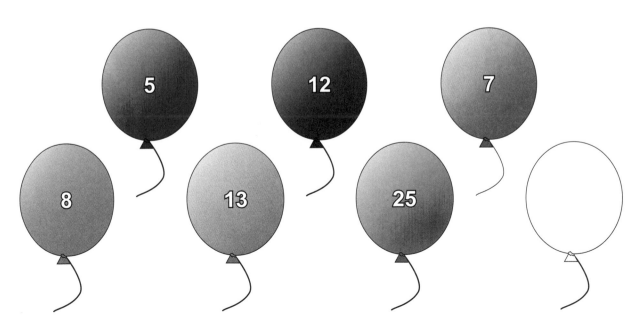

Place the eight tiles into the puzzle grid so that all adjacent numbers on each tile match up. Tiles may be rotated through 360 degrees, but none may be flipped over.

Place all twelve of the pieces into the grid. Any may be rotated or flipped over, but none may touch another, not even diagonally. The numbers outside the grid refer to the number of consecutive black squares; and each block is separated from the others by at least one white square. For instance, '3 2' could refer to a row with none, one or more white squares, then three black squares, then at least one white square, then two more black squares, followed by any number of white squares.

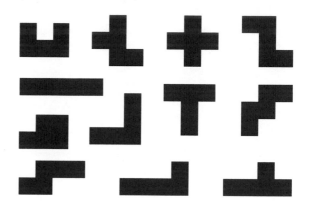

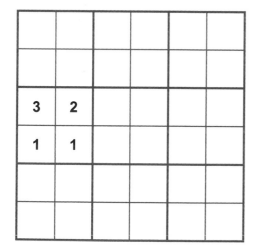

56

In the diagram below, which letter should replace the question mark?

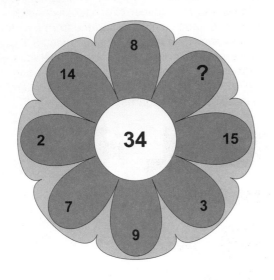

57

In the square below, change the positions of six numbers, one per horizontal row, vertical column and long diagonal line of six smaller squares, in such a way that the numbers in each row, column and long diagonal line total exactly 156. Any number may appear more than once in a row, column or line.

16	24	28	29	48	26
25	26	30	24	26	13
22	54	25	14	14	26
28	23	26	38	40	28
25	24	26	26	28	29
9	20	20	27	27	22

58

Every brick in this pyramid contains a number which is the sum of the two numbers below it, so that F=A+B, etc. Just work out the missing numbers!

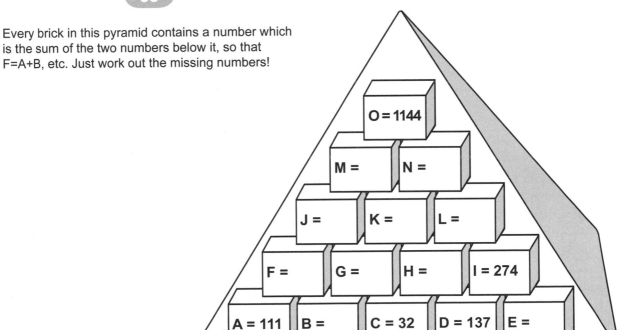

With the starter already given, can you fit all of the remaining listed numbers into this grid? Take care, this puzzle may not be as easy as it looks!

14	290	760	3904	83460
17	298	810	5651	92345
32	318	811	6702	93867
36	332	825	7184	95270
45	412	861	17446	153733
61	431	870	25336	204170
63	512	942	37830	209228
71	590	962	44822	504628
213	617	967	51836	590790
218 ✓	722	976	57110	640173
269	725	1125	59050	942478
283	748	3650	73524	956810

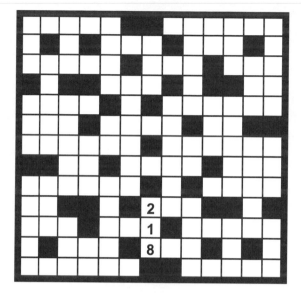

60

The chart gives directions to a hidden treasure behind the centre black square in the grid. Move the indicated number of spaces north, south, east and west (eg 4N means move four squares north) stopping at every square once only to arrive there. At which square should you start?

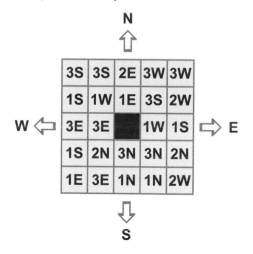

61

Fill the grid so that every horizontal row and vertical column contains the numbers 1-5. The 'greater than' or 'less than' signs indicate where a number is larger or smaller than that in the neighbouring square.

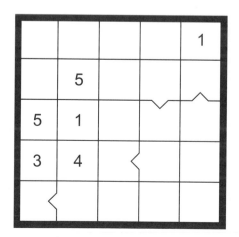

Each of the eight segments of the spider's web should be filled with a different number from 1 to 8, in such a way that every ring also contains a different number from 1 to 8.

The segments run from the outside of the spider's web to the centre, and the rings run all the way around.

Some numbers are already in place. Can you fill in the rest?

Every oval shape in this diagram contains a different letter of the alphabet from A to K inclusive. Use the clues to determine their locations. Reference in the clues to 'due' means in any location along the same horizontal or vertical line.

1 The B is next to and east of the I, which is next to and east of the C.

2 The D is next to and north of the K (which is not next to the H).

3 The E is further east than the A, which is further east than the F.

4 The J is next to and east of the G, which is due south of both the I and the K.

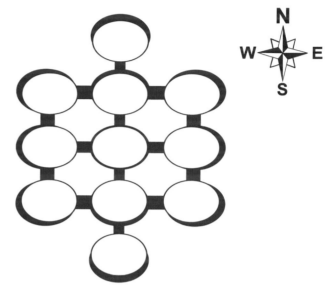

Fill the three empty circles with the symbols +, – and x in some order, to make a sum which totals the number in the centre. Each symbol must be used once and calculations are made in the direction of travel.

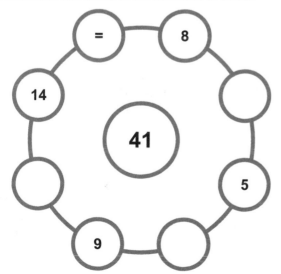

The numbers at the top and on the left side show the quantity of single-digit numbers (1-9) used in that row and column. The numbers at the bottom and on the right side show the sum of the digits. A number may appear more than once in a row or column, but no numbers are in squares that touch, even at a corner.

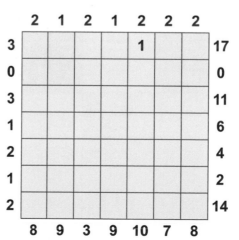

66

Using the numbers below, complete these six equations (three reading across and three reading downwards). Every number is used once.

```
1      3      4      5
   6      8      9
```

	+		−	2	=	11
x		−		x		
	x	7	−		=	1
+		x		+		
	−		x		=	16
=		=		=		
9		6		20		

67

In the grid below, which number should replace the question mark?

16	26	3	42	23	17	6
7	86	4	9	4	18	8
23	112	7	51	27	35	14
30	198	11	60	?	53	22
53	310	18	111	58	88	36
83	508	29	171	89	141	58
136	818	47	282	147	229	94

68

When the box below is folded to form a cube, just one of the five options (A, B, C, D or E) can be produced. Which?

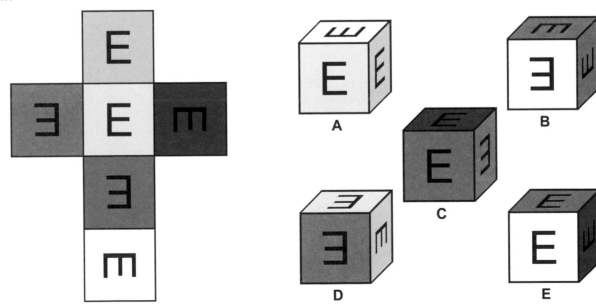

69

In this puzzle, an amateur coin collector has been out with his metal detector, searching for booty. He didn't have time to dig up all the coins he found, so has made a grid map, showing their locations, in the hope that if he loses the map, at least no-one else will understand it…

Those squares containing numbers are empty, but where a number appears in a square, it indicates how many coins are located in the squares (up to a maximum of eight) surrounding the numbered one, touching it at any corner or side. There is only one coin in any individual square.

Place a circle into every square containing a coin.

	3			1			1		1
1	3								
			4		4		2		
0		2		4		1		1	
	1						0		2
					3	1			
	1	0		2		2			2
2		1							3
			2	2	3		2		
	3							2	

70

Every row and column of this grid should contain one each of the letters A, B, C, D, E and F. Each of the six shapes (marked by thicker lines) should also contain one each of the letters A, B, C, D, E and F. Can you complete the grid?

			C	B	A
					D
	E				
F					

71

Each symbol stands for a different number. In order to reach the correct total at the end of each row and column, what is the value of the circle, cross, pentagon, square and star?

☆	■	✚	⬠	●	= 31
■	☆	■	⬠	☆	= 40
⬠	●	⬠	☆	✚	= 32
☆	☆	✚	✚	☆	= 29
☆	☆	●	●	●	= 36
= 42	= 40	= 23	= 32	= 31	

72

A standard set of 28 dominoes has been laid out as shown. Can you draw in the edges of them all? The checkbox is provided as an aid and the domino already placed will help.

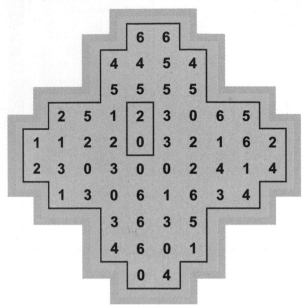

0-0	0-1	0-2	0-3	0-4	0-5	0-6
		✔				

1-1	1-2	1-3	1-4	1-5	1-6	2-2

2-3	2-4	2-5	2-6	3-3	3-4	3-5

3-6	4-4	4-5	4-6	5-5	5-6	6-6

73

Each of the small squares in the grid below contains either A, B or C. Every row and column has exactly two of each letter. Can you tell the letter in each square?

Across
1 The Bs are both between the As.
2 The Bs are further right than the Cs.
3 The Cs are both between the As.
4 The As are both between the Cs.
5 The Cs are both between the Bs.
6 The Cs are further right than the As.

Down
1 The Cs are in adjacent squares.
2 Each B is directly next to and below a C.
3 The Cs are lower than the Bs.
4 The As are in adjacent squares.
5 The As are lower than the Cs.
6 No two adjacent squares contain the same letter.

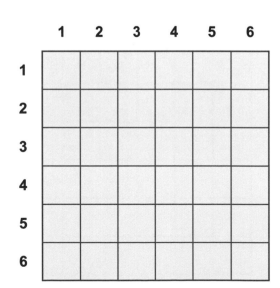

Every row and column in this grid originally contained one heart, one club, one diamond, one spade and two blank squares, although not necessarily in that order.

Every symbol with a black arrow refers to the first of the four symbols encountered when travelling in the direction of the arrow. Every symbol with a white arrow refers to the second of the four symbols encountered in the direction of the arrow.

Can you complete the original grid?

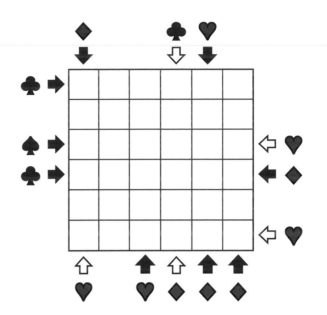

The blank squares below should be filled with whole numbers between 1 and 30 inclusive, any of which may occur more than once, or not at all.

The numbers in every horizontal row add up to the totals on the right, as do the two long diagonal lines; whilst those in every vertical column add up to the totals along the bottom.

							136
		3	21	6	22		97
20	8	21	30	3	6		102
5	6	17	5			4	85
13	7	17	29	29	15		138
			15	7	23	6	120
	23		3		27	15	124
23		17		14	11	20	141
119	122	125	129	84	130	98	122

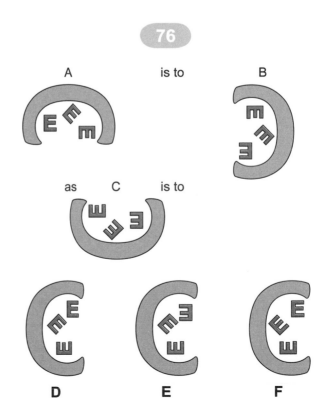

A is to B

as C is to

D   E   F

Can you place the hexagons into the grid, so that where any hexagon touches another along a straight line, the number in both triangles is the same? No rotation of any hexagon is allowed!

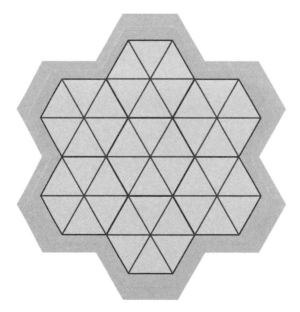

Twelve L-shapes like the ones here need to be inserted in the grid and each L has one hole in it.

There are three pieces of each of the four kinds shown here and any piece may be turned or flipped over before being put in the grid. No pieces of the same kind touch, even at a corner.

The pieces fit together so well that you cannot see any spaces between them; only the holes show.

Can you tell where the Ls are?

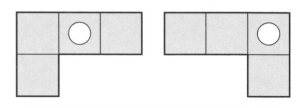
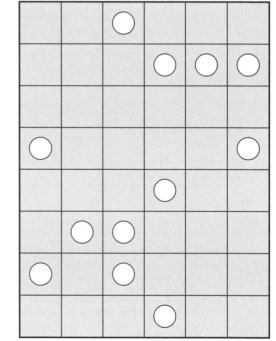
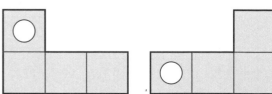

Given that scales A and B balance perfectly, how many hearts are needed to balance scale C?

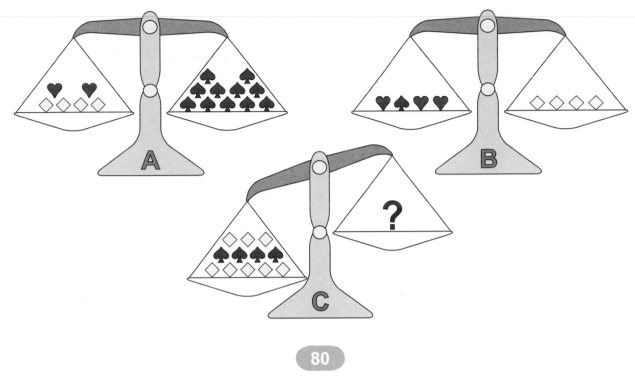

Which of the four lettered alternatives (A, B, C or D) fits most logically into the empty square?

12	19	17
9	4	1
6	5	11

3	1	10
12	12	6
12	15	13

15	6	11
5	10	14
7	12	4

?

4	9	16
15	5	3
8	13	10

A

17	3	12
7	13	5
2	12	12

B

17	7	3
2	11	13
8	10	13

C

8	10	17
15	8	3
4	10	8

D

S
E
C
T
I
O
N

3

123

81

The object of this puzzle is to trace a single path from the top left corner to the bottom right corner of the grid, travelling through all of the cells in either a horizontal, vertical or diagonal direction.

Every cell must be entered once only and your path should take you through the numbers in the sequence 1-2-3-4-1-2-3-4, etc.

Can you find the way?

1	1	2	3	2	3	1	2
3	2	4	3	4	1	4	3
1	4	2	4	3	2	4	1
4	2	1	3	2	4	1	2
1	3	3	4	1	4	2	3
3	2	1	2	1	1	3	4
4	2	3	4	3	4	2	1
1	2	4	1	2	3	3	4

82

The grid should be filled with numbers from 1 to 6, so that each number appears just once in every row and column. The clues refer to the digit totals in the squares, eg A 1 2 3 = 6 means that the numbers in squares A1, A2 and A3 add up to 6.

1 B C D 4 = 13

2 B C D 5 = 10

3 D E 6 = 5

4 A 3 4 = 10

5 B 1 2 = 10

6 C 1 2 = 8

7 D 1 2 = 4

8 E 3 4 = 7

9 F 3 4 = 6

10 E F 1 = 11

11 E F 2 = 6

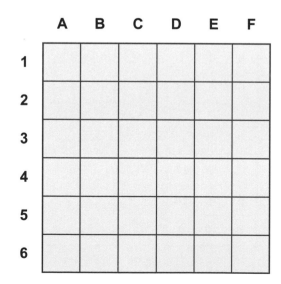

Can you fill each square in the bottom line with the correct digit?

Every square in the solution contains only one digit from each of the lettered lines above, although two or more squares in the solution may contain the same digit.

At the end of every row is a score, which shows:

a the number of digits placed in the correct finishing position on the bottom line, as indicated by a tick; and

b the number of digits which appear on the bottom line, but in a different position, as indicated by a cross.

SCORE

1	4	1	7	✓ ✗
1	4	4	5	✓ ✓
1	7	2	3	✓
0	0	5	0	✗ ✗
4	5	6	2	✗
				✓ ✓ ✓ ✓

Can you place the vessels into the diagram? Some parts of vessels or sea squares have already been filled in. A number to the right or below a row or column refers to the number of occupied squares in that row or column.

Any vessel may be positioned horizontally or vertically, but no part of a vessel touches part of any other vessel, either horizontally, vertically or diagonally.

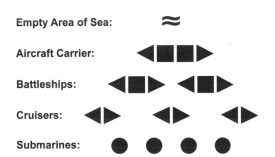

Empty Area of Sea: ≈

Aircraft Carrier: ◀■■▶

Battleships: ◀■▶ ◀■▶

Cruisers: ◀▶ ◀▶ ◀▶

Submarines: ● ● ● ●

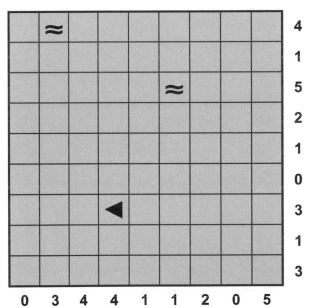

Column totals: 0 3 4 4 1 1 2 0 5

Row totals: 4 1 5 2 1 0 3 1 3

85

Draw a single continuous loop, by connecting the dots. No line may cross the path of another.

The figure inside each set of any four surrounding dots indicates the total number of surrounding lines.

```
.  .     .     .     .  .  .  .
   3     2     3     2  2
.  .  .  .  .  .  .  .  .  .  .
 2     0  2           0     2
.  .  .  .  .  .  .  .  .  .  .
      3     1                 2
.  .  .  .  .  .  .  .  .  .  .
 3  1           0  0     1
.  .  .  .  .  .  .  .  .  .  .
         1  2  2  2
.  .  .  .  .  .  .  .  .  .  .
   1     2        2  1  3
.  .  .  .  .  .  .  .  .  .  .
         0  1
.  .  .  .  .  .  .  .  .  .  .
      2  1  2        2
.  .  .  .  .  .  .  .  .  .  .
      2  1     2  2  0  1  2
.  .  .  .  .  .  .  .  .  .  .
 2     2
.  .  .  .  .  .  .  .  .  .  .
      1  3  2           1  2
.  .  .  .  .  .  .  .  .  .  .
   2     1     2  2  2
.  .  .  .  .  .  .  .  .  .  .
```

86

Each horizontal row and vertical column should contain different shapes and different numbers.

Every square will contain one number and one shape and no combination may be repeated anywhere else in the puzzle.

◇	○	☆	⬡	▢
1	2	3	4	5

3	1 (▢)	☆	2	
		3		◇
		2	1	
			○	3 (▢)
4				

87

Given that the letters are valued 1-26 according to their places in the alphabet, can you crack the mystery code to reveal the missing letter?

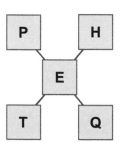

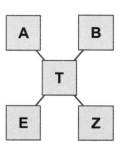

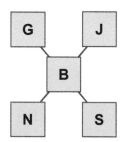

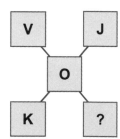

P H
E
T Q

A B
T
E Z

G J
B
N S

V J
O
K ?

A set of dominoes is to be placed in four rows as shown below. The numbers indicate which values are shown on all the dominoes in each column and the relevant half of the domino in every row. Find out where each domino is placed by carefully comparing rows and columns to determine the possible positions of certain dominoes: for instance, if any column contains only one 6, then the domino 6/6 isn't in that column.

A set of dominoes consists of:

0/0, 0/1, 0/2, 0/3, 0/4, 0/5, 0/6, 1/1, 1/2, 1/3, 1/4, 1/5, 1/6, 2/2,

2/3, 2/4, 2/5, 2/6, 3/3, 3/4, 3/5, 3/6, 4/4, 4/5, 4/6, 5/5, 5/6, 6/6.

	0, 1, 1, 1, 5, 5, 5, 6.	0, 1, 2, 3, 3, 3, 3, 3.	0, 1, 1, 4, 6, 6, 6, 6.	0, 0, 2, 4, 5, 5, 5, 6.	0, 1, 2, 3, 3, 4, 4, 6.	0, 1, 2, 4, 4, 4, 4, 5.	0, 2, 2, 2, 2, 3, 5, 6.
1, 2, 2, 5, 5, 6, 6. / 0, 1, 2, 2, 3, 3, 4.							
0, 0, 1, 1, 4, 6, 6. / 2, 3, 4, 4, 5, 5, 6.							
0, 1, 1, 4, 5, 5, 6. / 0, 1, 2, 3, 3, 5, 6.							
1, 2, 2, 3, 3, 5, 6. / 0, 0, 0, 3, 4, 4, 4.							

Place the eight tiles into the puzzle grid so that all adjacent numbers on each tile match up. Tiles may be rotated through 360 degrees, but none may be flipped over.

Place all twelve of the pieces into the grid. Any may be rotated or flipped over, but none may touch another, not even diagonally. The numbers outside the grid refer to the number of consecutive black squares; and each block is separated from the others by at least one white square. For instance, '3 2' could refer to a row with none, one or more white squares, then three black squares, then at least one white square, then two more black squares, followed by any number of white squares.

2	3
1	1

1	3
3	4

1	4
1	2

3	1
2	3

3	4
4	1

4	3
2	4

1	3
1	3

3	4
1	1

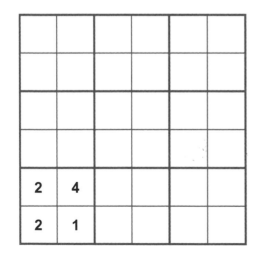

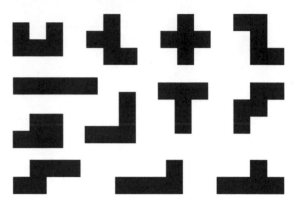

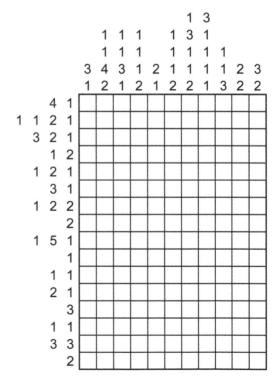

91

In the diagram below, which letter should replace the question mark?

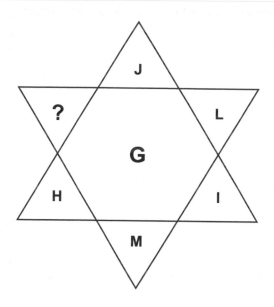

92

In the square below, change the positions of six numbers, one per horizontal row, vertical column and long diagonal line of six smaller squares, in such a way that the numbers in each row, column and long diagonal line total exactly 188. Any number may appear more than once in a row, column or line.

36	23	26	36	27	24
43	31	26	16	33	13
34	42	31	49	21	20
40	43	33	25	20	39
22	39	38	46	33	22
22	22	43	28	38	44

93

Every brick in this pyramid contains a number which is the sum of the two numbers below it, so that F=A+B, etc. Just work out the missing numbers!

O =

M = 552   N = 673

J =   K =   L =

F =   G =   H = 137   I =

A = 15   B =   C =   D = 120   E =

With the starter already given, can you fit all of the remaining listed numbers into this grid? Take care, this puzzle may not be as easy as it looks!

10	392	934	13330	73490
14	417	999	19029	76610
20	422	1739	24153	80090
29	497	2145	29540	83076
41	510	3477	30642	83760
63	526	3490	34674	85163
64	529 ✓	7152	35684	86022
91	640	8354	36780	91119
114	715	10549	39050	108020
161	831	10726	48237	410445
257	912	10800	71156	465760
378	924	12758	73045	600072

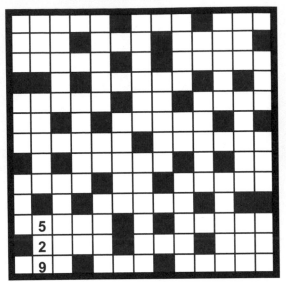

The chart gives directions to a hidden treasure behind the centre black square in the grid. Move the indicated number of spaces north, south, east and west (eg 4N means move four squares north) stopping at every square once only to arrive there. At which square should you start?

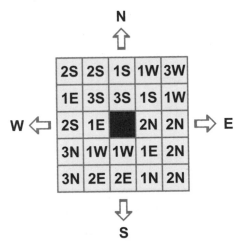

Fill the grid so that every horizontal row and vertical column contains the numbers 1-5. The 'greater than' or 'less than' signs indicate where a number is larger or smaller than that in the neighbouring square.

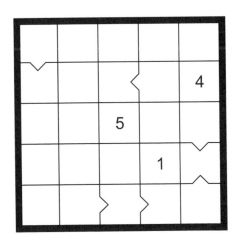

S E C T I O N

3

Each of the eight segments of the spider's web should be filled with a different number from 1 to 8, in such a way that every ring also contains a different number from 1 to 8.

The segments run from the outside of the spider's web to the centre, and the rings run all the way around.

Some numbers are already in place. Can you fill in the rest?

1

A standard set of 28 dominoes has been laid out as shown. Can you draw in the edges of them all? The checkbox is provided as an aid and the domino already placed will help.

0-0	0-1	0-2	0-3	0-4	0-5	0-6
			✓			

1-1	1-2	1-3	1-4	1-5	1-6	2-2

2-3	2-4	2-5	2-6	3-3	3-4	3-5

3-6	4-4	4-5	4-6	5-5	5-6	6-6

2

Given that scales A and B balance perfectly, how many diamonds are needed to balance scale C?

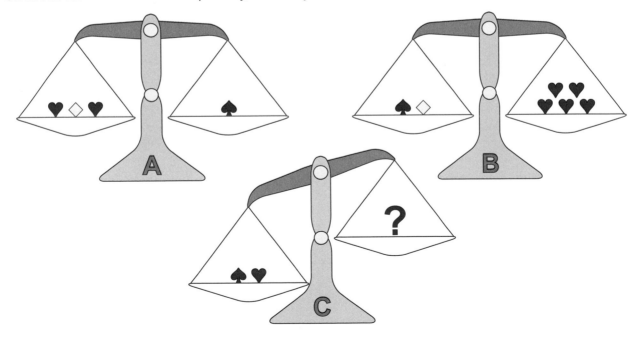

Every row and column in this grid originally contained one heart, one club, one diamond, one spade and two blank squares, although not necessarily in that order.

Every symbol with a black arrow refers to the first of the four symbols encountered when travelling in the direction of the arrow. Every symbol with a white arrow refers to the second of the four symbols encountered in the direction of the arrow.

Can you complete the original grid?

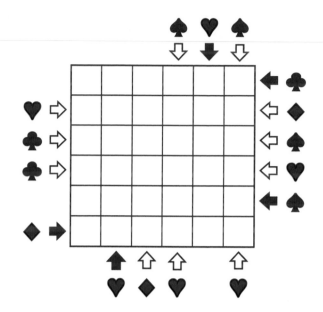

4

The blank squares below should be filled with whole numbers between 1 and 30 inclusive, any of which may occur more than once, or not at all.

The numbers in every horizontal row add up to the totals on the right, as do the two long diagonal lines; whilst those in every vertical column add up to the totals along the bottom.

							90
16			6	10	18	4	98
7	23	8			27	24	130
	6		21	10	22	21	104
		23	4	20	23		106
26	22		27	29	28	8	146
23			30	14		16	150
24		14		15	26	10	117
131	108	104	124	115	171	98	110

5

Draw in the missing hands on the final clock.

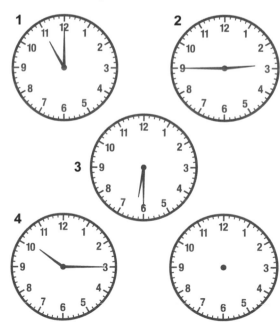

6

Can you place the hexagons into the grid, so that where any hexagon touches another along a straight line, the number in both triangles is the same? No rotation of any hexagon is allowed!

Hexagon 1: 1 / 5 3 / 6 2 / 4

Hexagon 2: 6 / 4 0 / 7 2 / 1

Hexagon 3: 1 / 2 4 / 0 3 / 7

Hexagon 4: 7 / 2 4 / 3 0 / 5

Hexagon 5: 1 / 0 7 / 3 5 / 2

Hexagon 6: 2 / 3 0 / 4 6 / 1

Hexagon 7: 5 / 2 3 / 6 4 / 1

7

Twelve L-shapes like the ones here need to be inserted in the grid and each L has one hole in it.

There are three pieces of each of the four kinds shown here and any piece may be turned or flipped over before being put in the grid. No pieces of the same kind touch, even at a corner.

The pieces fit together so well that you cannot see any spaces between them; only the holes show.

Can you tell where the Ls are?

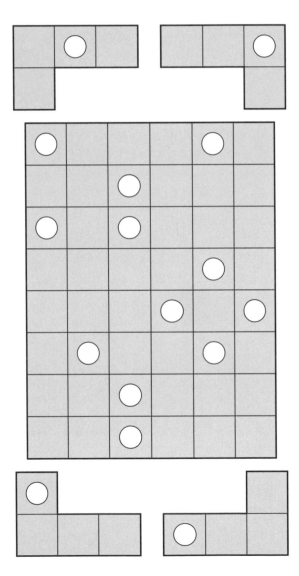

In this puzzle, an amateur coin collector has been out with his metal detector, searching for booty. He didn't have time to dig up all the coins he found, so has made a grid map, showing their locations, in the hope that if he loses the map, at least no-one else will understand it…

Those squares containing numbers are empty, but where a number appears in a square, it indicates how many coins are located in the squares (up to a maximum of eight) surrounding the numbered one, touching it at any corner or side. There is only one coin in any individual square.

Place a circle into every square containing a coin.

							1	0	
4		5		1					
2			2	1		2			
						1	1		1
1			1		3				
		1	1	2				2	
	0			2					
	2						4		3
		1					4		
1	2				3				3

The grid should be filled with numbers from 1 to 6, so that each number appears just once in every row and column. The clues refer to the digit totals in the squares, eg A 1 2 3 = 6 means that the numbers in squares A1, A2 and A3 add up to 6.

1 A 1 2 = 11

2 B 4 5 6 = 13

3 C 1 2 3 = 9

4 D 5 6 = 6

5 E 3 4 = 10

6 F 2 3 = 6

7 D E 1 = 4

8 D E 2 = 9

9 A B 3 = 9

10 C D 4 = 11

11 E F 5 = 11

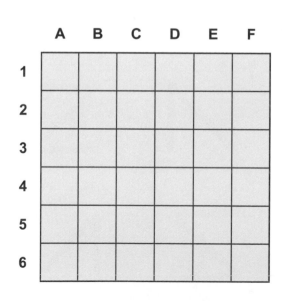

Each of the small squares in the grid below contains either A, B or C. Every row and column has exactly two of each letter. Can you tell the letter in each square?

Across

1 The As are further right than the Bs.
2 The Cs are further right than the As.
3 The As are both between the Cs.
4 The Cs are in adjacent squares.
5 The As are next to and right of the Bs.
6 The Bs are further right than the As.

Down

1 Each A is directly next to and below a C.
2 The Cs are both between the Bs.
3 No two adjacent squares contain the same letter.
4 The Bs are both between the As.
5 The As are both between the Cs.
6 The Bs are lower than the Cs.

	1	2	3	4	5	6
1						
2						
3						
4						
5						
6						

The object of this puzzle is to trace a single path from the top left corner to the bottom right corner of the grid, travelling through all of the cells in either a horizontal, vertical or diagonal direction.

Every cell must be entered once only and your path should take you through the numbers in the sequence 1-2-3-4-1-2-3-4, etc.

Can you find the way?

1	2	4	2	3	4	4	1
3	4	3	1	1	3	4	2
2	1	2	1	2	1	2	3
3	1	3	4	3	3	2	3
4	4	2	2	3	4	1	4
4	2	1	1	4	2	2	1
1	3	4	1	1	3	2	3
2	3	2	3	4	4	1	4

S E C T I O N

4

Can you place the vessels into the diagram? Some parts of vessels or sea squares have already been filled in. A number to the right or below a row or column refers to the number of occupied squares in that row or column.

Any vessel may be positioned horizontally or vertically, but no part of a vessel touches part of any other vessel, either horizontally, vertically or diagonally.

Empty Area of Sea: ≈

Aircraft Carrier: ◀■■▶

Battleships: ◀■▶ ◀■▶

Cruisers: ◀▶ ◀▶ ◀▶

Submarines: ● ● ● ●

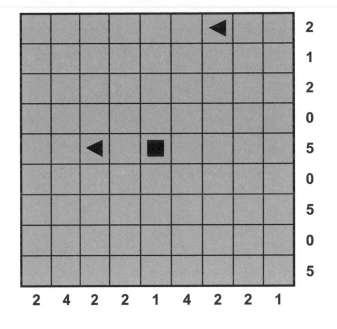

Column totals: 2 4 2 2 1 4 2 2 1

Row totals (top to bottom): 2 1 2 0 5 0 5 0 5

Can you fill each square in the bottom line with the correct digit?

Every square in the solution contains only one digit from each of the lettered lines above, although two or more squares in the solution may contain the same digit.

At the end of every row is a score, which shows:

a the number of digits placed in the correct finishing position on the bottom line, as indicated by a tick; and

b the number of digits which appear on the bottom line, but in a different position, as indicated by a cross.

SCORE

7	4	2	6	✓✓✓
6	2	2	4	✓✗
4	2	1	3	✗
5	6	6	4	✓✗
0	1	2	3	✓
				✓✓✓✓

14

Draw a single continuous loop, by connecting the dots. No line may cross the path of another.

The figure inside each set of any four surrounding dots indicates the total number of surrounding lines.

```
3  2      1           2        3

           2  0  1  1  1

2                          0

    2      1  2  3              1

    2                 3  3

       2  1  2        1         3

       0  0  1        2

       2  2  2                  3

       2                 1  0

          2  2  0  1

       1  1  1              0  3

    1              1  1
```

15

Each horizontal row and vertical column should contain different shapes and different numbers.

Every square will contain one number and one shape and no combination may be repeated anywhere else in the puzzle.

1   2   3   4   5

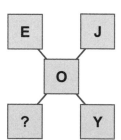

16

Given that the letters are valued 1-26 according to their places in the alphabet, can you crack the mystery code to reveal the missing letter?

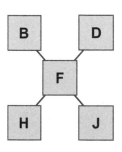

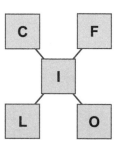

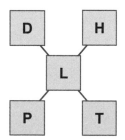

E   J

O

?   Y

A set of dominoes is to be placed in four rows as shown below. The numbers indicate which values are shown on all the dominoes in each column and the relevant half of the domino in every row. Find out where each domino is placed by carefully comparing rows and columns to determine the possible positions of certain dominoes: for instance, if any column contains only one 6, then the domino 6/6 isn't in that column.

A set of dominoes consists of:

0/0, 0/1, 0/2, 0/3, 0/4, 0/5, 0/6, 1/1, 1/2, 1/3, 1/4, 1/5, 1/6, 2/2,

2/3, 2/4, 2/5, 2/6, 3/3, 3/4, 3/5, 3/6, 4/4, 4/5, 4/6, 5/5, 5/6, 6/6.

0, 0, 0, 4, 5, 5, 6, 6.	0, 0, 1, 1, 2, 3, 4, 5.	1, 1, 2, 2, 3, 3, 6, 6.	0, 0, 2, 2, 4, 5, 5, 5.	0, 2, 3, 3, 4, 6, 6, 6.	2, 3, 3, 4, 4, 4, 5, 5.	1, 1, 1, 1, 2, 3, 4, 6.
0, 0, 1, 2, 3, 3, 4.						
0, 0, 1, 1, 3, 5, 6.						
0, 0, 2, 2, 5, 6, 6.						
1, 2, 2, 3, 3, 6, 6.						
0, 2, 2, 4, 4, 5, 5.						
0, 1, 1, 3, 4, 5, 5.						
1, 1, 2, 4, 5, 5, 6.						
3, 3, 4, 4, 4, 6, 6.						

18

Place the eight tiles into the puzzle grid so that all adjacent numbers on each tile match up. Tiles may be rotated through 360 degrees, but none may be flipped over.

3	1
1	3

3	3
1	4

4	3
4	1

4	4
4	3

1	1
1	3

1	3
3	3

3	3
4	4

1	3
1	2

2	2			
1	3			

19

Place all twelve of the pieces into the grid. Any may be rotated or flipped over, but none may touch another, not even diagonally. The numbers outside the grid refer to the number of consecutive black squares; and each block is separated from the others by at least one white square. For instance, '3 2' could refer to a row with none, one or more white squares, then three black squares, then at least one white square, then two more black squares, followed by any number of white squares.

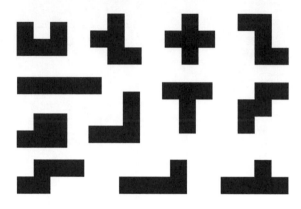

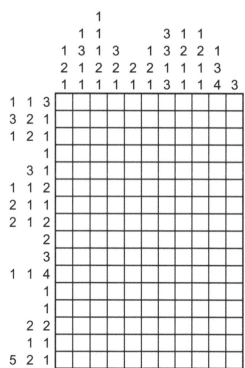

20

In the diagram below, which letter should replace the question mark?

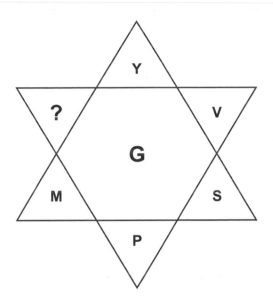

21

In the square below, change the positions of six numbers, one per horizontal row, vertical column and long diagonal line of six smaller squares, in such a way that the numbers in each row, column and long diagonal line total exactly 152. Any number may appear more than once in a row, column or line.

17	14	18	28	44	25
36	25	22	15	44	27
32	34	25	15	8	28
27	37	27	35	13	25
13	19	21	37	29	26
39	13	32	16	31	15

22

Every brick in this pyramid contains a number which is the sum of the two numbers below it, so that F=A+B, etc. Just work out the missing numbers!

O = 634

M =   N = 442

J =   K =   L =

F =   G =   H =   I = 224

A = 53   B =   C =   D = 85   E =

With the starter already given, can you fit all of the remaining listed numbers into this grid? Take care, this puzzle may not be as easy as it looks!

15	413	756	5557	31115
25	415	758	6010	36014
27	424	823	7125	37455
28	450	856	8175	38640
54	467	906	9050	64430
81	545	954	9437	71745
120	567	1040	13756	78616
140	574 ✓	1647	21213	95020
167	658	2117	22619	165467
325	719	2332	26456	348880
332	723	3326	29045	587775
412	728	3915	30459	895855

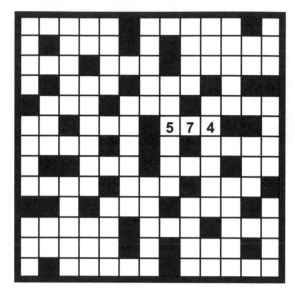

The chart gives directions to a hidden treasure behind the centre black square in the grid. Move the indicated number of spaces north, south, east and west (eg 4N means move four squares north) stopping at every square once only to arrive there. At which square should you start?

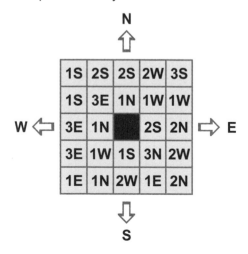

Fill the grid so that every horizontal row and vertical column contains the numbers 1-5. The 'greater than' or 'less than' signs indicate where a number is larger or smaller than that in the neighbouring square.

S
E
C
T
I
O
N

4

142

Each of the eight segments of the spider's web should be filled with a different number from 1 to 8, in such a way that every ring also contains a different number from 1 to 8.

The segments run from the outside of the spider's web to the centre, and the rings run all the way around.

Some numbers are already in place. Can you fill in the rest?

S E C T I O N

4

Every oval shape in this diagram contains a different letter of the alphabet from A to K inclusive. Use the clues to determine their locations. Reference in the clues to 'due' means in any location along the same horizontal or vertical line.

1   The B is due east of both the A and the G.

2   The C is next to the F, which is further east and further south than the E.

3   The G is next to and north of the I, which is next to and west of the C.

4   The J is due east of the H, due west of the K and due north of the D.

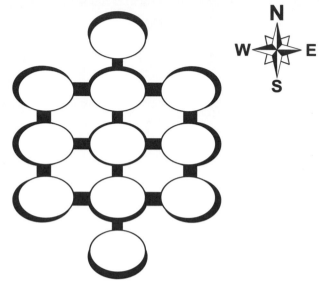

28

Fill the three empty circles with the symbols +, − and x in some order, to make a sum which totals the number in the centre. Each symbol must be used once and calculations are made in the direction of travel.

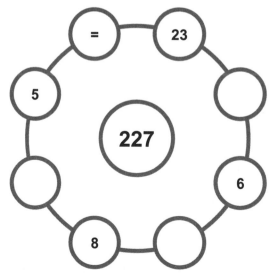

227

= 23 5 6 8

29

The numbers at the top and on the left side show the quantity of single-digit numbers (1-9) used in that row and column. The numbers at the bottom and on the right side show the sum of the digits. A number may appear more than once in a row or column, but no numbers are in squares that touch, even at a corner.

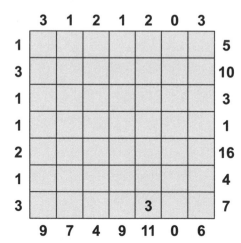

	3	1	2	1	2	0	3	
1								5
3								10
1								3
1								1
2								16
1								4
3				3				7
	9	7	4	9	11	0	6	

Using the numbers below, complete these six equations (three reading across and three reading downwards). Every number is used once.

```
      1       3       5
  6       7       8       9
┌─────┬─────┬─────┬─────┬─────┬─────┐
│     │  +  │     │  −  │  2  │  =  │ 14
├─────┼─────┼─────┼─────┼─────┤
│  −  │ ██  │  +  │ ██  │  x  │
├─────┼─────┼─────┼─────┼─────┤
│  4  │  −  │     │  x  │     │  =  │  6
├─────┼─────┼─────┼─────┼─────┤
│  +  │ ██  │  x  │ ██  │  +  │
├─────┼─────┼─────┼─────┼─────┤
│     │  x  │     │  +  │     │  =  │ 41
├─────┼─────┼─────┼─────┼─────┤
│  =  │     │  =  │     │  =  │
├─────┼─────┼─────┼─────┼─────┤
│ 11  │     │ 60  │     │ 13  │
└─────┴─────┴─────┴─────┴─────┘
```

In the grid below, which numbers should replace the question marks?

4	73	70	67	64	61	58
7	76	121	118	115	112	55
10	79	124	?	142	109	52
13	82	127	?	139	106	49
16	85	130	133	136	103	46
19	88	91	94	97	100	43
22	25	28	31	34	37	40

When the box below is folded to form a cube, just one of the five options (A, B, C, D or E) can be produced. Which?

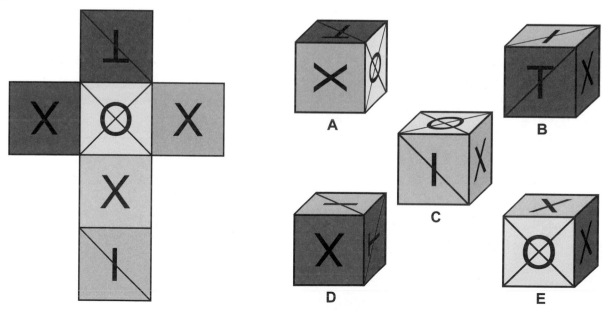

A

B

C

D

E

33

In this puzzle, an amateur coin collector has been out with his metal detector, searching for booty. He didn't have time to dig up all the coins he found, so has made a grid map, showing their locations, in the hope that if he loses the map, at least no-one else will understand it…

Those squares containing numbers are empty, but where a number appears in a square, it indicates how many coins are located in the squares (up to a maximum of eight) surrounding the numbered one, touching it at any corner or side. There is only one coin in any individual square.

Place a circle into every square containing a coin.

	3		2			1			
	4			2			2	4	2
	3		2		2				
2		1		3					
				2	1		0	2	
2		3					0		1
						1			
0				1					2
		0	1					3	
	1			2		2	2		

34

Each symbol stands for a different number. In order to reach the correct total at the end of each row and column, what is the value of the circle, cross, pentagon, square and star?

●	✚	●	⬠	☆	= 16
⬠	■	☆	✚	⬠	= 20
✚	☆	⬠	●	■	= 17
✚	✚	✚	■	☆	= 18
●	☆	■	⬠	✚	= 17
=12	=22	=17	=14	=23	

35

Every row and column of this grid should contain one each of the letters A, B, C, D, E and F. Each of the six shapes (marked by thicker lines) should also contain one each of the letters A, B, C, D, E and F. Can you complete the grid?

			C	B	A
			D		
	F				E

A standard set of 28 dominoes has been laid out as shown. Can you draw in the edges of them all? The checkbox is provided as an aid and the domino already placed will help.

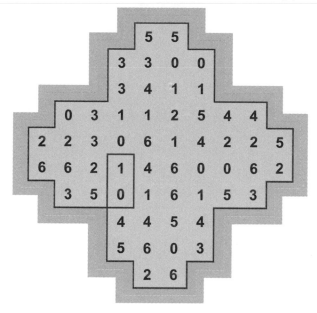

0-0	0-1	0-2	0-3	0-4	0-5	0-6
	✔					

1-1	1-2	1-3	1-4	1-5	1-6	2-2

2-3	2-4	2-5	2-6	3-3	3-4	3-5

3-6	4-4	4-5	4-6	5-5	5-6	6-6

Each of the small squares in the grid below contains either A, B or C. Every row and column has exactly two of each letter. Can you tell the letter in each square?

Across
1 No two adjacent squares contain the same letter.
2 The As are further right than the Cs.
3 The As are both between the Bs.
4 The Cs are in adjacent squares.
5 The Cs are both between the As.
6 The As are in adjacent squares.

Down
1 The Cs are in adjacent squares.
2 The Cs are in adjacent squares.
3 Each C is directly next to and below an A.
4 No two adjacent squares contain the same letter.
5 The Bs are both between the Cs.
6 The Cs are lower than the Bs.

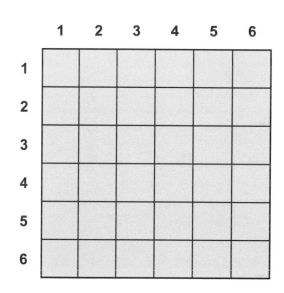

38

Every row and column in this grid originally contained one heart, one club, one diamond, one spade and two blank squares, although not necessarily in that order.

Every symbol with a black arrow refers to the first of the four symbols encountered when travelling in the direction of the arrow. Every symbol with a white arrow refers to the second of the four symbols encountered in the direction of the arrow.

Can you complete the original grid?

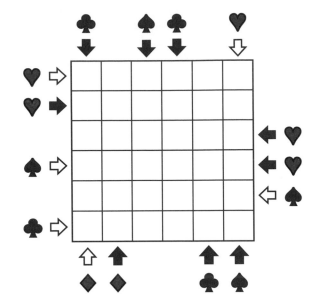

39

The blank squares below should be filled with whole numbers between 1 and 30 inclusive, any of which may occur more than once, or not at all.

The numbers in every horizontal row add up to the totals on the right, as do the two long diagonal lines; whilst those in every vertical column add up to the totals along the bottom.

40

							120
13	27		10	1	18	14	95
	13	5	30				136
28		10	3	7	9	29	97
	28			1	23	6	132
17		18	15	18	14		96
22			10	18	13	10	98
2	30	19		18		6	96
115	137	99	115	86	110	88	102

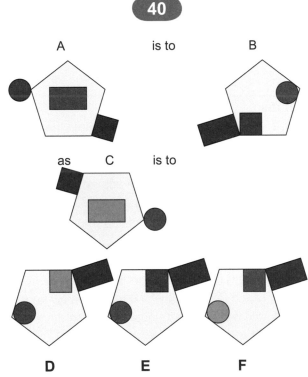

Can you place the hexagons into the grid, so that where any hexagon touches another along a straight line, the number in both triangles is the same? No rotation of any hexagon is allowed!

Twelve L-shapes like the ones here need to be inserted in the grid and each L has one hole in it.

There are three pieces of each of the four kinds shown here and any piece may be turned or flipped over before being put in the grid. No pieces of the same kind touch, even at a corner.

The pieces fit together so well that you cannot see any spaces between them; only the holes show.

Can you tell where the Ls are?

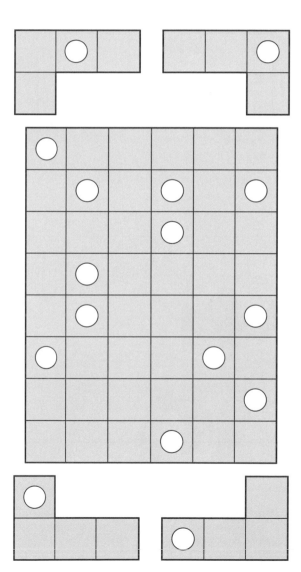

Which of the four lettered alternatives (A, B, C or D) fits most logically into the empty square?

F	M	Q
G	P	N
L	R	J

G	L	R
F	O	M
M	Q	K

H	K	S
E	N	L
N	P	L

?

J	I	T
D	L	K
O	P	N

A

I	J	T
D	M	K
O	O	M

B

I	J	T
D	L	K
O	O	M

C

J	I	T
D	M	K
O	P	N

D

Which four pieces can be fitted together to form an exact copy of this shape?

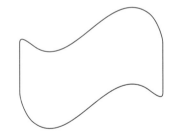

A
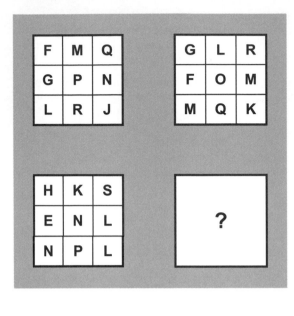

B

C

E
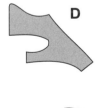

D

F

H
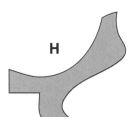

I

J

G

S
E
C
T
I
O
N

4

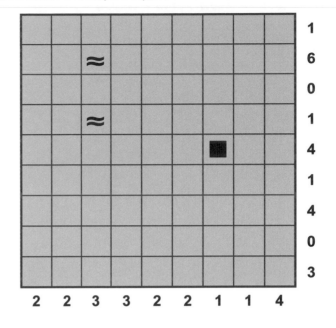

45

Can you place the vessels into the diagram? Some parts of vessels or sea squares have already been filled in. A number to the right or below a row or column refers to the number of occupied squares in that row or column.

Any vessel may be positioned horizontally or vertically, but no part of a vessel touches part of any other vessel, either horizontally, vertically or diagonally.

Empty Area of Sea: ≈

Aircraft Carrier: ◀■■▶

Battleships: ◀■▶ ◀■▶

Cruisers: ◀▶ ◀▶ ◀▶

Submarines: ● ● ● ●

Column totals: 2 2 3 3 2 2 1 1 4

Row totals: 1 6 0 1 4 1 4 0 3

46

Can you fill each square in the bottom line with the correct digit?

Every square in the solution contains only one digit from each of the lettered lines above, although two or more squares in the solution may contain the same digit.

At the end of every row is a score, which shows:

a the number of digits placed in the correct finishing position on the bottom line, as indicated by a tick; and

b the number of digits which appear on the bottom line, but in a different position, as indicated by a cross.

SCORE

2	7	2	1	✔✔
1	6	5	4	✘
6	4	0	0	✔
5	0	0	2	✔✘
3	0	0	1	✔✔
				✔✔✔✔

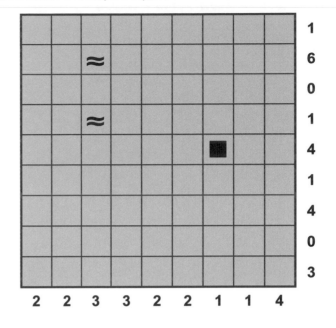

151

The grid should be filled with numbers from 1 to 6, so that each number appears just once in every row and column. The clues refer to the digit totals in the squares, eg A 1 2 3 = 6 means that the numbers in squares A1, A2 and A3 add up to 6.

1 B C D 5 = 13

2 C D 6 = 7

3 A 5 6 = 11

4 B 1 2 3 = 11

5 C 1 2 = 9

6 D 1 2 = 3

7 E 5 6 = 7

8 F 4 5 = 5

9 E F 1 = 9

10 E F 2 = 11

11 C D 3 = 6

	A	B	C	D	E	F
1						
2						
3						
4						
5						
6						

The object of this puzzle is to trace a single path from the top left corner to the bottom right corner of the grid, travelling through all of the cells in either a horizontal, vertical or diagonal direction.

Every cell must be entered once only and your path should take you through the numbers in the sequence 1-2-3-4-1-2-3-4, etc.

Can you find the way?

1	2	1	2	3	2	3	1
1	3	4	3	4	1	4	2
2	4	2	1	4	3	2	3
1	3	4	3	2	1	1	4
2	4	2	1	3	4	2	3
3	4	4	3	2	4	1	4
2	1	1	2	3	1	2	1
3	4	3	4	1	2	3	4

49

Draw a single continuous loop, by connecting the dots. No line may cross the path of another.

The figure inside each set of any four surrounding dots indicates the total number of surrounding lines.

```
 1     3  1        3
  2  2     1     0     1  2
  3  1  2     1        0
1     0  2     3     1
     1  2                 1
     1  2  2     1     3
1                 3
     2  2              0
        2  0        1     2
  2        1  2  2  1     1
     2  2           2  1
1              2     3  3  2
```

50

Each horizontal row and vertical column should contain different shapes and different numbers.

Every square will contain one number and one shape and no combination may be repeated anywhere else in the puzzle.

1   2   3   4   5

	5			
3		⬡		
	2	5		
☆			1	2
	◯		☆	

51

Given that the letters are valued 1-26 according to their places in the alphabet, can you crack the mystery code to reveal the missing letter?

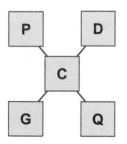

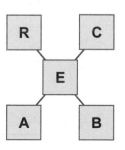

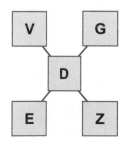

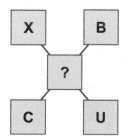

Which is the odd one out?

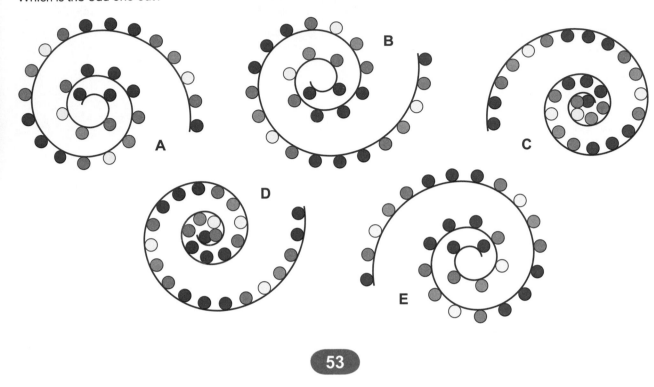

A B C D E

Which of the alternatives (A, B, C or D) is the missing piece?

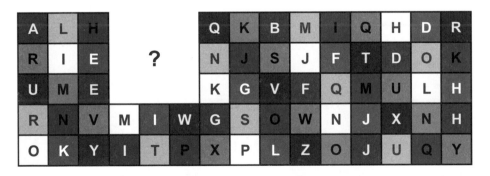

A B C D

54

Place the eight tiles into the puzzle grid so that all adjacent numbers on each tile match up. Tiles may be rotated through 360 degrees, but none may be flipped over.

2	4
2	3

4	2
1	4

3	2
3	2

2	4
3	4

2	3
2	2

2	4
2	2

2	2
1	2

4	1
3	3

				2	3
				4	1

55

Place all twelve of the pieces into the grid. Any may be rotated or flipped over, but none may touch another, not even diagonally. The numbers outside the grid refer to the number of consecutive black squares; and each block is separated from the others by at least one white square. For instance, '3 2' could refer to a row with none, one or more white squares, then three black squares, then at least one white square, then two more black squares, followed by any number of white squares.

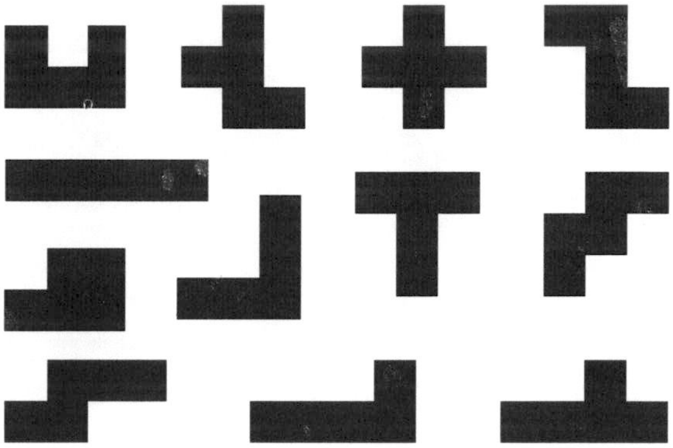

	3 3	2 1 1	3 1 2 1	1 1 2 2 2	1 1 1	1 1 3 1	1 1 1 1	2 3	2 2 1	1 2 5	2 2
2											
1											
2 3											
2											
4 1											
1 3											
1 1											
2 4 1											
1 1 3											
1 1 1											
3											
2 1 1											
2 1											
1 1 1 1											
1 3 1											
3 1 1											

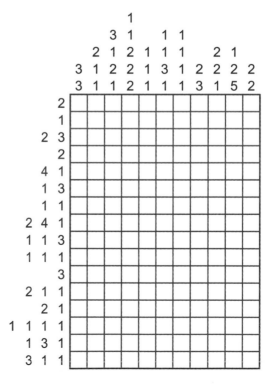

56

In the diagram below, which letter should replace the question mark?

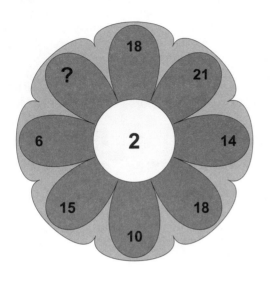

57

In the square below, change the positions of six numbers, one per horizontal row, vertical column and long diagonal line of six smaller squares, in such a way that the numbers in each row, column and long diagonal line total exactly 179. Any number may appear more than once in a row, column or line.

19	15	19	30	57	21
31	29	38	23	34	25
41	44	29	27	34	29
24	45	48	31	23	22
33	49	25	35	22	33
32	15	34	15	34	9

58

Every brick in this pyramid contains a number which is the sum of the two numbers below it, so that F=A+B, etc. Just work out the missing numbers!

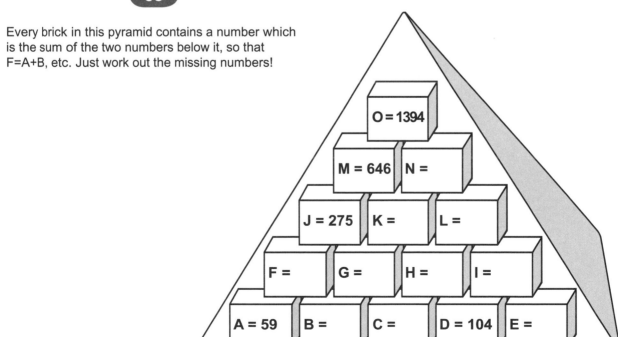

With the starter already given, can you fit all of the remaining listed numbers into this grid? Take care, this puzzle may not be as easy as it looks!

12	158	968	18826	71287
13	271	978	18847	71436
16	299	2868	19423	83135
20	346	3146	29444	96207
31	479	4429	35130	157460
32	635	4679	37657	261110
40	637	5228	54814	272080
43	678	6503	60298	420719
51	832 ✓	7592	62085	464711
57	861	7719	62418	475195
82	901	9561	65064	625250
84	944	9678	67131	768860

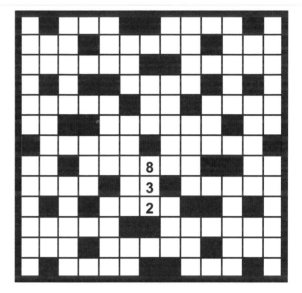

The chart gives directions to a hidden treasure behind the centre black square in the grid. Move the indicated number of spaces north, south, east and west (eg 4N means move four squares north) stopping at every square once only to arrive there. At which square should you start?

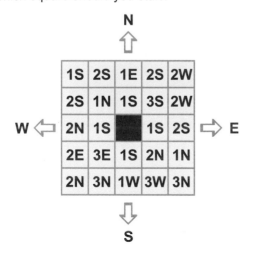

Fill the grid so that every horizontal row and vertical column contains the numbers 1-5. The 'greater than' or 'less than' signs indicate where a number is larger or smaller than that in the neighbouring square.

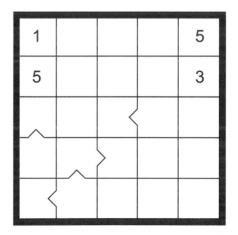

157

Each of the eight segments of the spider's web should be filled with a different number from 1 to 8, in such a way that every ring also contains a different number from 1 to 8.

The segments run from the outside of the spider's web to the centre, and the rings run all the way around.

Some numbers are already in place. Can you fill in the rest?

Every oval shape in this diagram contains a different letter of the alphabet from A to K inclusive. Use the clues to determine their locations. Reference in the clues to 'due' means in any location along the same horizontal or vertical line.

1 The A is next to and south of the D, which is due east of both the E and the G.

2 The B is further east than the F.

3 The I is next to and north of the K, which is next to and north of the E.

4 The J is next to and west of the C, which is further north than the H.

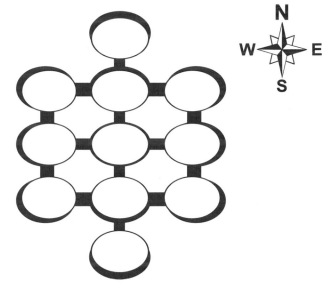

64

Fill the three empty circles with the symbols +, − and x in some order, to make a sum which totals the number in the centre. Each symbol must be used once and calculations are made in the direction of travel.

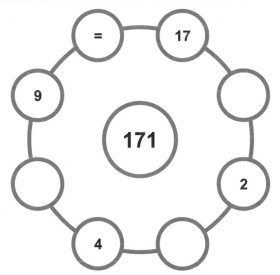

65

The numbers at the top and on the left side show the quantity of single-digit numbers (1-9) used in that row and column. The numbers at the bottom and on the right side show the sum of the digits. A number may appear more than once in a row or column, but no numbers are in squares that touch, even at a corner.

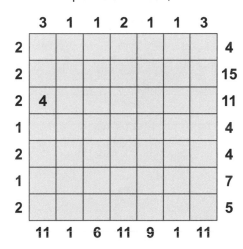

66

Using the numbers below, complete these six equations (three reading across and three reading downwards). Every number is used once.

1   2   3   4
5   6   7   8

	−		x		=	35
−	■	+	■	+		
	x	9	+		=	33
+	■	−	■	x		
	+		−		=	9
=		=		=		
12		6		22		

67

In the grid below, which number should replace the question mark?

4	24	120	480	1440	2880
7	42	210	840	2520	5040
2	12	60	240	720	1440
3	18	90	360	1080	2160
5	30	150	600	1800	3600
6	36	180	720	2160	?

68

When the box below is folded to form a cube, just one of the five options (A, B, C, D or E) can be produced. Which?

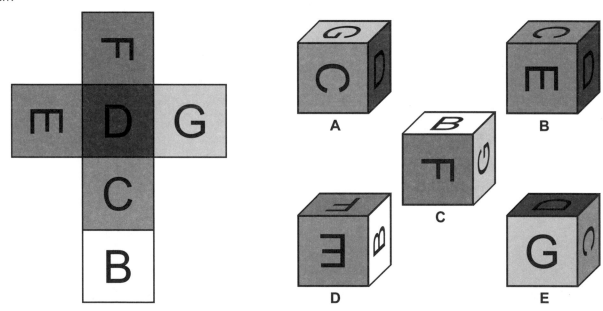

A

B

C

D

E

In this puzzle, an amateur coin collector has been out with his metal detector, searching for booty. He didn't have time to dig up all the coins he found, so has made a grid map, showing their locations, in the hope that if he loses the map, at least no-one else will understand it…

Those squares containing numbers are empty, but where a number appears in a square, it indicates how many coins are located in the squares (up to a maximum of eight) surrounding the numbered one, touching it at any corner or side. There is only one coin in any individual square.

Place a circle into every square containing a coin.

0	1			3		3		3	2
	2	3					5		
				5				3	
1	3					2			
	3			4				2	
		3							
		3	3			0			2
	1	1					0		
			3	2	2				0
1						0			

Every row and column of this grid should contain one each of the letters A, B, C, D, E and F. Each of the six shapes (marked by thicker lines) should also contain one each of the letters A, B, C, D, E and F. Can you complete the grid?

		C		B	A
				E	D
F					

Each symbol stands for a different number. In order to reach the correct total at the end of each row and column, what is the value of the circle, cross, pentagon, square and star?

Rows: = 11, = 15, = 14, = 18, = 12

Columns: = 15, = 11, = 14, = 15, = 15

A standard set of 28 dominoes has been laid out as shown. Can you draw in the edges of them all? The checkbox is provided as an aid and the domino already placed will help.

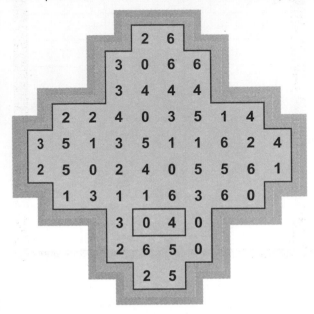

0-0	0-1	0-2	0-3	0-4	0-5	0-6
				✓		

1-1	1-2	1-3	1-4	1-5	1-6	2-2

2-3	2-4	2-5	2-6	3-3	3-4	3-5

3-6	4-4	4-5	4-6	5-5	5-6	6-6

73

Each of the small squares in the grid below contains either A, B or C. Every row and column has exactly two of each letter. Can you tell the letter in each square?

Across

1 The As are in adjacent squares.
2 The As are further right than the Bs.
3 No two adjacent squares contain the same letter.
4 The As are next to and right of the Cs.
5 The Cs are both between the Bs.
6 The Bs are in adjacent squares.

Down

1 The Cs are both between the As.
2 The Bs are in adjacent squares.
3 The As are both between the Bs.
4 The Bs are lower than the Cs.
5 The As are lower than the Bs.
6 The Bs are both between the Cs.

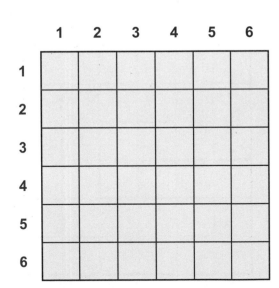

Every row and column in this grid originally contained one heart, one club, one diamond, one spade and two blank squares, although not necessarily in that order.

Every symbol with a black arrow refers to the first of the four symbols encountered when travelling in the direction of the arrow. Every symbol with a white arrow refers to the second of the four symbols encountered in the direction of the arrow.

Can you complete the original grid?

75

The blank squares below should be filled with whole numbers between 1 and 30 inclusive, any of which may occur more than once, or not at all.

The numbers in every horizontal row add up to the totals on the right, as do the two long diagonal lines; whilst those in every vertical column add up to the totals along the bottom.

76

							97
	3	14		12	2		61
28		19	27	3	15		106
7	14		3	3	3	20	69
	11	2	10	11		29	95
20			26	10	5	22	105
	27		23	5	24	21	128
8		5	5			19	87
102	69	84	97	67	92	140	94

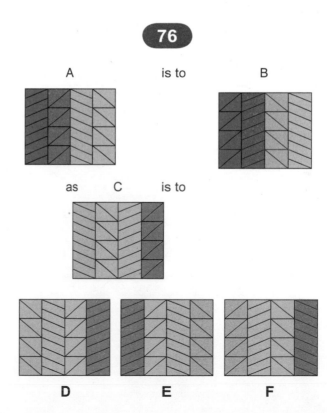

A is to B

as C is to

D   E   F

Can you place the hexagons into the grid, so that where any hexagon touches another along a straight line, the number in both triangles is the same? No rotation of any hexagon is allowed!

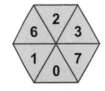
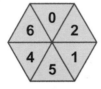

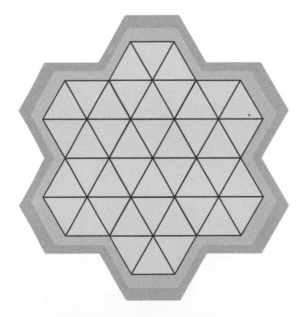

Twelve L-shapes like the ones here need to be inserted in the grid and each L has one hole in it.

There are three pieces of each of the four kinds shown here and any piece may be turned or flipped over before being put in the grid. No pieces of the same kind touch, even at a corner.

The pieces fit together so well that you cannot see any spaces between them; only the holes show.

Can you tell where the Ls are?

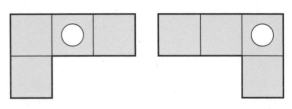
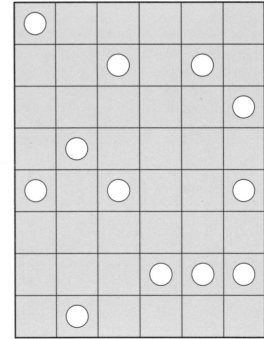

S E C T I O N

4

Given that scales A and B balance perfectly, how many hearts are needed to balance scale C?

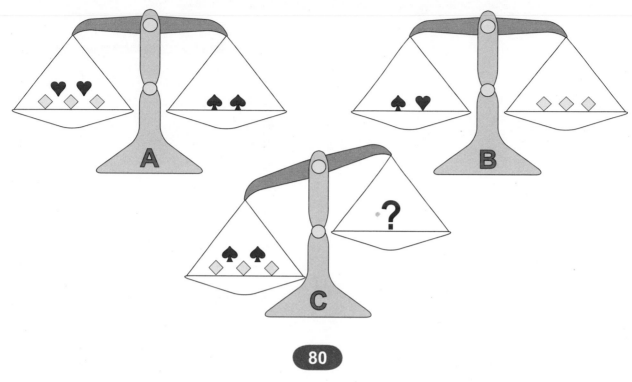

Which of the four lettered alternatives (A, B, C or D) fits most logically into the empty square?

19	12	6
8	13	17
9	10	15

16	17	11
13	10	14
6	15	12

18	19	13
15	12	16
6	17	14

A

18	14	13
15	21	16
8	17	14

B

21	14	8
10	15	19
11	12	17

?

18	14	13
15	18	16
8	19	14

C

18	19	13
15	12	16
8	17	14

D

The object of this puzzle is to trace a single path from the top left corner to the bottom right corner of the grid, travelling through all of the cells in either a horizontal, vertical or diagonal direction.

Every cell must be entered once only and your path should take you through the numbers in the sequence 1-2-3-4-1-2-3-4, etc.

Can you find the way?

1	1	2	1	2	4	1	2
2	3	4	3	4	3	4	3
2	1	4	2	1	4	2	1
3	1	3	3	4	3	1	2
4	2	3	1	2	1	3	4
2	1	4	2	4	3	2	1
3	4	3	3	1	2	2	3
4	1	2	4	3	4	1	4

82

The grid should be filled with numbers from 1 to 6, so that each number appears just once in every row and column. The clues refer to the digit totals in the squares, eg A 1 2 3 = 6 means that the numbers in squares A1, A2 and A3 add up to 6.

1 A 1 2 = 4

2 B 5 6 = 6

3 C 1 2 = 6

4 D 2 3 4 = 11

5 E 3 4 = 7

6 F 3 4 5 = 14

7 D E 1 = 7

8 E F 2 = 10

9 A B 3 = 6

10 A B 4 = 8

11 C D 5 = 6

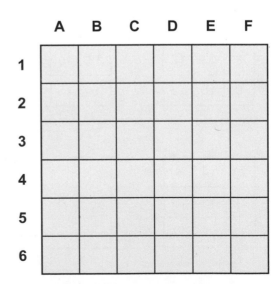

Can you fill each square in the bottom line with the correct digit?

Every square in the solution contains only one digit from each of the lettered lines above, although two or more squares in the solution may contain the same digit.

At the end of every row is a score, which shows:

a the number of digits placed in the correct finishing position on the bottom line, as indicated by a tick; and

b the number of digits which appear on the bottom line, but in a different position, as indicated by a cross.

SCORE

5	5	4	1	✗ ✗
7	4	4	2	✔ ✗
7	4	3	0	✔ ✔
7	0	5	7	✔ ✗
2	6	5	4	✔ ✗
				✔ ✔ ✔ ✔

Can you place the vessels into the diagram? Some parts of vessels or sea squares have already been filled in. A number to the right or below a row or column refers to the number of occupied squares in that row or column.

Any vessel may be positioned horizontally or vertically, but no part of a vessel touches part of any other vessel, either horizontally, vertically or diagonally.

Empty Area of Sea: ≈

Aircraft Carrier: ◀■■▶

Battleships: ◀■▶ ◀■▶

Cruisers: ◀▶ ◀▶ ◀▶

Submarines: ● ● ● ●

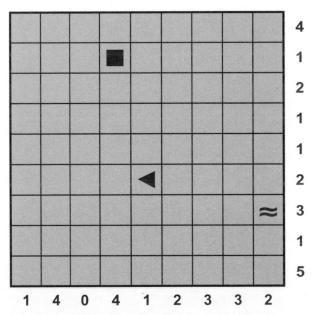

S
E
C
T
I
O
N

4

85

Draw a single continuous loop, by connecting the dots. No line may cross the path of another.

The figure inside each set of any four surrounding dots indicates the total number of surrounding lines.

```
  1  1              2  2
        0  3        1  0
 2     1        3  0
        0              3  2
 1           0     2     1
     0     3  1
     2     2  1  1  2  1  0  1
           2           2
 3        0  2     3  2
           3        0        1
     3  2  2           3     3
 1              2  1
```

86

Each horizontal row and vertical column should contain different shapes and different numbers.

Every square will contain one number and one shape and no combination may be repeated anywhere else in the puzzle.

1   2   3   4   5

5				
		5		
	3 (hexagon)	4	1	☆
		5	(hexagon)	1 (square)
	○	1		

87

Given that the letters are valued 1-26 according to their places in the alphabet, can you crack the mystery code to reveal the missing letter?

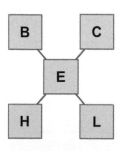

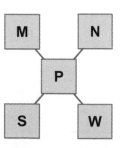

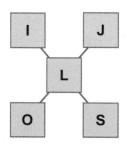

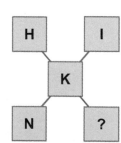

A set of dominoes is to be placed in four rows as shown below. The numbers indicate which values are shown on all the dominoes in each column and the relevant half of the domino in every row. Find out where each domino is placed by carefully comparing rows and columns to determine the possible positions of certain dominoes: for instance, if any column contains only one 6, then the domino 6/6 isn't in that column.

A set of dominoes consists of:

0/0, 0/1, 0/2, 0/3, 0/4, 0/5, 0/6, 1/1, 1/2, 1/3, 1/4, 1/5, 1/6, 2/2,

2/3, 2/4, 2/5, 2/6, 3/3, 3/4, 3/5, 3/6, 4/4, 4/5, 4/6, 5/5, 5/6, 6/6.

0, 2, 2, 3, 3, 4, 4, 4.	2, 4, 5, 5, 5, 6, 6, 6.	0, 1, 1, 3, 5, 5, 5, 6.	0, 0, 0, 1, 1, 2, 3, 3.	1, 1, 3, 3, 4, 4, 4, 6.	0, 1, 1, 2, 2, 2, 3, 6.	0, 0, 2, 4, 5, 5, 6, 6.

0, 0, 1, 1, 2, 5, 6.

0, 2, 3, 3, 5, 5, 6.

0, 1, 1, 2, 3, 6, 6.

1, 1, 2, 2, 4, 4, 6.

0, 0, 1, 1, 2, 3, 4.

2, 2, 3, 5, 5, 5, 6.

0, 3, 3, 4, 4, 4, 5.

0, 3, 4, 4, 5, 6, 6.

Place the eight tiles into the puzzle grid so that all adjacent numbers on each tile match up. Tiles may be rotated through 360 degrees, but none may be flipped over.

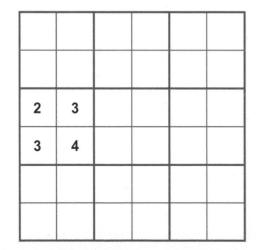

Place all twelve of the pieces into the grid. Any may be rotated or flipped over, but none may touch another, not even diagonally. The numbers outside the grid refer to the number of consecutive black squares; and each block is separated from the others by at least one white square. For instance, '3 2' could refer to a row with none, one or more white squares, then three black squares, then at least one white square, then two more black squares, followed by any number of white squares.

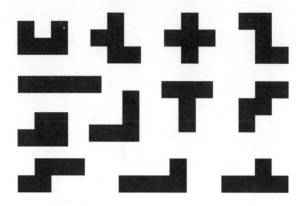

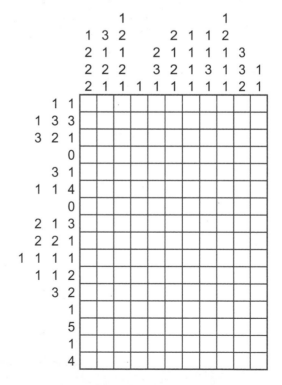

SECTION 4

91

In the diagram below, which letter should replace the question mark?

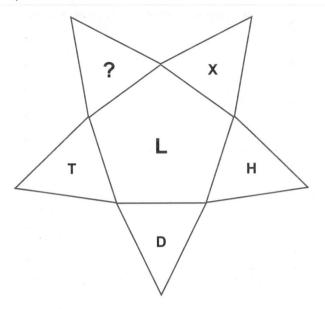

92

In the square below, change the positions of six numbers, one per horizontal row, vertical column and long diagonal line of six smaller squares, in such a way that the numbers in each row, column and long diagonal line total exactly 133. Any number may appear more than once in a row, column or line.

18	14	25	17	24	33
13	26	28	36	26	13
28	24	16	12	16	30
16	31	22	32	18	17
23	22	15	10	23	32
27	14	20	31	35	11

93

Every brick in this pyramid contains a number which is the sum of the two numbers below it, so that F=A+B, etc. Just work out the missing numbers!

O =

M =   N = 413

J = 395   K = 299   L =

F =   G =   H =   I =

A =   B = 127   C =   D = 08   E =

With the starter already given, can you fit all of the remaining listed numbers into this grid? Take care, this puzzle may not be as easy as it looks!

12	153	570	1738	42895
14	166	627	2240	81126
26	249	681	2659	96448
31	286	690	5247	98722
51	312	777	5342	417268
57	318	795	6513	621447
60	324	826	7288	677949
61	410	835	7500	751875
62	436	837✓	8398	912418
63	450	898	9025	916526
76	485	914	22548	968225
94	503	935	23088	987545

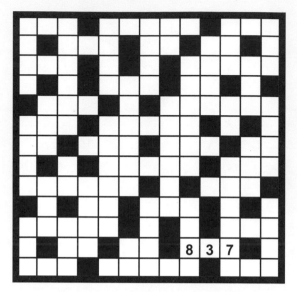

The chart gives directions to a hidden treasure behind the centre black square in the grid. Move the indicated number of spaces north, south, east and west (eg 4N means move four squares north) stopping at every square once only to arrive there. At which square should you start?

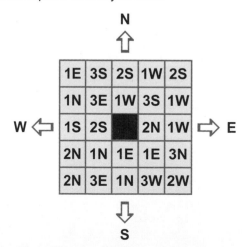

Fill the grid so that every horizontal row and vertical column contains the numbers 1-5. The 'greater than' or 'less than' signs indicate where a number is larger or smaller than that in the neighbouring square.

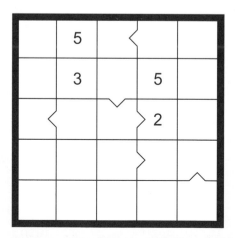

SECTION 4

Each of the eight segments of the spider's web should be filled with a different number from 1 to 8, in such a way that every ring also contains a different number from 1 to 8.

The segments run from the outside of the spider's web to the centre, and the rings run all the way around.

Some numbers are already in place. Can you fill in the rest?

1

A standard set of 28 dominoes has been laid out as shown. Can you draw in the edges of them all? The checkbox is provided as an aid and the domino already placed will help.

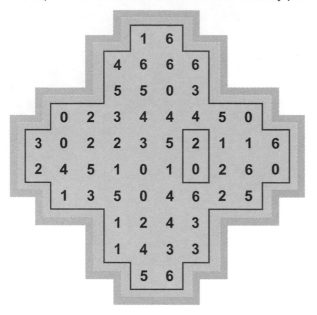

0-0	0-1	0-2	0-3	0-4	0-5	0-6
		✓				

1-1	1-2	1-3	1-4	1-5	1-6	2-2

2-3	2-4	2-5	2-6	3-3	3-4	3-5

3-6	4-4	4-5	4-6	5-5	5-6	6-6

2

Given that scales A and B balance perfectly, how many hearts are needed to balance scale C?

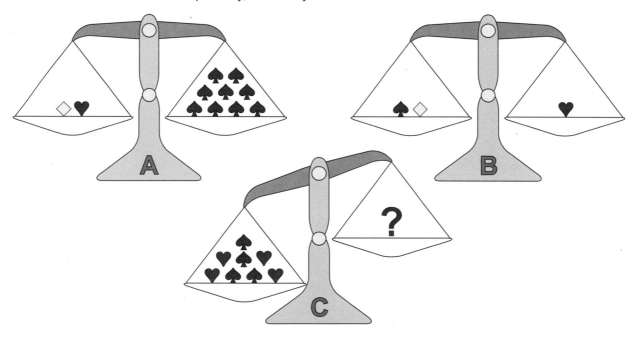

Every row and column in this grid originally contained one heart, one club, one diamond, one spade and two blank squares, although not necessarily in that order.

Every symbol with a black arrow refers to the first of the four symbols encountered when travelling in the direction of the arrow. Every symbol with a white arrow refers to the second of the four symbols encountered in the direction of the arrow.

Can you complete the original grid?

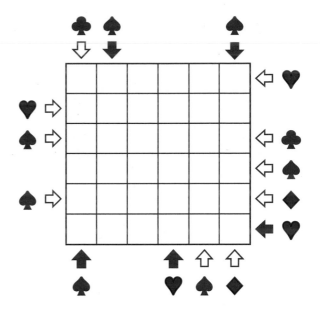

4

The blank squares below should be filled with whole numbers between 1 and 30 inclusive, any of which may occur more than once, or not at all.

The numbers in every horizontal row add up to the totals on the right, as do the two long diagonal lines; whilst those in every vertical column add up to the totals along the bottom.

							61
		13	19	16		1	88
14	7			25	10	17	94
		16	30	6	11	16	95
22			2	15	11		96
8	2	23	10		7	26	101
9		17	28		12	21	121
4	11		7		10	18	90
78	49	119	106	131	82	120	94

5

Draw in the missing hands on the final clock.

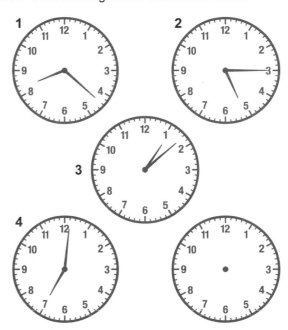

Can you place the hexagons into the grid, so that where any hexagon touches another along a straight line, the number in both triangles is the same? No rotation of any hexagon is allowed!

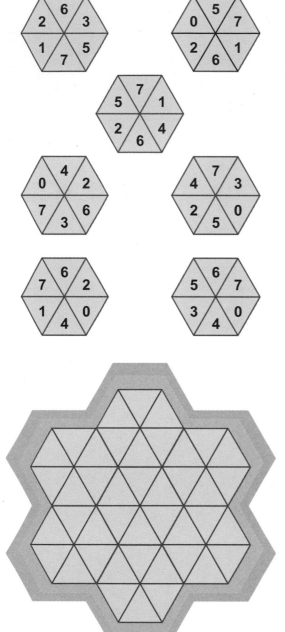

Twelve L-shapes like the ones here need to be inserted in the grid and each L has one hole in it.

There are three pieces of each of the four kinds shown here and any piece may be turned or flipped over before being put in the grid. No pieces of the same kind touch, even at a corner.

The pieces fit together so well that you cannot see any spaces between them; only the holes show.

Can you tell where the Ls are?

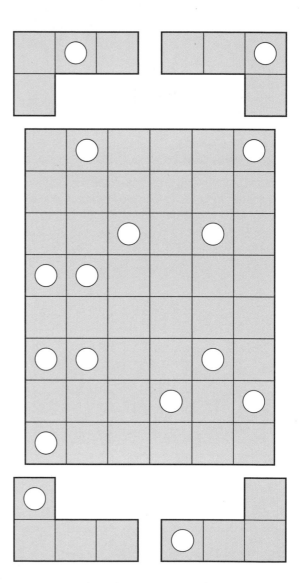

In this puzzle, an amateur coin collector has been out with his metal detector, searching for booty. He didn't have time to dig up all the coins he found, so has made a grid map, showing their locations, in the hope that if he loses the map, at least no-one else will understand it…

Those squares containing numbers are empty, but where a number appears in a square, it indicates how many coins are located in the squares (up to a maximum of eight) surrounding the numbered one, touching it at any corner or side. There is only one coin in any individual square.

Place a circle into every square containing a coin.

	0				2			1	
			2						2
0		0			3				2
	2			1	1			4	
1				1		1		4	
			3			2			
	2				2			3	4
1		0			2	3		4	3
	1		1	1	3		5		
1								3	

The grid should be filled with numbers from 1 to 6, so that each number appears just once in every row and column. The clues refer to the digit totals in the squares, eg A 1 2 3 = 6 means that the numbers in squares A1, A2 and A3 add up to 6.

1 F 3 4 5 = 11

2 C D E 1 = 6

3 B C 2 = 7

4 A B 3 = 4

5 B C 4 = 6

6 D E 5 = 11

7 D E 6 = 8

8 A 4 5 = 3

9 B 5 6 = 6

10 C 5 6 = 9

11 D 2 3 = 6

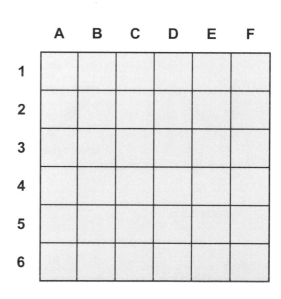

Each of the small squares in the grid below contains either A, B or C. Every row and column has exactly two of each letter. Can you tell the letter in each square?

Across

1 No two adjacent squares contain the same letter.

2 The Cs are next to and right of the As.

3 No two adjacent squares contain the same letter.

4 The Bs are next to and right of the Cs.

5 The Cs are both between the As.

Down

1 No two adjacent squares contain the same letter.

2 The Bs are both between the Cs.

3 The As are in adjacent squares.

4 The Bs are in adjacent squares.

5 The Bs are both between the As.

	1	2	3	4	5	6
1						
2						
3						
4						
5						
6						

The object of this puzzle is to trace a single path from the top left corner to the bottom right corner of the grid, travelling through all of the cells in either a horizontal, vertical or diagonal direction.

Every cell must be entered once only and your path should take you through the numbers in the sequence 1-2-3-4-1-2-3-4, etc.

Can you find the way?

1	2	1	2	1	2	4	1
4	2	3	4	3	4	3	2
1	3	1	4	1	3	3	1
3	2	3	2	4	2	4	2
4	1	3	4	1	2	1	3
2	4	2	3	2	3	4	4
3	1	2	3	2	1	2	1
4	1	4	1	3	4	3	4

12

Can you place the vessels into the diagram? Some parts of vessels or sea squares have already been filled in. A number to the right or below a row or column refers to the number of occupied squares in that row or column.

Any vessel may be positioned horizontally or vertically, but no part of a vessel touches part of any other vessel, either horizontally, vertically or diagonally.

Empty Area of Sea: ≈

Aircraft Carrier: ◄■■■►

Battleships: ◄■► ◄■►

Cruisers: ◄► ◄► ◄►

Submarines: ● ● ● ●

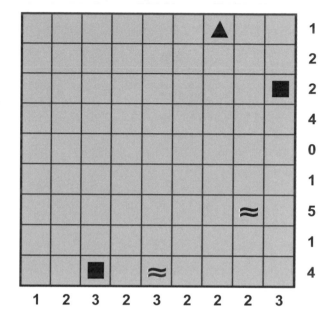

1
2
2
4
0
1
5
1
4

1 2 3 2 3 2 2 2 3

13

Can you fill each square in the bottom line with the correct digit?

Every square in the solution contains only one digit from each of the lettered lines above, although two or more squares in the solution may contain the same digit.

At the end of every row is a score, which shows:

a the number of digits placed in the correct finishing position on the bottom line, as indicated by a tick; and

b the number of digits which appear on the bottom line, but in a different position, as indicated by a cross.

SCORE

5	4	3	2	✓
0	1	7	2	✗ ✗
0	4	6	6	✗
0	7	3	1	✗ ✗
6	0	2	0	✓ ✓
				✓ ✓ ✓ ✓

179

14

Draw a single continuous loop, by connecting the dots. No line may cross the path of another.

The figure inside each set of any four surrounding dots indicates the total number of surrounding lines.

```
  2          3   3      3   1
  2     1          1   1   2
  1              3   1      3
     1   2                1   1
     1          1   1   3
     1      2   1   1      0      1
     1   2      3   2
     3   1      1          1
        0      1   1          3   2
  1                      1      1
  2     3      0                2
  1         2   1   1      2   1
```

15

Each horizontal row and vertical column should contain different shapes and different numbers.

Every square will contain one number and one shape and no combination may be repeated anywhere else in the puzzle.

1   2   3   4   5

2		⬡	◇	◯
5		2	4	
			3	
3		◇	◯	
☆		3	5	

16

Given that the letters are valued 1-26 according to their places in the alphabet, can you crack the mystery code to reveal the missing letter?

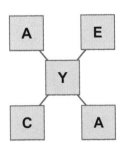

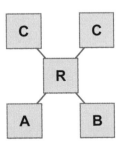

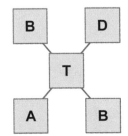

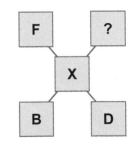

A set of dominoes is to be placed in four rows as shown below. The numbers indicate which values are shown on all the dominoes in each column and the relevant half of the domino in every row. Find out where each domino is placed by carefully comparing rows and columns to determine the possible positions of certain dominoes: for instance, if any column contains only one 6, then the domino 6/6 isn't in that column.

A set of dominoes consists of:

0/0, 0/1, 0/2, 0/3, 0/4, 0/5, 0/6, 1/1, 1/2, 1/3, 1/4, 1/5, 1/6, 2/2,

2/3, 2/4, 2/5, 2/6, 3/3, 3/4, 3/5, 3/6, 4/4, 4/5, 4/6, 5/5, 5/6, 6/6.

	0, 1, 1, 2, 3, 3, 4, 5.	1, 2, 2, 2, 4, 5, 6, 6.	0, 0, 0, 2, 2, 4, 5, 5.	1, 3, 3, 3, 5, 6, 6, 6.	0, 1, 1, 4, 4, 4, 5, 6.	2, 2, 3, 3, 3, 5, 6, 6.	0, 0, 0, 1, 1, 4, 4, 5.
0, 1, 2, 2, 2, 4, 6.							
0, 2, 3, 3, 4, 4, 5.							
0, 1, 1, 1, 2, 4, 6.							
0, 2, 4, 5, 6, 6, 6.							
1, 2, 2, 3, 3, 4, 5.							
0, 1, 1, 3, 3, 4, 5.							
0, 0, 0, 5, 5, 6, 6.							
1, 3, 3, 4, 5, 5, 6.							

S
E
C
T
I
O
N

Place the eight tiles into the puzzle grid so that all adjacent numbers on each tile match up. Tiles may be rotated through 360 degrees, but none may be flipped over.

Place all twelve of the pieces into the grid. Any may be rotated or flipped over, but none may touch another, not even diagonally. The numbers outside the grid refer to the number of consecutive black squares; and each block is separated from the others by at least one white square. For instance, '3 2' could refer to a row with none, one or more white squares, then three black squares, then at least one white square, then two more black squares, followed by any number of white squares.

3	4
1	1

3	1
3	2

4	4
4	3

3	2
1	2

4	2
1	2

2	1
4	1

3	1
2	4

4	1
3	3

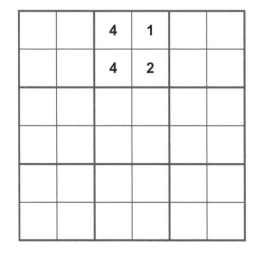

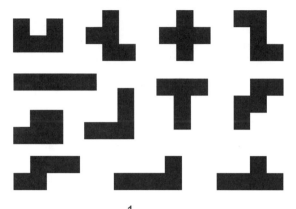

S E C T I O N

5

In the diagram below, which letter should replace the question mark?

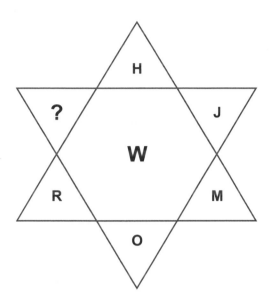

In the square below, change the positions of six numbers, one per horizontal row, vertical column and long diagonal line of six smaller squares, in such a way that the numbers in each row, column and long diagonal line total exactly 184. Any number may appear more than once in a row, column or line.

35	33	27	36	28	31
46	20	17	17	34	63
31	50	40	14	14	29
32	22	34	30	38	30
18	33	41	49	30	10
35	23	19	44	28	23

Every brick in this pyramid contains a number which is the sum of the two numbers below it, so that F=A+B, etc. Just work out the missing numbers!

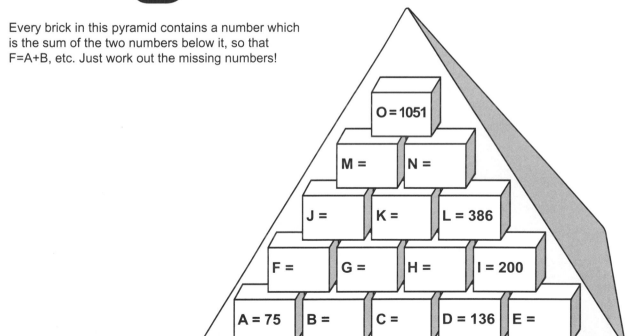

23

With the starter already given, can you fit all of the remaining listed numbers into this grid? Take care, this puzzle may not be as easy as it looks!

16	260	960	6327	72887
20	278	962	6429	83041
23	288	1269	7318	107970
25	367	1643	7501	178499
32	445	2115	8170	198090
38	619	2600	8195	223983
41	710	4123	8216	335778
42	712	4705	8292	506729
62	794	5026	8488	699802
98	847	5188	9378	746820
167 ✓	880	6137	47868	777186
169	958	6288	51858	953116

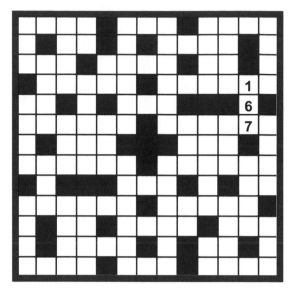

24

The chart gives directions to a hidden treasure behind the centre black square in the grid. Move the indicated number of spaces north, south, east and west (eg 4N means move four squares north) stopping at every square once only to arrive there. At which square should you start?

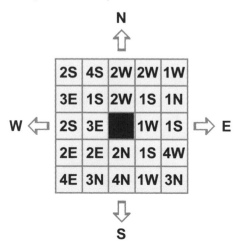

25

Fill the grid so that every horizontal row and vertical column contains the numbers 1-5. The 'greater than' or 'less than' signs indicate where a number is larger or smaller than that in the neighbouring square.

184

Each of the eight segments of the spider's web should be filled with a different number from 1 to 8, in such a way that every ring also contains a different number from 1 to 8.

The segments run from the outside of the spider's web to the centre, and the rings run all the way around.

Some numbers are already in place. Can you fill in the rest?

Every oval shape in this diagram contains a different letter of the alphabet from A to K inclusive. Use the clues to determine their locations. Reference in the clues to 'due' means in any location along the same horizontal or vertical line.

1 The B is due south of the G and due west of the I.

2 The E is due south of the A and due west of the B.

3 The G is due south of the F and due west of the J.

4 The H is due north of the D and due east of the A.

5 The J is due south of the C and due east of the K.

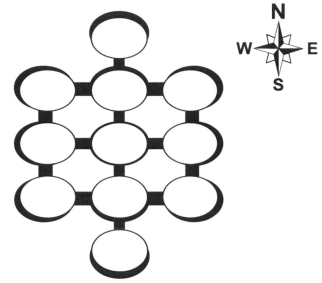

Fill the three empty circles with the symbols +, − and x in some order, to make a sum which totals the number in the centre. Each symbol must be used once and calculations are made in the direction of travel.

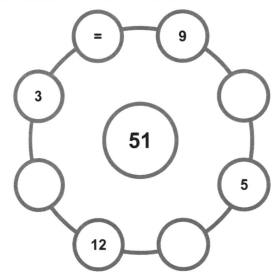

The numbers at the top and on the left side show the quantity of single-digit numbers (1-9) used in that row and column. The numbers at the bottom and on the right side show the sum of the digits. A number may appear more than once in a row or column, but no numbers are in squares that touch, even at a corner.

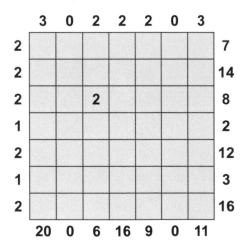

5

Using the numbers below, complete these six equations (three reading across and three reading downwards). Every number is used once.

1	2	3	5
6	7	8	9

	+		−		=	2
x		+		−		
4	x		+		=	39
+		−		x		
	−		x		=	30
=		=		=		
12		14		15		

In the grid below, which number should replace the question mark?

13	18	10	15	7	12	4
41	49	44	52	47	55	50
32	37	29	34	26	31	23
29	37	32	40	35	43	38
19	24	16	21	13	18	10
19	27	22	30	25	33	28
?	46	38	43	35	40	32

When the box below is folded to form a cube, just one of the five options (A, B, C, D or E) can be produced. Which?

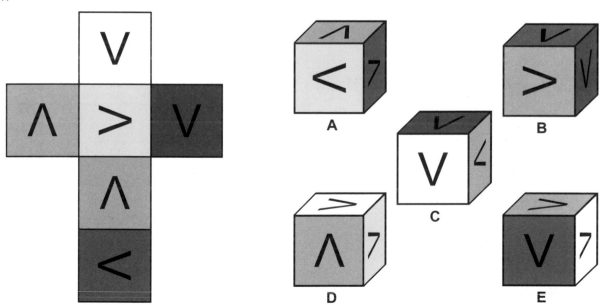

S
E
C
T
I
O
N

5

187

33

In this puzzle, an amateur coin collector has been out with his metal detector, searching for booty. He didn't have time to dig up all the coins he found, so has made a grid map, showing their locations, in the hope that if he loses the map, at least no-one else will understand it…

Those squares containing numbers are empty, but where a number appears in a square, it indicates how many coins are located in the squares (up to a maximum of eight) surrounding the numbered one, touching it at any corner or side. There is only one coin in any individual square.

Place a circle into every square containing a coin.

1			1				2		
	2			3		3			3
0		1	1						2
	1				2			3	4
			1			2			
		0	2				4		
	2					4		4	
				2				5	
	0		1	3			1		
		1						1	

34

Each symbol stands for a different number. In order to reach the correct total at the end of each row and column, what is the value of the circle, cross, pentagon, square and star?

cross	cross	star	star	pentagon	= 34
circle	circle	square	square	star	= 37
star	circle	star	square	circle	= 38
cross	circle	star	cross	star	= 38
square	cross	cross	cross	circle	= 35
= 37	= 32	= 42	= 39	= 32	

35

Every row and column of this grid should contain one each of the letters A, B, C, D, E and F. Each of the six shapes (marked by thicker lines) should also contain one each of the letters A, B, C, D, E and F. Can you complete the grid?

D		C		B	A
	E				
F					

A standard set of 28 dominoes has been laid out as shown. Can you draw in the edges of them all? The checkbox is provided as an aid and the domino already placed will help.

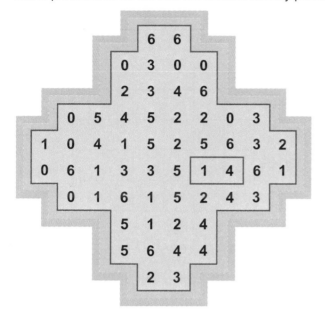

0-0	0-1	0-2	0-3	0-4	0-5	0-6

1-1	1-2	1-3	1-4	1-5	1-6	2-2
			✓			

2-3	2-4	2-5	2-6	3-3	3-4	3-5

3-6	4-4	4-5	4-6	5-5	5-6	6-6

37

Each of the small squares in the grid below contains either A, B or C. Every row and column has exactly two of each letter. Can you tell the letter in each square?

Across

1 No two adjacent squares contain the same letter.
2 The Cs are both between the As.
3 No two adjacent squares contain the same letter.
6 The Bs are both between the Cs.

Down

1 The Cs are both between the As.
2 The Bs are lower than the As.
4 The Cs are lower than the Bs.
6 Each C is directly next to and below an A.

Every row and column in this grid originally contained one heart, one club, one diamond, one spade and two blank squares, although not necessarily in that order.

Every symbol with a black arrow refers to the first of the four symbols encountered when travelling in the direction of the arrow. Every symbol with a white arrow refers to the second of the four symbols encountered in the direction of the arrow.

Can you complete the original grid?

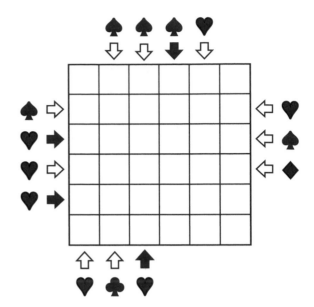

The blank squares below should be filled with whole numbers between 1 and 30 inclusive, any of which may occur more than once, or not at all.

The numbers in every horizontal row add up to the totals on the right, as do the two long diagonal lines; whilst those in every vertical column add up to the totals along the bottom.

							106
27		26	29	4			112
10	23			2	2	22	112
30	29	10		5		10	114
		2		1	24	19	100
	18	22	23	5	29	2	102
27	18	2			7	19	83
	3	5		21	21	18	111
156	97	91	149	42	102	97	113

A is to B

as C is to

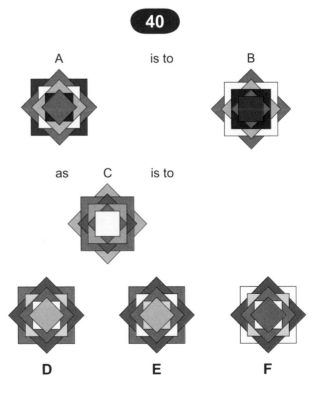

S
E
C
T
I
O
N

5

Can you place the hexagons into the grid, so that where any hexagon touches another along a straight line, the number in both triangles is the same? No rotation of any hexagon is allowed!

Twelve L-shapes like the ones here need to be inserted in the grid and each L has one hole in it.

There are three pieces of each of the four kinds shown here and any piece may be turned or flipped over before being put in the grid. No pieces of the same kind touch, even at a corner.

The pieces fit together so well that you cannot see any spaces between them; only the holes show.

Can you tell where the Ls are?

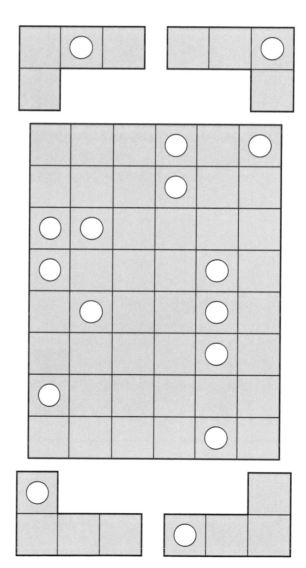

Which of the four lettered alternatives (A, B, C or D) fits most logically into the empty square?

12	4	15
1	12	3
21	15	11

6	11	14
2	6	8
28	7	12

3	20	8
9	2	5
10	29	8

?

11	16	4
7	5	3
14	18	15

A

9	15	7
3	7	6
17	15	14

B

17	9	5
1	3	12
13	15	19

C

12	14	7
10	2	4
16	11	20

D

Which four pieces can be fitted together to form an exact copy of this shape?

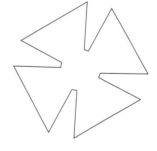

A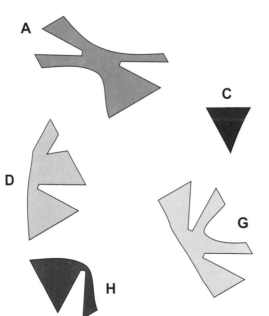

B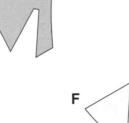

C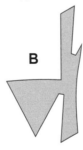

D

E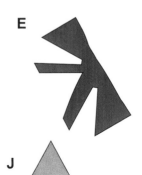

F

G

H

I

J

Can you place the vessels into the diagram? Some parts of vessels or sea squares have already been filled in. A number to the right or below a row or column refers to the number of occupied squares in that row or column.

Any vessel may be positioned horizontally or vertically, but no part of a vessel touches part of any other vessel, either horizontally, vertically or diagonally.

Empty Area of Sea:

Aircraft Carrier:

Battleships:

Cruisers:

Submarines:

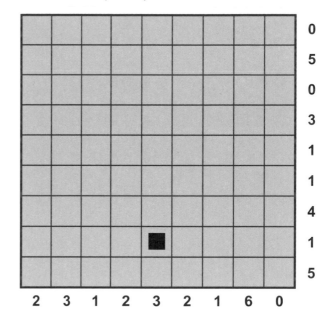

| 0 |
| 5 |
| 0 |
| 3 |
| 1 |
| 1 |
| 4 |
| 1 |
| 5 |

2 3 1 2 3 2 1 6 0

Can you fill each square in the bottom line with the correct digit?

Every square in the solution contains only one digit from each of the lettered lines above, although two or more squares in the solution may contain the same digit.

At the end of every row is a score, which shows:

   a the number of digits placed in the correct finishing position on the bottom line, as indicated by a tick; and

   b the number of digits which appear on the bottom line, but in a different position, as indicated by a cross.

SCORE

2	2	7	1	✓
2	3	2	2	✓
5	7	4	6	✓✓✗
5	0	0	1	✗
7	3	0	2	✗
				✓✓✓✓

S
E
C
T
I
O
N

5

193

The grid should be filled with numbers from 1 to 6, so that each number appears just once in every row and column. The clues refer to the digit totals in the squares, eg A 1 2 3 = 6 means that the numbers in squares A1, A2 and A3 add up to 6.

1 A 3 4 5 = 11

2 B 2 3 = 7

3 C 1 2 = 8

4 D 4 5 6 = 6

5 E 3 4 = 5

6 F 4 5 = 10

7 D E 1 = 11

8 D E 2 = 5

9 C D 3 = 11

10 B C 4 = 5

11 B C 5 = 9

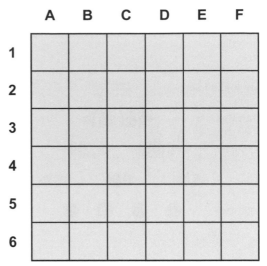

The object of this puzzle is to trace a single path from the top left corner to the bottom right corner of the grid, travelling through all of the cells in either a horizontal, vertical or diagonal direction.

Every cell must be entered once only and your path should take you through the numbers in the sequence 1-2-3-4-1-2-3-4, etc.

Can you find the way?

1	2	4	3	4	2	3	1
1	4	3	1	2	1	4	2
2	3	2	1	4	2	4	3
3	2	3	4	3	1	2	3
4	1	4	1	2	4	1	4
1	3	2	4	1	3	2	1
3	2	3	3	2	3	2	3
4	1	2	4	1	4	1	4

S E C T I O N

5

49

Draw a single continuous loop, by connecting the dots. No line may cross the path of another.

The figure inside each set of any four surrounding dots indicates the total number of surrounding lines.

```
3       0                   3

            1       2       0

    1   3       3       1           1

  1   0       1               0       1

  2       0       3   1               1

  2       1   1   2           0

  2   2   1       2   2

            1       1               1

      3   2   2   1       1   0       1

  2           2               2

  2               2           2

  1   2   2   2   2   3       3       1
```

50

Each horizontal row and vertical column should contain different shapes and different numbers.

Every square will contain one number and one shape and no combination may be repeated anywhere else in the puzzle.

| 1 | 2 | 3 | 4 | 5 |

			5	
			1	☆5
	2			
		○1	◇	3
◇5			⬡	

51

Given that the letters are valued 1-26 according to their places in the alphabet, can you crack the mystery code to reveal the missing letter?

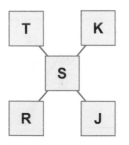
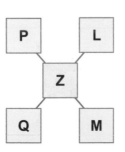
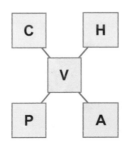
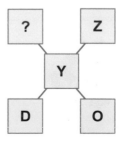

Which is the odd one out?

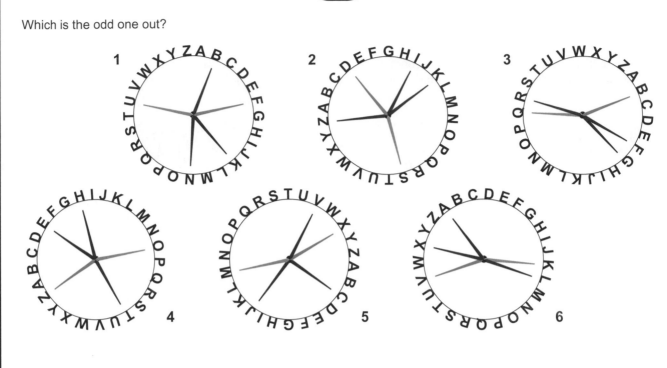

Which of the alternatives (A, B, C or D) comes next?

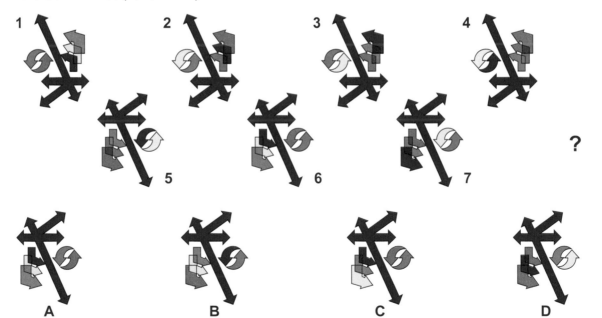

Place the eight tiles into the puzzle grid so that all adjacent numbers on each tile match up. Tiles may be rotated through 360 degrees, but none may be flipped over.

1	3
3	2

4	2
4	2

4	1
2	2

2	2
4	1

2	1
1	3

4	3
2	2

4	2
4	3

1	2
2	4

4	3				
2	1				

Place all twelve of the pieces into the grid. Any may be rotated or flipped over, but none may touch another, not even diagonally. The numbers outside the grid refer to the number of consecutive black squares; and each block is separated from the others by at least one white square. For instance, '3 2' could refer to a row with none, one or more white squares, then three black squares, then at least one white square, then two more black squares, followed by any number of white squares.

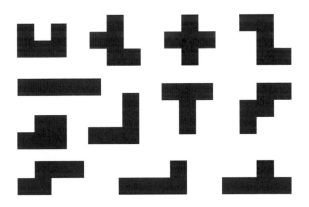

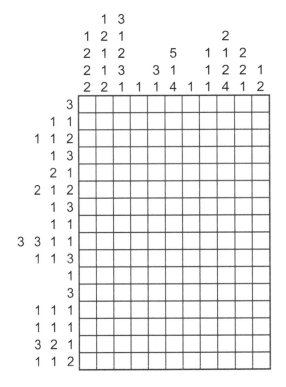

56

In the diagram below, which number should replace the question mark?

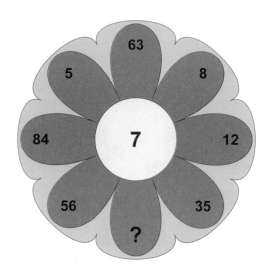

57

In the square below, change the positions of six numbers, one per horizontal row, vertical column and long diagonal line of six smaller squares, in such a way that the numbers in each row, column and long diagonal line total exactly 141. Any number may appear more than once in a row, column or line.

34	21	12	30	48	14
27	23	21	10	29	34
26	43	23	19	15	20
23	25	26	21	12	28
13	33	30	34	10	27
23	14	3	21	30	24

58

Every brick in this pyramid contains a number which is the sum of the two numbers below it, so that F=A+B, etc. Just work out the missing numbers!

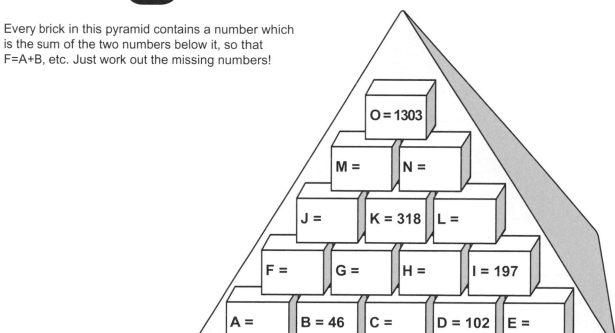

With the starter already given, can you fit all of the remaining listed numbers into this grid? Take care, this puzzle may not be as easy as it looks!

22	222 ✓	672	4333	70455
28	224	763	5812	85129
32	378	832	6242	88913
38	407	844	7891	94842
42	487	846	13331	224844
64	490	891	22574	301246
73	515	901	28455	430448
88	562	921	34051	513284
146	574	936	38914	647925
189	591	998	38997	668357
193	645	2036	46785	811238
207	666	4273	51891	873876

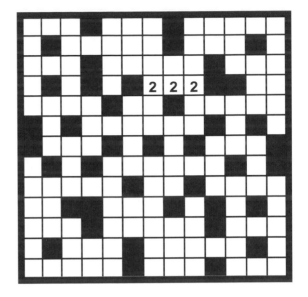

The chart gives directions to a hidden treasure behind the centre black square in the grid. Move the indicated number of spaces north, south, east and west (eg 4N means move four squares north) stopping at every square once only to arrive there. At which square should you start?

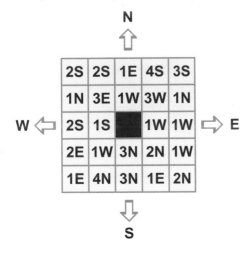

Fill the grid so that every horizontal row and vertical column contains the numbers 1-5. The 'greater than' or 'less than' signs indicate where a number is larger or smaller than that in the neighbouring square.

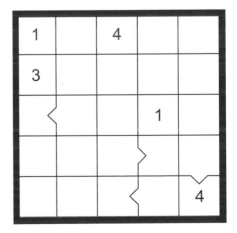

Each of the eight segments of the spider's web should be filled with a different number from 1 to 8, in such a way that every ring also contains a different number from 1 to 8.

The segments run from the outside of the spider's web to the centre, and the rings run all the way around.

Some numbers are already in place. Can you fill in the rest?

Every oval shape in this diagram contains a different letter of the alphabet from A to K inclusive. Use the clues to determine their locations. Reference in the clues to 'due' means in any location along the same horizontal or vertical line.

1   The A is due north of the J and due west of the K.

2   The B is due north of the I and further west than the D (which is further south than the A).

3   The G is due north of the E and due east of the F.

4   The J is due west of the C and due south of the H (which is further north than the B).

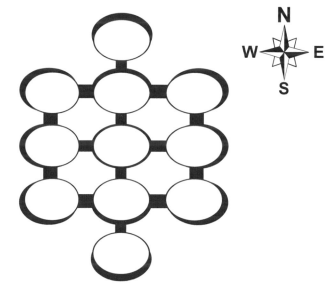

64

Fill the three empty circles with the symbols +, − and x in some order, to make a sum which totals the number in the centre. Each symbol must be used once and calculations are made in the direction of travel.

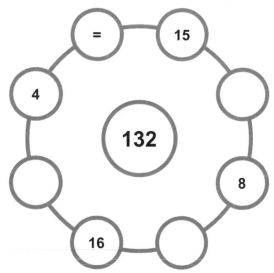

65

The numbers at the top and on the left side show the quantity of single-digit numbers (1-9) used in that row and column. The numbers at the bottom and on the right side show the sum of the digits. A number may appear more than once in a row or column, but no numbers are in squares that touch, even at a corner.

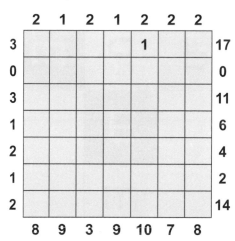

	2	1	2	1	2	2	2	
3					1			17
0								0
3								11
1								6
2								4
1								2
2								14
	8	9	3	9	10	7	8	

66

Using the numbers below, complete these six equations (three reading across and three reading downwards). Every number is used once.

1	2	4	5
6	7	8	9

	+		x		=	64
−	■	−	■	x		
	x	3	+		=	9
+	■	x	■	−		
	−		x		=	24
=		=		=		
11		12		16		

67

In the grid below, which number should replace the question mark?

111	93	83	70	62	42	33
95	79	71	60	54	36	29
78	64	58	49	45	29	24
62	50	46	39	37	23	20
45	35	33	28	28	16	15
29	21	21	18	20	10	11
12	6	8	?	11	3	6

68

When the box below is folded to form a cube, just one of the five options (A, B, C, D or E) can be produced. Which?

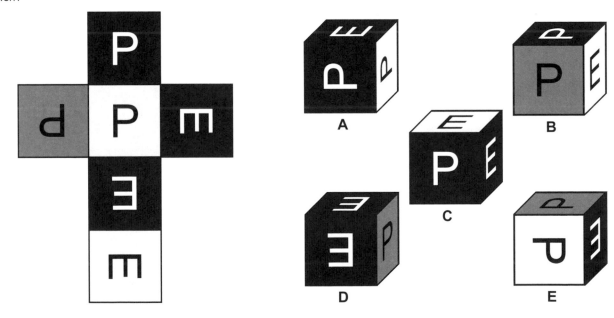

A

B

C

D

E

69

In this puzzle, an amateur coin collector has been out with his metal detector, searching for booty. He didn't have time to dig up all the coins he found, so has made a grid map, showing their locations, in the hope that if he loses the map, at least no-one else will understand it…

Those squares containing numbers are empty, but where a number appears in a square, it indicates how many coins are located in the squares (up to a maximum of eight) surrounding the numbered one, touching it at any corner or side. There is only one coin in any individual square.

Place a circle into every square containing a coin.

2					2			2	1
	3		2			2	2		2
2		4		3					
				4					
2					1	1	1	2	
	3				1				0
			3					0	
			2		3				
1	3								0
1			2	1			0		

70

Every row and column of this grid should contain one each of the letters A, B, C, D, E and F. Each of the six shapes (marked by thicker lines) should also contain one each of the letters A, B, C, D, E and F. Can you complete the grid?

D			C	B	A
F					E

71

Each symbol stands for a different number. In order to reach the correct total at the end of each row and column, what is the value of the circle, cross, pentagon, square and star?

Row totals: = 23, = 15, = 17, = 22, = 24

Column totals: 26   18   12   26   19

A standard set of 28 dominoes has been laid out as shown. Can you draw in the edges of them all? The check-box is provided as an aid and the domino already placed will help.

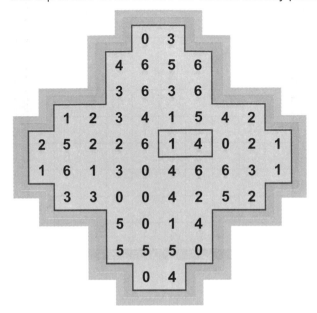

0-0	0-1	0-2	0-3	0-4	0-5	0-6

1-1	1-2	1-3	1-4	1-5	1-6	2-2
			✔			

2-3	2-4	2-5	2-6	3-3	3-4	3-5

3-6	4-4	4-5	4-6	5-5	5-6	6-6

73

Each of the small squares in the grid below contains either A, B or C. Every row and column has exactly two of each letter. Can you tell the letter in each square?

Across
1 The Bs are further right than the As.
2 The As are next to and right of the Cs.
3 The Cs are both between the Bs.
5 The As are further right than the Cs.
6 The As are next to and right of the Bs.

Down
1 Each C is directly next to and below an A.
2 The Bs are lower than the Cs.
3 No two adjacent squares contain the same letter.
4 No two adjacent squares contain the same letter.
6 The As are lower than the Bs.

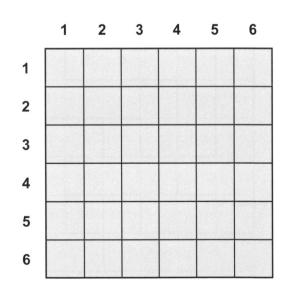

Every row and column in this grid originally contained one heart, one club, one diamond, one spade and two blank squares, although not necessarily in that order.

Every symbol with a black arrow refers to the first of the four symbols encountered when travelling in the direction of the arrow. Every symbol with a white arrow refers to the second of the four symbols encountered in the direction of the arrow.

Can you complete the original grid?

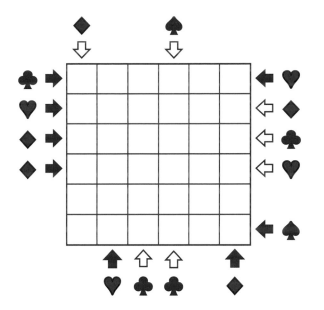

75

The blank squares below should be filled with whole numbers between 1 and 30 inclusive, any of which may occur more than once, or not at all.

The numbers in every horizontal row add up to the totals on the right, as do the two long diagonal lines; whilst those in every vertical column add up to the totals along the bottom.

							97
		15	27	6			117
	27	23	8			28	137
	11	14		25	24		124
19		26	10	6	6	6	93
9		7	13	4	16	21	71
11	13		11	24	12	12	99
24		22		11	26	4	94
117	**99**	**137**	**87**	**108**	**106**	**81**	**88**

76

A   is to   B

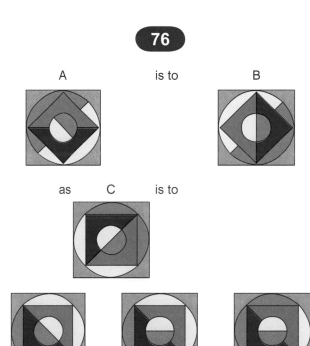

as   C   is to

D   E   F

Can you place the hexagons into the grid, so that where any hexagon touches another along a straight line, the number in both triangles is the same? No rotation of any hexagon is allowed!

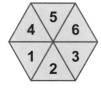
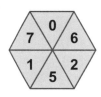

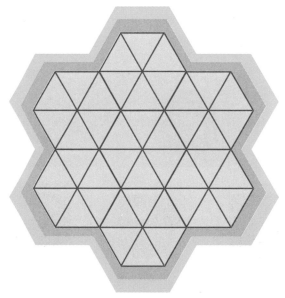

Twelve L-shapes like the ones here need to be inserted in the grid and each L has one hole in it.

There are three pieces of each of the four kinds shown here and any piece may be turned or flipped over before being put in the grid. No pieces of the same kind touch, even at a corner.

The pieces fit together so well that you cannot see any spaces between them; only the holes show.

Can you tell where the Ls are?

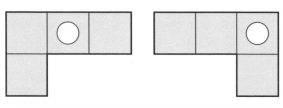
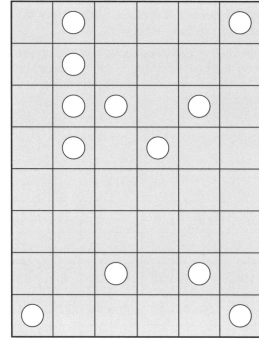
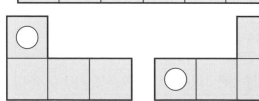

Given that scales A and B balance perfectly, how many hearts are needed to balance scale C?

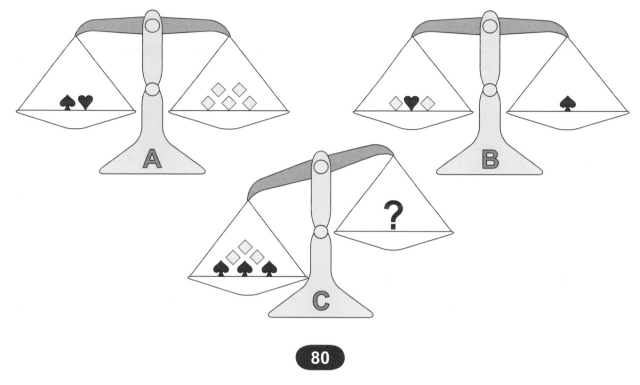

Which of the four lettered alternatives (A, B, C or D) fits most logically into the empty square?

16	51	12
26	17	19
20	34	43

11	54	7
21	20	22
15	29	46

14	49	10
24	15	17
18	32	41

?

9	52	5
19	18	20
13	27	44

A

5	52	9
19	18	22
13	27	44

B

9	52	5
19	18	22
13	27	44

C

9	52	5
19	18	20
13	27	42

D

The object of this puzzle is to trace a single path from the top left corner to the bottom right corner of the grid, travelling through all of the cells in either a horizontal, vertical or diagonal direction.

Every cell must be entered once only and your path should take you through the numbers in the sequence 1-2-3-4-1-2-3-4, etc.

Can you find the way?

1	3	2	3	2	3	4	1
2	4	4	1	4	1	2	3
2	1	2	3	4	3	1	4
3	1	4	3	1	2	3	4
4	2	1	2	3	1	2	1
3	4	1	2	4	1	4	2
4	3	2	4	2	1	2	3
1	2	3	1	3	4	3	4

82

The grid should be filled with numbers from 1 to 6, so that each number appears just once in every row and column. The clues refer to the digit totals in the squares, eg A 1 2 3 = 6 means that the numbers in squares A1, A2 and A3 add up to 6.

1 A 2 3 = 6

2 B 3 4 = 10

3 C 5 6 = 6

4 D 4 5 6 = 7

5 E 5 6 = 9

6 F 1 2 3 = 7

7 C D 1 = 11

8 C D 2 = 9

9 D E 3 = 11

10 E F 4 = 5

11 A B 5 = 9

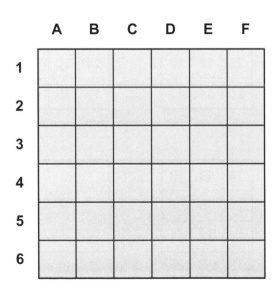

Can you fill each square in the bottom line with the correct digit?

Every square in the solution contains only one digit from each of the lettered lines above, although two or more squares in the solution may contain the same digit.

At the end of every row is a score, which shows:

a the number of digits placed in the correct finishing position on the bottom line, as indicated by a tick; and

b the number of digits which appear on the bottom line, but in a different position, as indicated by a cross.

SCORE

0	5	4	7	✓ ✗
7	5	7	7	✓ ✓
3	0	7	7	✓ ✓ ✓
2	7	2	2	✗
6	2	1	1	✗
				✓ ✓ ✓ ✓

84

Can you place the vessels into the diagram? Some parts of vessels or sea squares have already been filled in. A number to the right or below a row or column refers to the number of occupied squares in that row or column.

Any vessel may be positioned horizontally or vertically, but no part of a vessel touches part of any other vessel, either horizontally, vertically or diagonally.

Empty Area of Sea: ≈

Aircraft Carrier: ◀■■▶

Battleships: ◀■▶   ◀■▶

Cruisers: ◀▶   ◀▶   ◀▶

Submarines: ● ● ● ●

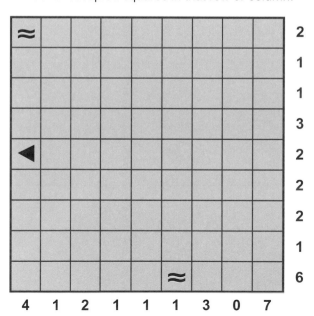

Draw a single continuous loop, by connecting the dots. No line may cross the path of another.

The figure inside each set of any four surrounding dots indicates the total number of surrounding lines.

```
2           1  2  3        2
2  1        3        1  2  1        3
2  2  2           1  3
                  0  1  2  2        2
1                 2        3        2
         2
1        0                    3
                  3
      1  0  1  2              0
1  3        2        3        0  2  2
            1
3  2              1           1     1
```

Each horizontal row and vertical column should contain different shapes and different numbers.

Every square will contain one number and one shape and no combination may be repeated anywhere else in the puzzle.

1   2   3   4   5

	◇3	★	5	4
		⬡		
				2
	4	1		◇
○			⬡	

Given that the letters are valued 1-26 according to their places in the alphabet, can you crack the mystery code to reveal the missing letter?

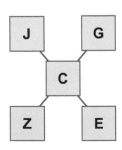
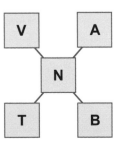
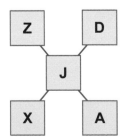
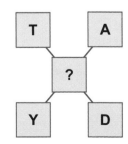

A set of dominoes is to be placed in four rows as shown below. The numbers indicate which values are shown on all the dominoes in each column and the relevant half of the domino in every row. Find out where each domino is placed by carefully comparing rows and columns to determine the possible positions of certain dominoes: for instance, if any column contains only one 6, then the domino 6/6 isn't in that column.

A set of dominoes consists of:

0/0, 0/1, 0/2, 0/3, 0/4, 0/5, 0/6, 1/1, 1/2, 1/3, 1/4, 1/5, 1/6, 2/2,

2/3, 2/4, 2/5, 2/6, 3/3, 3/4, 3/5, 3/6, 4/4, 4/5, 4/6, 5/5, 5/6, 6/6.

	1, 1, 2, 2, 2, 4, 4, 6.	2, 2, 3, 3, 3, 5, 5, 6.	2, 3, 3, 3, 4, 5, 6, 6.	0, 1, 4, 4, 5, 5, 5, 6.	0, 1, 1, 1, 4, 4, 6, 6.	0, 0, 0, 0, 1, 2, 3, 4.	0, 0, 1, 2, 3, 5, 5, 6.
0, 1, 2, 2, 3, 4, 5.							
0, 0, 1, 2, 2, 5, 6.							
0, 1, 3, 3, 6, 6, 6.							
0, 1, 1, 4, 4, 4, 6.							
0, 3, 4, 4, 4, 5, 5.							
0, 2, 2, 3, 4, 5, 5.							
1, 2, 2, 3, 3, 3, 6.							
0, 1, 1, 5, 5, 6, 6.							

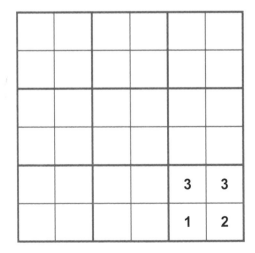

89

Place the eight tiles into the puzzle grid so that all adjacent numbers on each tile match up. Tiles may be rotated through 360 degrees, but none may be flipped over.

Tiles:

1	1
4	1

3	1
3	1

4	2
2	1

4	2
1	4

1	2
3	1

4	1
1	3

1	2
4	2

1	1
3	1

Grid contains: 3 3 / 1 2 in the lower right.

90

Place all twelve of the pieces into the grid. Any may be rotated or flipped over, but none may touch another, not even diagonally. The numbers outside the grid refer to the number of consecutive black squares; and each block is separated from the others by at least one white square. For instance, '3 2' could refer to a row with none, one or more white squares, then three black squares, then at least one white square, then two more black squares, followed by any number of white squares.

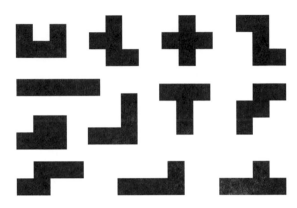

Column clues (top):

```
          1
          1   2   2       1
          4 2 1 3 1     1 4
      3 1 1 1 2 2 1 3 3 1 2
      3 1 1 1 1 1 1 1 2 3 2
```

Row clues (left):
```
1 2 2
1 3 2 1
1 1 1 1
    3 1
      1
    2 3
1 1 1
    1 2
2 1 1
1 2 3
    1 2
    3 1
    1 1
    5 1
      2
      1
```

In the diagram below, which letter should replace the question mark?

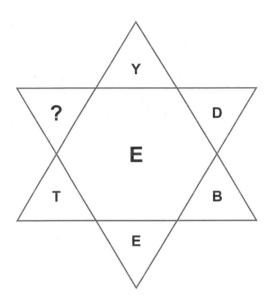

In the square below, change the positions of six numbers, one per horizontal row, vertical column and long diagonal line of six smaller squares, in such a way that the numbers in each row, column and long diagonal line total exactly 180. Any number may appear more than once in a row, column or line.

26	36	9	12	27	26
44	56	26	33	10	56
51	11	8	52	42	12
12	16	58	6	35	48
16	11	23	22	54	57
26	53	52	11	17	26

Every brick in this pyramid contains a number which is the sum of the two numbers below it, so that F=A+B, etc. Just work out the missing numbers!

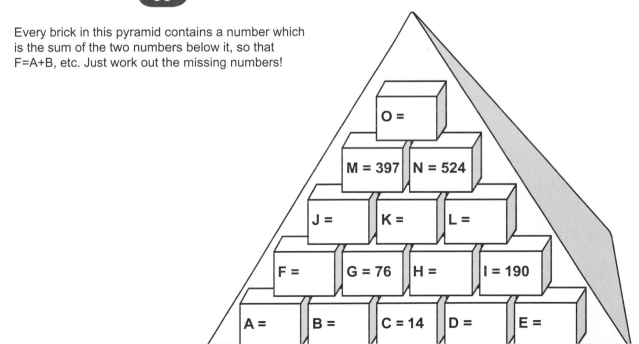

94

With the starter already given, can you fit all of the remaining listed numbers into this grid? Take care, this puzzle may not be as easy as it looks!

25 ✓	408	835	40382	71974
34	470	859	42789	75134
42	501	2627	43385	75386
43	522	5549	43589	83717
52	527	6257	47042	85423
55	627	6955	52778	87349
62	750	7632	54278	97338
72	759	7891	61342	97805
169	777	12345	62889	428526
232	789	13425	64184	859349
238	806	17893	65321	890751
369	827	31351	69887	935045

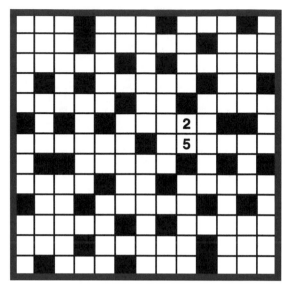

95

The chart gives directions to a hidden treasure behind the centre black square in the grid. Move the indicated number of spaces north, south, east and west (eg 4N means move four squares north) stopping at every square once only to arrive there. At which square should you start?

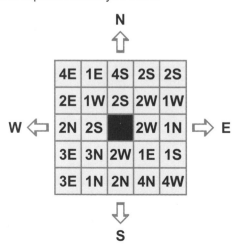

96

Fill the grid so that every horizontal row and vertical column contains the numbers 1-5. The 'greater than' or 'less than' signs indicate where a number is larger or smaller than that in the neighbouring square.

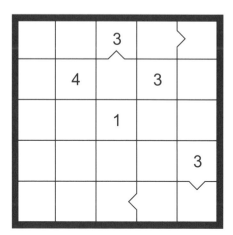

Each of the eight segments of the spider's web should be filled with a different number from 1 to 8, in such a way that every ring also contains a different number from 1 to 8.

The segments run from the outside of the spider's web to the centre, and the rings run all the way around.

Some numbers are already in place. Can you fill in the rest?

A standard set of 28 dominoes has been laid out as shown. Can you draw in the edges of them all? The checkbox is provided as an aid and the domino already placed will help.

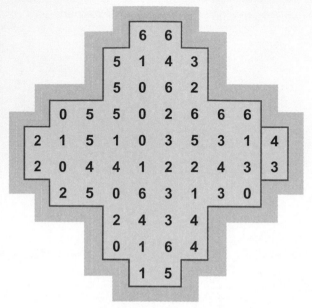

0-0	0-1	0-2	0-3	0-4	0-5	0-6

1-1	1-2	1-3	1-4	1-5	1-6	2-2

2-3	2-4	2-5	2-6	3-3	3-4	3-5
					✓	

3-6	4-4	4-5	4-6	5-5	5-6	6-6

Given that scales A and B balance perfectly, how many hearts are needed to balance scale C?

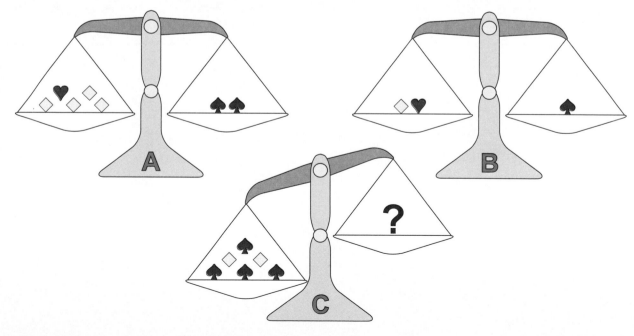

Every row and column in this grid originally contained one heart, one club, one diamond, one spade and two blank squares, although not necessarily in that order.

Every symbol with a black arrow refers to the first of the four symbols encountered when travelling in the direction of the arrow. Every symbol with a white arrow refers to the second of the four symbols encountered in the direction of the arrow.

Can you complete the original grid?

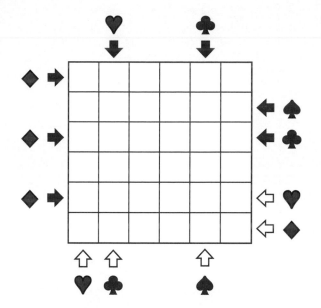

4

The blank squares below should be filled with whole numbers between 1 and 30 inclusive, any of which may occur more than once, or not at all.

The numbers in every horizontal row add up to the totals on the right, as do the two long diagonal lines; whilst those in every vertical column add up to the totals along the bottom.

							111
15		30			5	9	114
	5		12		20		110
	7	5	10	7	5	8	45
8		30		28		19	135
	17		25	1	1	28	117
6	18	24	5		11	2	91
7	14	4		5	12	2	68
89	89	125	123	87	76	91	65

5

Draw in the missing hands on the final clock.

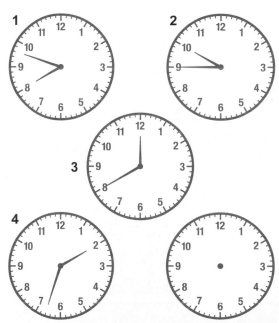

Can you place the hexagons into the grid, so that where any hexagon touches another along a straight line, the number in both triangles is the same? No rotation of any hexagon is allowed!

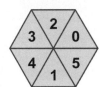

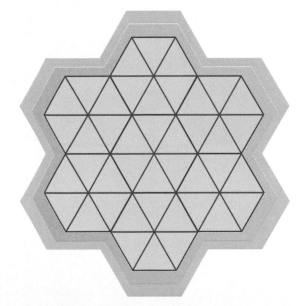

Twelve L-shapes like the ones here need to be inserted in the grid and each L has one hole in it.

There are three pieces of each of the four kinds shown here and any piece may be turned or flipped over before being put in the grid. No pieces of the same kind touch, even at a corner.

The pieces fit together so well that you cannot see any spaces between them; only the holes show.

Can you tell where the Ls are?

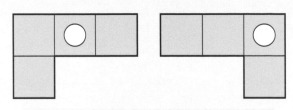

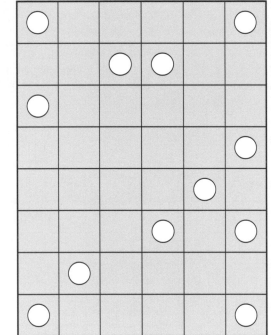

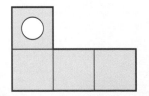
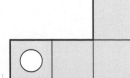

In this puzzle, an amateur coin collector has been out with his metal detector, searching for booty. He didn't have time to dig up all the coins he found, so has made a grid map, showing their locations, in the hope that if he loses the map, at least no-one else will understand it…

Those squares containing numbers are empty, but where a number appears in a square, it indicates how many coins are located in the squares (up to a maximum of eight) surrounding the numbered one, touching it at any corner or side. There is only one coin in any individual square.

Place a circle into every square containing a coin.

3							0	
		3	3	1				
	4	4			1	2			0
			4					
	5		6		1				
								1	
	1					2			1
	0			2	2		1	1	
		2			3			1	
	2			1				1	

The grid should be filled with numbers from 1 to 6, so that each number appears just once in every row and column. The clues refer to the digit totals in the squares, eg A 1 2 3 = 6 means that the numbers in squares A1, A2 and A3 add up to 6.

1 D E 5 = 5

2 C D 6 = 5

3 A 4 5 = 7

4 B 5 6 = 11

5 C 4 5 = 4

6 D 1 2 = 7

7 E 2 3 = 5

8 F 5 6 = 6

9 E F 1 = 8

10 A B C 2 = 6

11 B C D 3 = 11

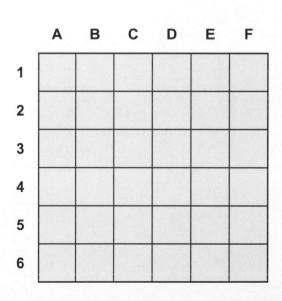

10

Each of the small squares in the grid below contains either A, B or C. Every row and column has exactly two of each letter. Can you tell the letter in each square?

Across

1　The As are both between the Cs.

3　The Cs are both between the As.

4　The Cs are next to and right of the Bs.

5　No two adjacent squares
　contain the same letter.

6　The Cs are both between the Bs.

Down

2　The Cs are lower than the As.

3　The Bs are both between the Cs.

4　The As are in adjacent squares.

5　The As are in adjacent squares.

6　The As are both between the Cs.

	1	2	3	4	5	6
1						
2						
3						
4						
5						
6						

11

The object of this puzzle is to trace a single path from the top left corner to the bottom right corner of the grid, travelling through all of the cells in either a horizontal, vertical or diagonal direction.

Every cell must be entered once only and your path should take you through the numbers in the sequence 1-2-3-4-1-2-3-4, etc.

Can you find the way?

1	2	3	4	4	1	2	3
4	3	1	2	3	2	4	1
1	2	3	4	1	1	3	2
4	2	2	2	3	4	4	3
1	3	1	4	1	1	4	2
3	2	2	3	2	4	1	3
4	2	1	3	4	3	1	4
1	3	4	1	2	2	3	4

Can you place the vessels into the diagram? Some parts of vessels or sea squares have already been filled in. A number to the right or below a row or column refers to the number of occupied squares in that row or column.

Any vessel may be positioned horizontally or vertically, but no part of a vessel touches part of any other vessel, either horizontally, vertically or diagonally.

Empty Area of Sea: ≈

Aircraft Carrier: ◀■■■▶

Battleships: ◀■▶ ◀■■▶

Cruisers: ◀■▶ ◀■▶ ◀■▶

Submarines: ● ● ● ●

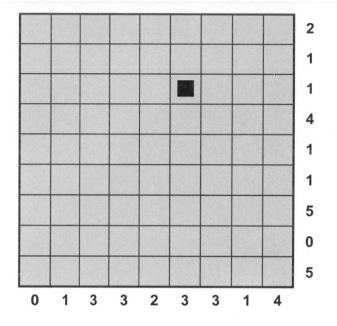

| 2 |
| 1 |
| 1 |
| 4 |
| 1 |
| 1 |
| 5 |
| 0 |
| 5 |

0 1 3 3 2 3 3 1 4

13

Can you fill each square in the bottom line with the correct digit?

Every square in the solution contains only one digit from each of the lettered lines above, although two or more squares in the solution may contain the same digit.

At the end of every row is a score, which shows:

a the number of digits placed in the correct finishing position on the bottom line, as indicated by a tick; and

b the number of digits which appear on the bottom line, but in a different position, as indicated by a cross.

SCORE

5	2	5	4	✔✔
6	1	6	1	✗
3	5	5	5	✔✔✗
3	7	6	5	✔✗
7	0	5	5	✔✔
				✔✔✔✔

Draw a single continuous loop, by connecting the dots. No line may cross the path of another.

The figure inside each set of any four surrounding dots indicates the total number of surrounding lines.

```
1       1   2   2           2   2
        2   0           0       1   2
                                    1
        2   2               2
2       1           3       3   2   2
1                       1   2
    0   2   1   3           2   1
1       1               2   2       1
    1       3       0
            0               1
                        1       1
2   1       1       1   3   2   2
```

Each horizontal row and vertical column should contain different shapes and different numbers.

Every square will contain one number and one shape and no combination may be repeated anywhere else in the puzzle.

| 1 | 2 | 3 | 4 | 5 |

The grid:

	⬡		5	
3				2
☐	☆			
②			◇	
	2		④	

Given that the letters are valued 1-26 according to their places in the alphabet, can you crack the mystery code to reveal the missing letter?

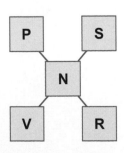

P, S / N / V, R

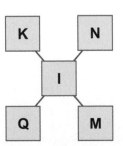

K, N / I / Q, M

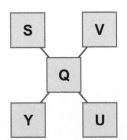

S, V / Q / Y, U

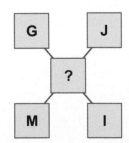

G, J / ? / M, I

A set of dominoes is to be placed in four rows as shown below. The numbers indicate which values are shown on all the dominoes in each column and the relevant half of the domino in every row. Find out where each domino is placed by carefully comparing rows and columns to determine the possible positions of certain dominoes: for instance, if any column contains only one 6, then the domino 6/6 isn't in that column.

A set of dominoes consists of:

0/0, 0/1, 0/2, 0/3, 0/4, 0/5, 0/6, 1/1, 1/2, 1/3, 1/4, 1/5, 1/6, 2/2,

2/3, 2/4, 2/5, 2/6, 3/3, 3/4, 3/5, 3/6, 4/4, 4/5, 4/6, 5/5, 5/6, 6/6.

?	0, 3, 3, 5, 5, 5, 6, 6.	0, 1, 2, 2, 3, 3, 4, 4.	0, 1, 2, 2, 2, 5, 5, 6.	0, 1, 3, 3, 3, 4, 4, 5.	0, 2, 3, 4, 4, 4, 6, 6.	0, 1, 1, 2, 2, 5, 6, 6.	0, 0, 1, 1, 1, 4, 5, 6.
1, 2, 2, 2, 3, 6, 6. **0, 1, 4, 4, 5, 5, 5.**							
0, 0, 0, 2, 2, 4, 5. **0, 0, 2, 3, 3, 4, 5.**							
1, 3, 3, 5, 6, 6, 6. **0, 0, 1, 2, 2, 3, 6.**							
3, 4, 4, 5, 5, 6, 6. **1, 1, 1, 1, 3, 4, 4.**							

Place the eight tiles into the puzzle grid so that all adjacent numbers on each tile match up. Tiles may be rotated through 360 degrees, but none may be flipped over.

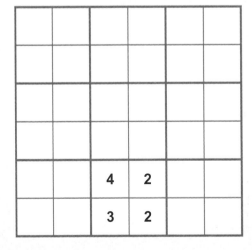

Place all twelve of the pieces into the grid. Any may be rotated or flipped over, but none may touch another, not even diagonally. The numbers outside the grid refer to the number of consecutive black squares; and each block is separated from the others by at least one white square. For instance, '3 2' could refer to a row with none, one or more white squares, then three black squares, then at least one white square, then two more black squares, followed by any number of white squares.

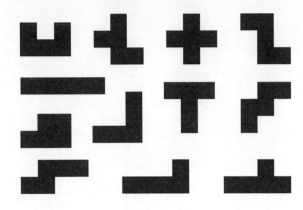

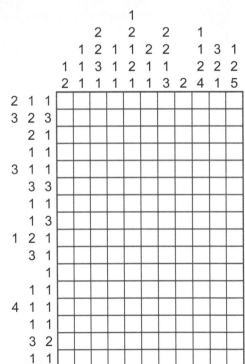

In the diagram below, which letter should replace the question mark?

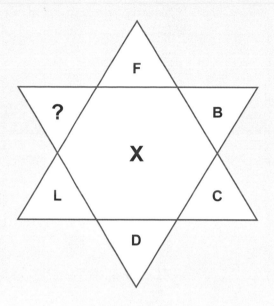

In the square below, change the positions of six numbers, one per horizontal row, vertical column and long diagonal line of six smaller squares, in such a way that the numbers in each row, column and long diagonal line total exactly 169. Any number may appear more than once in a row, column or line.

33	24	22	29	28	50
34	28	16	20	29	25
35	43	28	22	12	25
27	37	29	34	17	16
30	36	32	28	43	24
27	25	25	25	36	20

Every brick in this pyramid contains a number which is the sum of the two numbers below it, so that F=A+B, etc. Just work out the missing numbers!

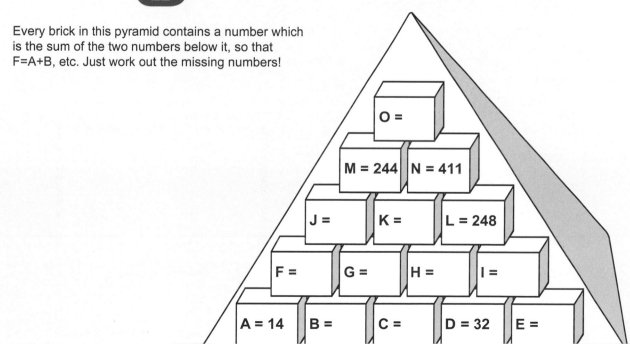

With the starter already given, can you fit all of the remaining listed numbers into this grid? Take care, this puzzle may not be as easy as it looks!

33	416	904	7849	64897
41 ✓	468	928	8590	69839
58	615	933	8591	75809
75	655	945	8890	75891
90	678	967	9389	78955
92	699	970	9756	89175
152	715	2572	14009	97198
201	779	3167	18539	98501
255	789	4279	42695	131835
270	808	4529	42789	628321
341	852	6838	44377	759266
371	890	7158	50181	789126

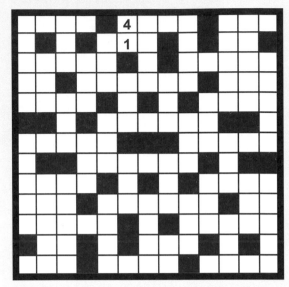

24

The chart gives directions to a hidden treasure behind the centre black square in the grid. Move the indicated number of spaces north, south, east and west (eg 4N means move four squares north) stopping at every square once only to arrive there. At which square should you start?

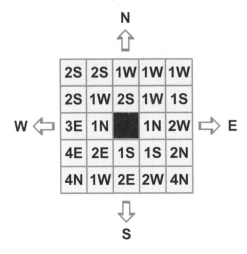

25

Fill the grid so that every horizontal row and vertical column contains the numbers 1-5. The 'greater than' or 'less than' signs indicate where a number is larger or smaller than that in the neighbouring square.

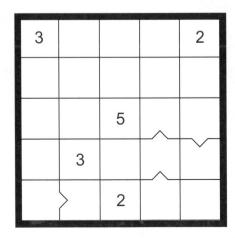

Each of the eight segments of the spider's web should be filled with a different number from 1 to 8, in such a way that every ring also contains a different number from 1 to 8.

The segments run from the outside of the spider's web to the centre, and the rings run all the way around.

Some numbers are already in place. Can you fill in the rest?

Every oval shape in this diagram contains a different letter of the alphabet from A to K inclusive. Use the clues to determine their locations. Reference in the clues to 'due' means in any location along the same horizontal or vertical line.

1 The C is next to and north of the B, which is next to and west of the K, which is further north than the A.

2 The D is next to and east of the J, which is next to and south of the E.

3 The F and the D are both due north of the G.

4 The H is next to and south of the I, which is next to and east of the A.

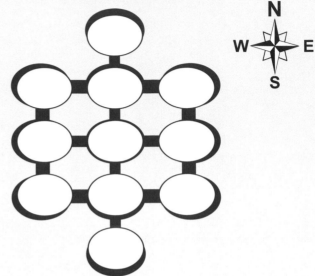

Fill the three empty circles with the symbols +, – and x in some order, to make a sum which totals the number in the centre. Each symbol must be used once and calculations are made in the direction of travel.

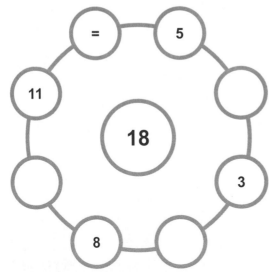

The numbers at the top and on the left side show the quantity of single-digit numbers (1-9) used in that row and column. The numbers at the bottom and on the right side show the sum of the digits. A number may appear more than once in a row or column, but no numbers are in squares that touch, even at a corner.

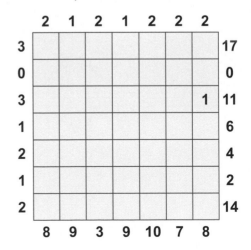

S
E
C
T
I
O
N

6

228

Using the numbers below, complete these six equations (three reading across and three reading downwards). Every number is used once.

	1		2		3		4
	5		6		7		

	+		−		=	10
x	■	−	■	+		
8	−		x		=	9
−	■	+	■	x		
	x		+	9	=	21
=		=		=		
30		8		36		

In the grid below, which number should replace the question mark?

7	8	10	7	6	10	13
14	11	11	12	15	9	8
8	7	11	6	7	9	14
7	18	4	19	8	16	1
9	6	12	5	8	8	15
21	4	18	?	22	2	15
5	10	8	9	4	12	11

When the box below is folded to form a cube, just one of the five options (A, B, C, D or E) can be produced. Which?

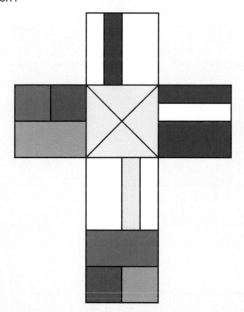

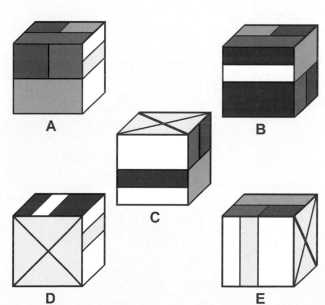

A

B

C

D

E

33

In this puzzle, an amateur coin collector has been out with his metal detector, searching for booty. He didn't have time to dig up all the coins he found, so has made a grid map, showing their locations, in the hope that if he loses the map, at least no-one else will understand it…

Those squares containing numbers are empty, but where a number appears in a square, it indicates how many coins are located in the squares (up to a maximum of eight) surrounding the numbered one, touching it at any corner or side. There is only one coin in any individual square.

Place a circle into every square containing a coin.

	2			0			1
3		2	0			3	1
			1	1	3		
2	5	3					1
	4			3			
			2				
0		4	3			1	0
						0	
	0			5			1
		0				3	

34

Each symbol stands for a different number. In order to reach the correct total at the end of each row and column, what is the value of the circle, cross, pentagon, square and star?

pentagon	cross	square	circle	pentagon	= 19
square	circle	cross	pentagon	square	= 14
pentagon	pentagon	cross	star	cross	= 28
pentagon	star	star	pentagon	star	= 36
circle	square	star	circle	square	= 14

21   21   25   24   20

35

Every row and column of this grid should contain one each of the letters A, B, C, D, E and F. Each of the six shapes (marked by thicker lines) should also contain one each of the letters A, B, C, D, E and F. Can you complete the grid?

			B	A	
	C				
		D			
E					
			F		

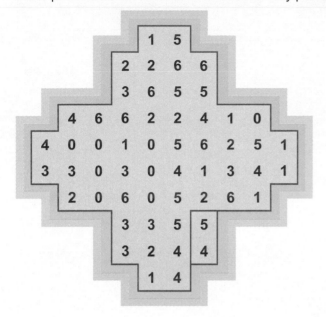

A standard set of 28 dominoes has been laid out as shown. Can you draw in the edges of them all? The check-box is provided as an aid and the domino already placed will help.

0-0	0-1	0-2	0-3	0-4	0-5	0-6

1-1	1-2	1-3	1-4	1-5	1-6	2-2

2-3	2-4	2-5	2-6	3-3	3-4	3-5

3-6	4-4	4-5	4-6	5-5	5-6	6-6
		✔				

Each of the small squares in the grid below contains either A, B or C. Every row and column has exactly two of each letter. Can you tell the letter in each square?

Across

1 The Bs are further right than the As.
2 No two adjacent squares contain the same letter.
4 The Cs are next to and right of the Bs.
5 No two adjacent squares contain the same letter.
6 The Cs are both between the Bs.

Down

1 Each C is directly next to and below a B.
2 The Bs are lower than the Cs.
3 The As are in adjacent squares.
5 The As are both between the Cs.
6 The Bs are in adjacent squares.

Every row and column in this grid originally contained one heart, one club, one diamond, one spade and two blank squares, although not necessarily in that order.

Every symbol with a black arrow refers to the first of the four symbols encountered when travelling in the direction of the arrow. Every symbol with a white arrow refers to the second of the four symbols encountered in the direction of the arrow.

Can you complete the original grid?

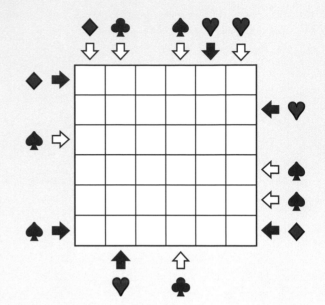

The blank squares below should be filled with whole numbers between 1 and 30 inclusive, any of which may occur more than once, or not at all.

The numbers in every horizontal row add up to the totals on the right, as do the two long diagonal lines; whilst those in every vertical column add up to the totals along the bottom.

							119
	30	1			20	13	111
27				15	24	26	134
13	10		3	30			88
	14	13	28		8	29	95
	17		30	2	25	28	124
27		23	9	19	11	11	107
6	10	22		2	6	23	80
98	90	98	113	99	109	132	93

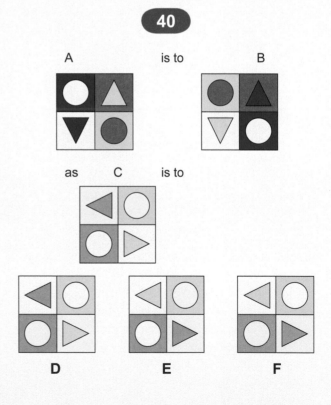

S
E
C
T
I
O
N

Can you place the hexagons into the grid, so that where any hexagon touches another along a straight line, the number in both triangles is the same? No rotation of any hexagon is allowed!

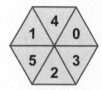

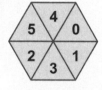

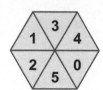

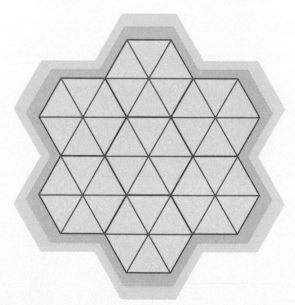

Twelve L-shapes like the ones here need to be inserted in the grid and each L has one hole in it.

There are three pieces of each of the four kinds shown here and any piece may be turned or flipped over before being put in the grid. No pieces of the same kind touch, even at a corner.

The pieces fit together so well that you cannot see any spaces between them; only the holes show.

Can you tell where the Ls are?

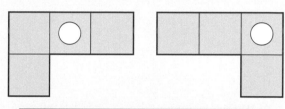

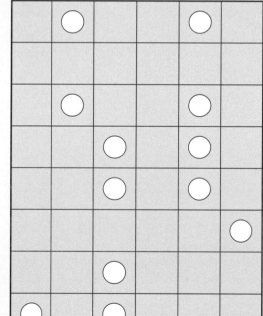

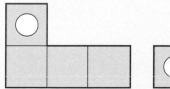

43

Which of the four lettered alternatives (A, B, C or D) fits most logically into the empty square?

6	11	5
5	32	3
12	13	9

14	3	7
9	32	16
3	4	8

9	1	16
14	32	7
3	10	4

?

12	7	16
3	32	3
1	20	5

A

3	11	12
4	32	8
12	9	5

B

6	11	7
13	32	8
10	1	9

C

6	7	15
10	32	9
11	8	10

D

44

Which four pieces can be fitted together to form an exact copy of this shape?

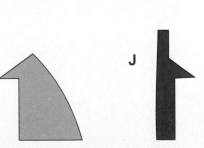
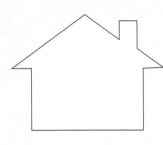
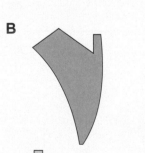
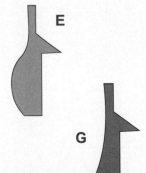
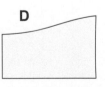
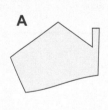
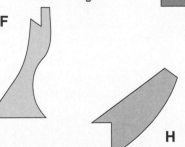

A

B

C

D

E

F

G

H

I

J

Can you place the vessels into the diagram? Some parts of vessels or sea squares have already been filled in. A number to the right or below a row or column refers to the number of occupied squares in that row or column.

Any vessel may be positioned horizontally or vertically, but no part of a vessel touches part of any other vessel, either horizontally, vertically or diagonally.

Empty Area of Sea: ≈

Aircraft Carrier: ◄▮▮▮►

Battleships: ◄▮▮► ◄▮▮►

Cruisers: ◄▮► ◄▮► ◄▮►

Submarines: ● ● ● ●

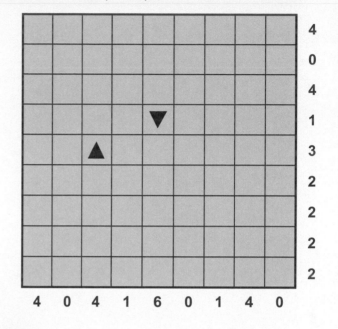

Columns: 4 0 4 1 6 0 1 4 0

Rows: 4 0 4 1 3 2 2 2 2

Can you fill each square in the bottom line with the correct digit?

Every square in the solution contains only one digit from each of the lettered lines above, although two or more squares in the solution may contain the same digit.

At the end of every row is a score, which shows:

a the number of digits placed in the correct finishing position on the bottom line, as indicated by a tick; and

b the number of digits which appear on the bottom line, but in a different position, as indicated by a cross.

				SCORE
5	6	7	5	✔ ✗
5	4	7	7	✔ ✔
5	3	2	7	✔
4	7	1	0	✔
2	3	1	7	✔
				✔ ✔ ✔ ✔

The grid should be filled with numbers from 1 to 6, so that each number appears just once in every row and column. The clues refer to the digit totals in the squares, eg A 1 2 3 = 6 means that the numbers in squares A1, A2 and A3 add up to 6.

1 B C D 6 = 15

2 A 2 3 4 = 11

3 B 1 2 = 9

4 C 2 3 = 10

5 D 3 4 = 5

6 E 4 5 = 10

7 F 5 6 = 9

8 C D 1 = 3

9 D E 2 = 6

10 E F 3 = 9

11 B C 4 = 8

	A	B	C	D	E	F
1						
2						
3						
4						
5						
6						

The object of this puzzle is to trace a single path from the top left corner to the bottom right corner of the grid, travelling through all of the cells in either a horizontal, vertical or diagonal direction.

Every cell must be entered once only and your path should take you through the numbers in the sequence 1-2-3-4-1-2-3-4, etc.

Can you find the way?

1	2	3	4	1	2	3	4
1	4	1	2	4	3	2	1
2	3	3	2	3	4	1	2
3	2	1	4	1	1	3	4
4	2	2	3	4	3	2	3
1	1	3	1	4	2	1	4
3	2	4	3	4	3	2	3
4	1	2	1	2	4	1	4

SECTION 6

49

Draw a single continuous loop, by connecting the dots. No line may cross the path of another.

The figure inside each set of any four surrounding dots indicates the total number of surrounding lines.

```
.  .  .  .  .  .  .  .  .  .  .  .  .  .
      .  .  .  .  .  1  .  .  1  .  .  .
   .  0  2  2  .  .  .  .  .  .  1  2  .
      .  .  .  .  1  3  2  .  2  .  .  .
   .  2  2  2  2  .  2  .  .  .  2  .  .
      1  1  0  .  .  .  .  .  1  .  .  .
   .  .  .  .  2  1  1  2  .  .  .  .  .
   2  2  1  .  2  2  .  .  1  .  .  .
   2  .  .  .  .  .  .  0  .  1  .  .
   2  .  .  0  .  1  .  1  .  .  .  .
      1  1  .  .  .  2  2  0  .  .  .
         .  1  .  .  .  .  .  1  .  .
   3  .  1  .  1  1  3  .  2  .  .  .
   .  .  .  .  .  .  .  .  .  .  .  .
```

50

Each horizontal row and vertical column should contain different shapes and different numbers.

Every square will contain one number and one shape and no combination may be repeated anywhere else in the puzzle.

◇	○	☆	⬡	▢
1	2	3	4	5

2	☆1	○	5	
		2		◇
		1		
		⬡	☆	○2
3	5			

51

Given that the letters are valued 1-26 according to their places in the alphabet, can you crack the mystery code to reveal the missing letter?

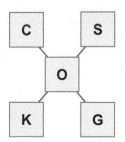
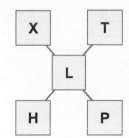
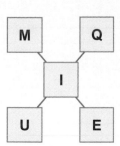
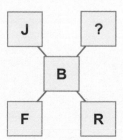

Which is the odd one out?

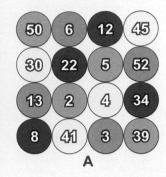

A

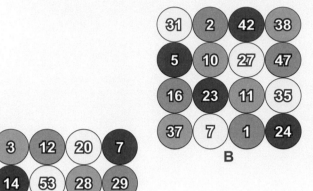

B

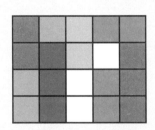

C

D

Which of the alternatives (A, B, C or D) comes next in this sequence?

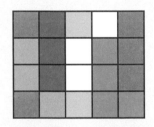

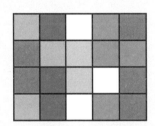

?

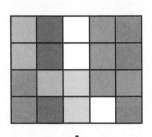

A

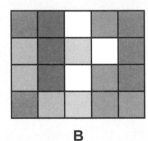

B

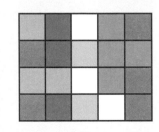

C

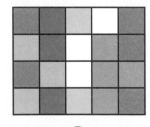

D

Place the eight tiles into the puzzle grid so that all adjacent numbers on each tile match up. Tiles may be rotated through 360 degrees, but none may be flipped over.

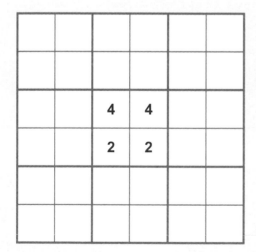

Place all twelve of the pieces into the grid. Any may be rotated or flipped over, but none may touch another, not even diagonally. The numbers outside the grid refer to the number of consecutive black squares; and each block is separated from the others by at least one white square. For instance, '3 2' could refer to a row with none, one or more white squares, then three black squares, then at least one white square, then two more black squares, followed by any number of white squares.

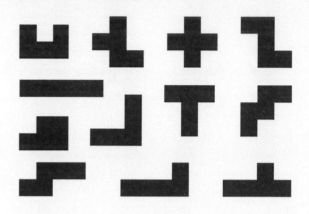

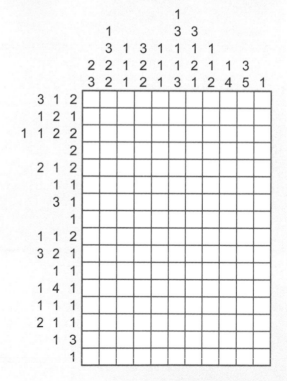

56

In the diagram below, which letter should replace the question mark?

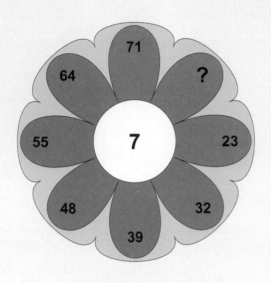

71
64
?
55
7
23
48
32
39

57

In the square below, change the positions of six numbers, one per horizontal row, vertical column and long diagonal line of six smaller squares, in such a way that the numbers in each row, column and long diagonal line total exactly 176. Any number may appear more than once in a row, column or line.

29	35	38	20	16	27
33	31	13	23	29	46
29	16	25	29	34	17
33	14	38	31	28	37
24	31	44	46	25	14
27	38	23	35	18	60

58

Every brick in this pyramid contains a number which is the sum of the two numbers below it, so that F=A+B, etc. Just work out the missing numbers!

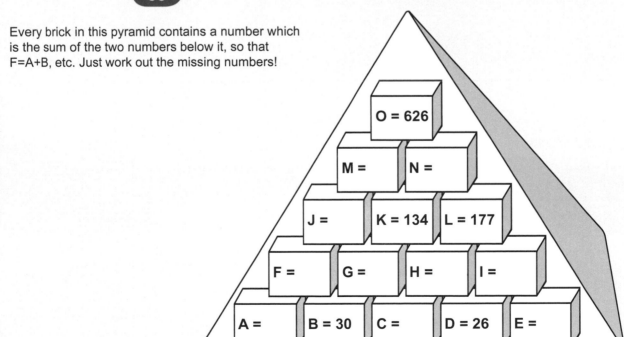

O = 626

M =   N =

J =   K = 134   L = 177

F =   G =   H =   I =

A =   B = 30   C =   D = 26   E =

With the starter already given, can you fit all of the remaining listed numbers into this grid? Take care, this puzzle may not be as easy as it looks!

15	263	892	15762	83725
24	334	934	22729	83850
32	416	1702	28194	86425
42	424	3125	30003	86676
43	427	4432	34653	141670
52	443	6528	44176	420042
55	516	6879	47690	421841
59	610	7045	50823	464184
60	634	7212	61452	541760
62 ✓	740	7389	62594	580594
71	741	7980	73524	835000
73	840	9876	77032	988447

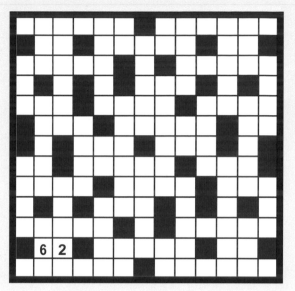

The chart gives directions to a hidden treasure behind the centre black square in the grid. Move the indicated number of spaces north, south, east and west (eg 4N means move four squares north) stopping at every square once only to arrive there. At which square should you start?

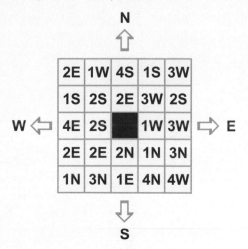

Fill the grid so that every horizontal row and vertical column contains the numbers 1-5. The 'greater than' or 'less than' signs indicate where a number is larger or smaller than that in the neighbouring square.

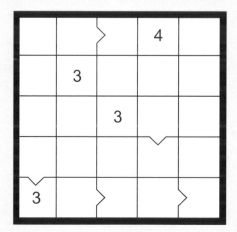

Each of the eight segments of the spider's web should be filled with a different number from 1 to 8, in such a way that every ring also contains a different number from 1 to 8.

The segments run from the outside of the spider's web to the centre, and the rings run all the way around.

Some numbers are already in place. Can you fill in the rest?

Every oval shape in this diagram contains a different letter of the alphabet from A to K inclusive. Use the clues to determine their locations. Reference in the clues to 'due' means in any location along the same horizontal or vertical line.

1 The E is next to and south of the G, which is next to and west of the H.

2 The H is next to and south of the B, which is next to and east of the K.

3 The J is next to and west of the C, which is next to and south of the F.

4 The K is next to and east of the A, which is next to and north of the I.

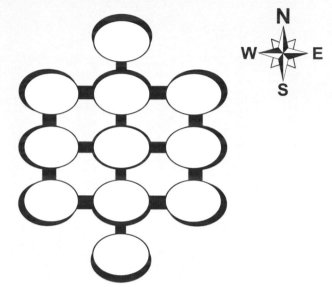

Fill the three empty circles with the symbols +, − and x in some order, to make a sum which totals the number in the centre. Each symbol must be used once and calculations are made in the direction of travel.

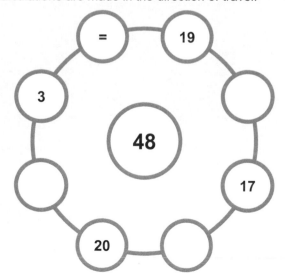

The numbers at the top and on the left side show the quantity of single-digit numbers (1-9) used in that row and column. The numbers at the bottom and on the right side show the sum of the digits. A number may appear more than once in a row or column, but no numbers are in squares that touch, even at a corner.

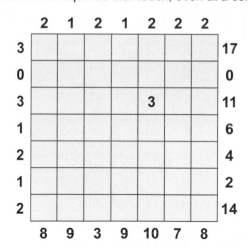

66

Using the numbers below, complete these six equations (three reading across and three reading downwards). Every number is used once.

1	2	3	5
6	7	8	9

	−	4	x		=	24
+		x		−		
	+		x		=	20
x		−		+		
	−		+		=	9
=		=		=		
45		33		11		

67

In the grid below, which number should replace the question mark?

32	27	22	17	12	7	2
41	38	35	32	29	26	23
26	22	18	14	10	6	2
87	76	65	54	43	32	21
60	51	42	33	24	15	6
14	12	10	8	6	4	2
57	49	41	33	25	17	?

68

When the box below is folded to form a cube, just one of the five options (A, B, C, D or E) can be produced. Which?

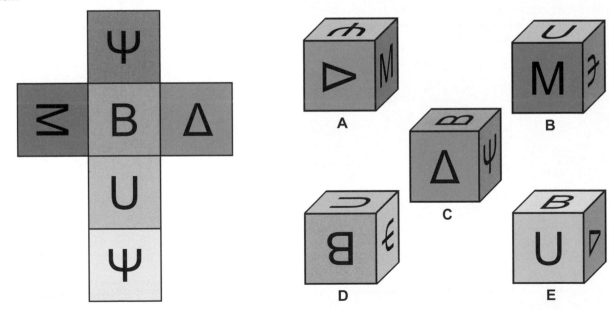

A

B

C

D

E

In this puzzle, an amateur coin collector has been out with his metal detector, searching for booty. He didn't have time to dig up all the coins he found, so has made a grid map, showing their locations, in the hope that if he loses the map, at least no-one else will understand it…

Those squares containing numbers are empty, but where a number appears in a square, it indicates how many coins are located in the squares (up to a maximum of eight) surrounding the numbered one, touching it at any corner or side. There is only one coin in any individual square.

Place a circle into every square containing a coin.

1			1				4	3	
		0		3					
			2		6		6		2
1	2	3		4					
1				3		2		1	
									1
		1			0		0		
	0					1	2	2	1
	1			2	2				
1				1				2	

Every row and column of this grid should contain one each of the letters A, B, C, D, E and F. Each of the six shapes (marked by thicker lines) should also contain one each of the letters A, B, C, D, E and F. Can you complete the grid?

		A			
					B
D	C				
		E			
					F

Each symbol stands for a different number. In order to reach the correct total at the end of each row and column, what is the value of the circle, cross, pentagon, square and star?

cross	cross	cross	star	circle	= 29
cross	circle	star	cross	circle	= 30
square	star	cross	circle	star	= 29
pentagon	circle	cross	circle	square	= 28
cross	pentagon	star	star	cross	= 35
= 26	= 34	= 31	= 33	= 27	

A standard set of 28 dominoes has been laid out as shown. Can you draw in the edges of them all? The checkbox is provided as an aid and the domino already placed will help.

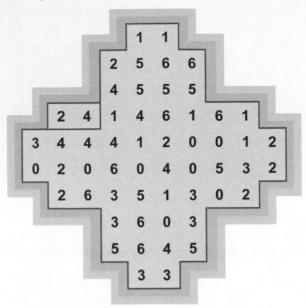

0-0	0-1	0-2	0-3	0-4	0-5	0-6

1-1	1-2	1-3	1-4	1-5	1-6	2-2

2-3	2-4	2-5	2-6	3-3	3-4	3-5
	✔					

3-6	4-4	4-5	4-6	5-5	5-6	6-6

Each of the small squares in the grid below contains either A, B or C. Every row and column has exactly two of each letter. Can you tell the letter in each square?

Across
1   The As are further right than the Cs.
3   The Bs are next to and right of the As.
5   The Cs are next to and right of the As.
6   The Cs are both between the Bs.

Down
2   The Bs are both between the Cs.
3   The Bs are in adjacent squares.
4   The Bs are lower than the Cs.
5   The Cs are both between the Bs.

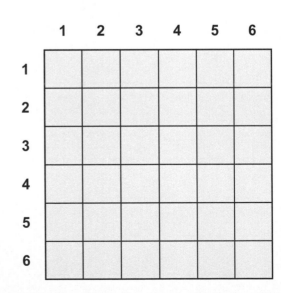

Every row and column in this grid originally contained one heart, one club, one diamond, one spade and two blank squares, although not necessarily in that order.

Every symbol with a black arrow refers to the first of the four symbols encountered when travelling in the direction of the arrow. Every symbol with a white arrow refers to the second of the four symbols encountered in the direction of the arrow.

Can you complete the original grid?

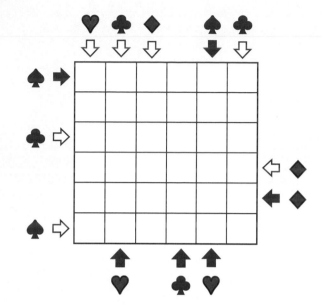

75

The blank squares below should be filled with whole numbers between 1 and 30 inclusive, any of which may occur more than once, or not at all.

The numbers in every horizontal row add up to the totals on the right, as do the two long diagonal lines; whilst those in every vertical column add up to the totals along the bottom.

76

							132
19	13		12		17	5	105
14	5	17			9	18	79
2	24	27		30		30	148
	15	19	28		11	24	112
15	3		4	21	15	15	88
18			26	11	17		120
	15	14	28	29			136
98	103	123	120	120	109	115	128

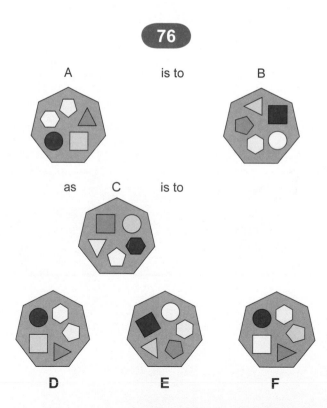

A   is to   B

as   C   is to

D   E   F

Can you place the hexagons into the grid, so that where any hexagon touches another along a straight line, the number in both triangles is the same? No rotation of any hexagon is allowed!

Twelve L-shapes like the ones here need to be inserted in the grid and each L has one hole in it.

There are three pieces of each of the four kinds shown here and any piece may be turned or flipped over before being put in the grid. No pieces of the same kind touch, even at a corner.

The pieces fit together so well that you cannot see any spaces between them; only the holes show.

Can you tell where the Ls are?

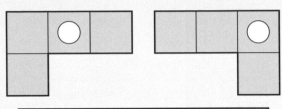

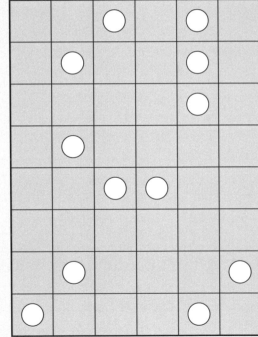

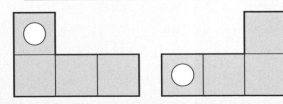

S E C T I O N

6

Given that scales A and B balance perfectly, how many spades are needed to balance scale C?

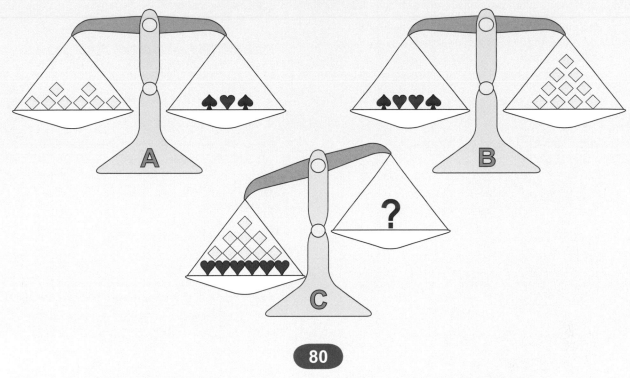

Which of the four lettered alternatives (A, B, C or D) fits most logically into the empty square?

28	31	27
24	29	26
23	25	30

30	27	29
20	25	22
25	21	32

34	18	33
11	16	14
29	13	36

A

34	18	33
11	17	14
29	12	36

B

32	23	31
16	21	18
27	17	34

?

34	19	33
12	16	14
29	13	36

C

34	19	33
12	17	14
29	13	36

D

The object of this puzzle is to trace a single path from the top left corner to the bottom right corner of the grid, travelling through all of the cells in either a horizontal, vertical or diagonal direction.

Every cell must be entered once only and your path should take you through the numbers in the sequence 1-2-3-4-1-2-3-4, etc.

Can you find the way?

1	2	3	2	3	4	1	3
1	4	1	4	4	3	2	4
2	3	2	3	1	2	2	1
3	1	4	2	4	1	3	4
1	4	1	2	3	2	1	2
3	2	4	3	4	1	1	3
1	4	2	3	2	1	2	4
2	3	4	1	3	4	3	4

The grid should be filled with numbers from 1 to 6, so that each number appears just once in every row and column. The clues refer to the digit totals in the squares, eg A 1 2 3 = 6 means that the numbers in squares A1, A2 and A3 add up to 6.

1 C D 5 = 10

2 C D E 6 = 6

3 A 3 4 5 = 9

4 B 4 5 = 6

5 C 1 2 = 5

6 D 3 4 = 8

7 E 2 3 = 11

8 F 4 5 = 3

9 D E 1 = 9

10 A B 2 = 7

11 B C 3 = 10

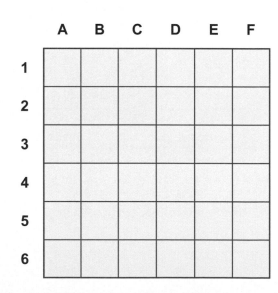

Can you fill each square in the bottom line with the correct digit?

Every square in the solution contains only one digit from each of the lettered lines above, although two or more squares in the solution may contain the same digit.

At the end of every row is a score, which shows:

   a the number of digits placed in the correct finishing position on the bottom line, as indicated by a tick; and

   b the number of digits which appear on the bottom line, but in a different position, as indicated by a cross.

SCORE

0	4	2	0	✓ ✗ ✗
0	4	2	4	✓ ✗
4	5	0	3	✓
6	0	2	2	✓ ✗ ✗
7	2	1	1	✓
				✓ ✓ ✓ ✓

Can you place the vessels into the diagram? Some parts of vessels or sea squares have already been filled in. A number to the right or below a row or column refers to the number of occupied squares in that row or column.

Any vessel may be positioned horizontally or vertically, but no part of a vessel touches part of any other vessel, either horizontally, vertically or diagonally.

Empty Area of Sea: ≈

Aircraft Carrier: ◀▮▮▶

Battleships: ◀▮▶ ◀▮▶

Cruisers: ◀▶ ◀▶ ◀▶

Submarines: ● ● ● ●

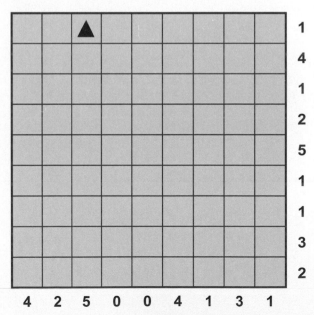

85

Draw a single continuous loop, by connecting the dots. No line may cross the path of another.

The figure inside each set of any four surrounding dots indicates the total number of surrounding lines.

```
. . . . . . . . . . .
            2   2       2
. . . . . . . . . . .
        3   2               0   2
. . . . . . . . . . .
      0           1       0
. . . . . . . . . . .
  1           2   1     3   1
. . . . . . . . . . .
    2   2   2               1
. . . . . . . . . . .
  1   1           1   2   2       2
. . . . . . . . . . .
            2   2           1
. . . . . . . . . . .
    1       1       2       1
. . . . . . . . . . .
  1   0   1   0       1       2
. . . . . . . . . . .
                1       3   2   2
. . . . . . . . . . .
                1       2   2
. . . . . . . . . . .
  2   1   1       1           3
. . . . . . . . . . .
```

86

Each horizontal row and vertical column should contain different shapes and different numbers.

Every square will contain one number and one shape and no combination may be repeated anywhere else in the puzzle.

1   2   3   4   5

		⬡		☆5
⬡5	◇2		◯	1
	5		☆	
	⬡4			2

87

Given that the letters are valued 1-26 according to their places in the alphabet, can you crack the mystery code to reveal the missing letter?

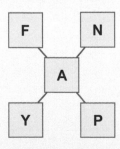

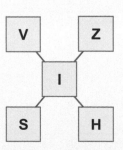

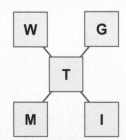

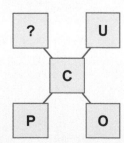

Place the eight tiles into the puzzle grid so that all adjacent numbers on each tile match up. Tiles may be rotated through 360 degrees, but none may be flipped over.

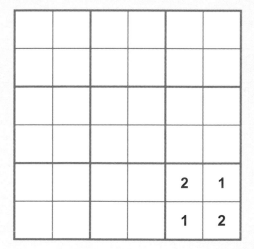

Place all twelve of the pieces into the grid. Any may be rotated or flipped over, but none may touch another, not even diagonally. The numbers outside the grid refer to the number of consecutive black squares; and each block is separated from the others by at least one white square. For instance, '3 2' could refer to a row with none, one or more white squares, then three black squares, then at least one white square, then two more black squares, followed by any number of white squares.

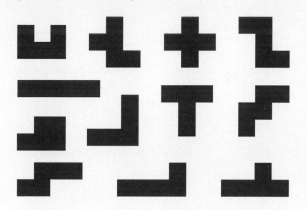

90

In the diagram below, which letter should replace the question mark?

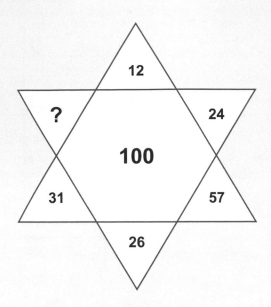

12

?

24

100

31

57

26

91

In the square below, change the positions of six numbers, one per horizontal row, vertical column and long diagonal line of six smaller squares, in such a way that the numbers in each row, column and long diagonal line total exactly 195. Any number may appear more than once in a row, column or line.

41	32	23	30	37	47
44	32	31	17	41	36
55	34	28	22	15	37
8	60	35	42	22	35
17	28	40	43	33	32
28	24	34	19	53	15

92

Every brick in this pyramid contains a number which is the sum of the two numbers below it, so that F=A+B, etc. Just work out the missing numbers!

O = 978

M =   N =

J =   K = 225   L =

F =   G =   H =   I = 147

A = 137   B =   C = 52   D =   E =

With the starter already given, can you fit all of the remaining listed numbers into this grid? Take care, this puzzle may not be as easy as it looks!

21 ✓	147	423	1261	20794
27	152	448	1353	35514
34	155	486	1729	54180
36	163	520	2610	67394
43	179	588	2974	240809
45	180	617	3873	253874
58	198	619	4519	282014
68	260	635	6795	329495
71	265	638	9008	391095
72	267	744	9670	399739
76	349	820	20365	928609
88	410	879	20405	960710

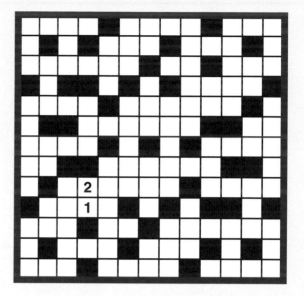

The chart gives directions to a hidden treasure behind the centre black square in the grid. Move the indicated number of spaces north, south, east and west (eg 4N means move four squares north) stopping at every square once only to arrive there. At which square should you start?

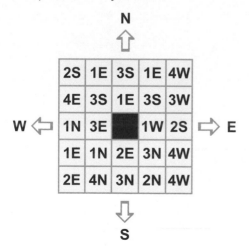

Fill the grid so that every horizontal row and vertical column contains the numbers 1-5. The 'greater than' or 'less than' signs indicate where a number is larger or smaller than that in the neighbouring square.

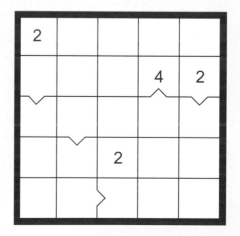

Each of the eight segments of the spider's web should be filled with a different number from 1 to 8, in such a way that every ring also contains a different number from 1 to 8.

The segments run from the outside of the spider's web to the centre, and the rings run all the way around.

Some numbers are already in place. Can you fill in the rest?

No 1

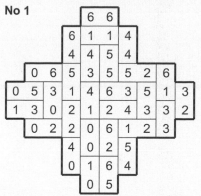

No 2

5: Replacing the value of the diamond from scale A into scale B gives 1 spade + 1 spade + 1 heart = 2 hearts, so 2 spades = 1 heart. Converting the hearts value in scale A to spades gives 1 spade + 2 spades = 1 diamond, so 3 spades = 1 diamond. Therefore 1 diamond + 1 heart = 5 spades.

No 3

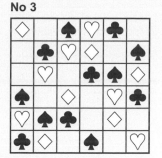

No 4

116

23	7	15	2	17	17	7	88
8	13	11	8	1	24	6	71
22	5	21	16	23	18	28	133
16	22	19	11	6	23	15	112
2	24	4	21	14	17	17	99
5	23	29	6	25	21	8	117
24	2	30	16	2	11	30	115
100	96	129	80	88	131	111	133

No 5

Clocks gain 52½ minutes each time.

No 6

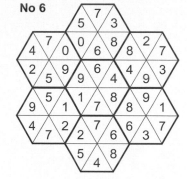

No 7

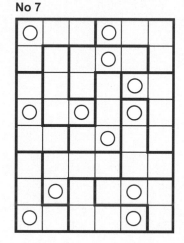

No 8

1			●	3				
●		2		●		●	1	0
	●	2	●	3	●	3	2	
	1	3			4	4	●	1
2		2	●	●	●	●		
●	●	3		●		5	4	●
3			●	2	2	●	3	0
●							●	
2		1	●	4	●			1
●			2	●	●	2		

No 9

2	3	5	6	1	4
3	1	4	5	2	6
1	4	6	3	5	2
5	2	3	4	6	1
4	6	1	2	3	5
6	5	2	1	4	3

No 10

C	B	B	C	A	A
A	C	C	B	B	A
A	B	A	C	C	B
C	A	C	A	B	B
B	A	A	B	C	C
B	C	B	A	A	C

No 11

1	5	6	1	1	3
2	4	2	6	2	4
3	3	4	5	1	5
4	5	3	2	2	6
1	6	4	1	4	3
2	3	5	6	5	6

No 12

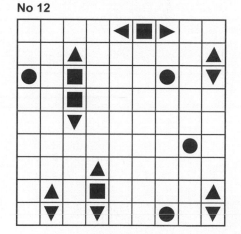

No 13

3467

No 16

The value of the letter in the central square is the sum total of the values of the letters in the other squares. Thus the missing value is 21, so the missing letter is U.

No 14

```
3 2 1 . 1 1 1 . 3 .
3 . 0 1 . . 0 0 2 .
3 . 3 3 . 2 1 . 1 1
2 1 2 . 2 . . 1 . .
1 . 3 . . 3 3 1 . .
. . . . . 1 . . 1 .
. . . . 1 2 . . 2 2
1 0 3 . . . . . . .
. 3 2 1 . . . . . .
2 . . . 1 1 0 0 2 .
2 2 . 2 2 . . 1 1 .
```

No 19

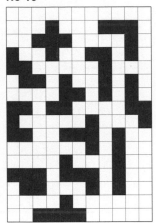

No 15

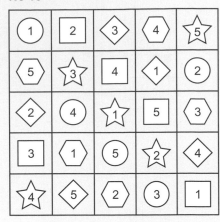

No 17

| 4 | 6 | 6 | 6 | 5 | 4 | 0 |
| 2 | 2 | 4 | 3 | 5 | 3 | 0 |

| 5 | 2 | 5 | 5 | 2 | 4 | 6 |
| 2 | 3 | 6 | 1 | 0 | 1 | 0 |

| 4 | 3 | 5 | 1 | 5 | 1 | 1 |
| 0 | 0 | 3 | 1 | 0 | 0 | 6 |

| 4 | 1 | 6 | 3 | 2 | 4 | 1 |
| 5 | 2 | 6 | 3 | 2 | 4 | 3 |

No 18

3	1	1	4	4	1
2	2	2	3	3	1
2	2	2	3	3	1
3	4	4	3	3	1
3	4	4	3	3	1
2	2	2	4	4	1

No 20

G – Assign a number to each letter according to its place in the alphabet, so B=2, D=4, F=6, J=10 and L=12, making a total of 34. The total in the centre is 41, so the missing letter is G (=7).

No 21

28	12	18	25	31	36
39	25	23	14	**25**	24
36	**32**	25	19	13	25
16	36	25	31	19	**23**
13	27	**34**	29	23	24
18	18	25	**32**	39	18

No 22

A=118, B=99, C=25, D=10, E=24, F=217, G=124, H=35, I=34, J=341, K=159, L=69, M=500, N=228, O=728.

No 23

2	3	6	7		2	7	3		5	6	3	8
1		3	0		9		4	3	2	6		6
6	2	0		6	2	8	5		1	1		1
	7	8	9	0	6		6	7	8	3	4	0
7	2		1		3	5	7			9		
6	3	6	4	3	0		9	3	6	7	3	5
4		7	3	8			6	2	5			1
6	2	7	5	8	3		7	6	3	8	9	0
	4			6	2	8		4		1	5	
1	7	2	8	5	5		7	3	9	8	0	
5		8	0		4	2	7	7		4	2	6
9		5	3	7	8		3		6	6		1
4	6	3	8		9	0	9		4	7	8	4

No 24

1S	2E	2E	1S	2S
2E	2S	1N	2W	2S
2N	1W	■	1W	1N
1S	1W	1S	1W	1W
1E	2N	2E	2N	1W

No 25

3	2	4	5	1
2	1	3	4	5
4	5	2	1	3
1	4	5	3	2
5	3	1	2	4

No 26

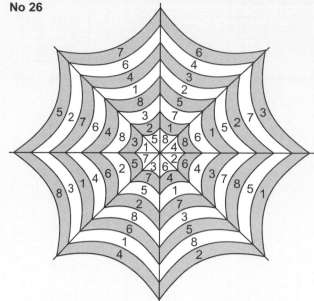

No 27

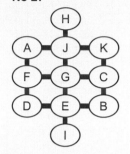

No 28

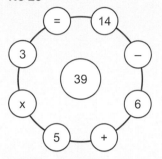

No 29

3					1
		6		9	
4					7
			4		
	1				3
		7			
4				1	

No 30

6	–	2	x	5	=	20
+	■	x	■	+		
3	x	9	+	4	=	31
x	■	+	■	–		
8	–	7	+	1	=	2
=		=		=		
72		25		8		

No 31

22 – All of the numbers in any row across total 162.

No 32

A

No 34

Circle = 3, cross = 1, pentagon = 4, square = 9, star = 6.

No 35

E	D	F	C	B	A
C	E	B	A	F	D
B	A	D	E	C	F
F	B	C	D	A	E
D	C	A	F	E	B
A	F	E	B	D	C

No 33

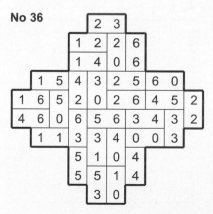

No 36

			2	3					
		1	2	2	6				
		1	4	0	6				
	1	5	4	3	2	5	6	0	
1	6	5	2	0	2	6	4	5	2
4	6	0	6	5	6	3	4	3	2
	1	1	3	3	4	0	0	3	
		5	1	0	4				
		5	5	1	4				
			3	0					

259

No 37

B	A	B	A	C	C
B	C	C	B	A	A
A	B	C	C	A	B
C	B	A	A	C	B
C	A	B	C	B	A
A	C	A	B	B	C

No 40

F (269 x 2 = 538)

No 38

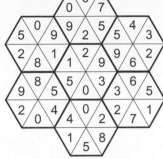

No 41

No 39

123

18	7	3	26	23	24	27	128
11	29	18	4	25	1	30	118
1	21	10	24	10	6	22	94
25	4	24	12	18	12	18	113
22	20	27	26	17	9	30	151
11	16	24	1	15	5	13	85
30	22	11	18	15	28	7	131

118	119	117	111	123	85	147	98

No 42

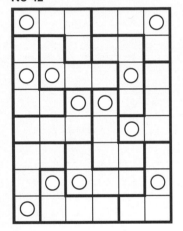

No 45

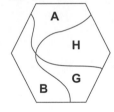

No 43

D - The top row of each contains the digits 4, 6 and 9 which ascend in numerical order (469, 496, 649), as do the digits 3, 5 and 7 (357, 375, 537) of the middle row, as do the digits 4, 6 and 8 (468, 486, 648) of the bottom row.

No 44

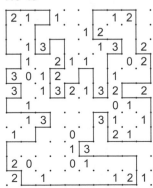

A

H

G

B

No 46

1344

No 47

1	3	2	4	5	6
3	2	1	5	6	4
5	6	3	2	4	1
4	5	6	3	1	2
6	4	5	1	2	3
2	1	4	6	3	5

No 48

1	6	1	2	4	5
2	5	4	3	3	6
3	4	5	6	2	1
5	4	4	1	3	2
6	3	5	3	4	5
1	2	6	1	2	6

No 49

No 50

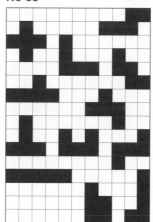

No 51

The sum total of the values of the letters in the top left and bottom right squares equals that of the value of the letter in the central square, as does the sum total of the values of the letters in the top right and bottom left squares. Thus the missing value is 17, so the missing letter is Q.

No 52

E - From top to bottom the sections follow the sequence of the colours of the rainbow.

No 53

A – The small pieces rotate 45°.

No 54

2	3	3	2	2	3
1	2	2	4	4	3
1	2	2	4	4	3
1	4	4	2	2	2
1	4	4	2	2	2
1	4	4	3	3	3

No 56

26 – The two numbers on opposite petals total the number in the centre.

No 58

A=73, B=14, C=67, D=16, E=55, F=87, G=81, H=83, I=71, J=168, K=164, L=154, M=332, N=318, O=650.

No 55

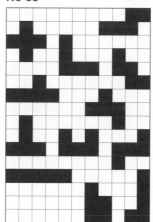

No 57

21	10	33	19	**58**	21
32	27	23	34	27	19
23	45	27	**37**	12	18
36	**41**	27	17	10	31
27	27	**23**	28	27	30
23	12	29	27	28	**43**

No 59

4	5	3		7	5	4		1	2	3	0	7
5		7	5	4	7	5		8	9	0		4
4	3	4		6	0	0	7	0		1	1	1
2		0	3		6	5	3			2	0	
4	1	6	2		5	7		7	5	1	2	0
	4		5	7	3	8	6	2		2		1
	3	1	5		3		1		7	8	3	
1		6		7	8	3	8	2	0			0
8	5	7	8	1		4	9		4	1	5	5
6	1			4	1	6		8		3		6
9	0	1		5	0	0	1	3		6	2	7
8		5	8	1			5	9	1	0	9		3
8	5	9	0	1		8	5	9		7	5	1

No 60

2S	2E	2W	1W	**1S**
1E	1N	2S	2S	2W
1E	2E		1N	2W
2N	1S	1W	1E	1N
1N	2E	2W	1E	2W

No 61

4	3	5	2	1
2	1	4	3	5
3	2	1	5	4
5	4	3	1	2
1	5	2	4	3

No 62

No 63

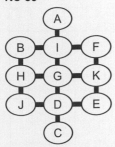

No 64

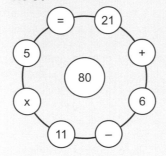

No 65

	9			7		1
		1		3		7
6						
		2			2	
2						
			9		5	

No 66

4	+	9	−	6	=	7
x	■	x	■	−		
7	−	1	x	3	=	18
−	■	−	■	+		
2	x	5	−	8	=	2
=		=		=		
26		4		11		

No 67

63 – All of the numbers in any column down total 267.

No 68

A

No 69

	0		●		1	●	2	3	●
			3	3			●		●
●	2		●	●	2		1		1
		●	3		●				1
0		2					2	●	
		1	●		1	1		●	3
0				4	●			4	●
			●	●	3	●	●	●	
2	2		●				4	3	
●	●		2	●	1		●	1	

No 70

F	D	E	C	B	A
A	F	B	D	E	C
B	C	D	F	A	E
E	B	C	A	D	F
D	A	F	E	C	B
C	E	A	B	F	D

No 71

Circle = 5, cross = 7, pentagon = 3, square = 8, star = 6.

No 72

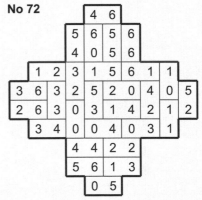

No 73

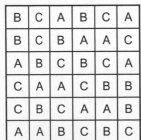

No 74

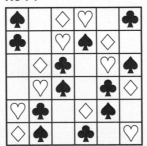

No 75

28	13	2	13	19	28	21	124
22	13	27	2	24	3	27	118
18	2	17	10	19	2	16	84
7	28	15	5	6	10	12	83
29	25	14	5	17	5	4	99
7	21	5	11	20	2	24	90
27	30	10	6	13	13	16	115
138	132	90	52	118	63	120	98

110

No 76

E

No 78

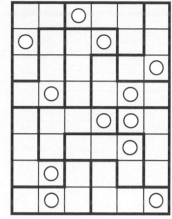

No 77

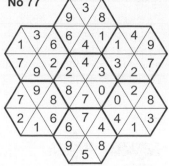

No 79

11: Replacing the 3 spades value from scale B into scale A gives 1 diamond + 2 hearts + 3 diamonds = 4 hearts, thus 4 diamonds + 2 hearts = 4 hearts, so 4 diamonds = 2 hearts, thus 2 diamonds = 1 heart. Converting the hearts value to diamonds in scale B gives 1 diamond + 4 diamonds = 3 spades, so 5 diamonds = 3 spades. Thus 3 spades + 3 hearts = 5 diamonds + 6 diamonds = 11 diamonds.

No 80

B - Reading from left to right, top to bottom, each letter moves forward two places in the alphabet every time.

No 81

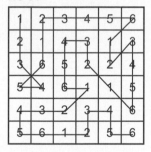

No 82

4	2	6	5	1	3
5	4	2	3	6	1
1	6	5	4	3	2
3	1	4	2	5	6
2	3	1	6	4	5
6	5	3	1	2	4

No 83

5252

No 84

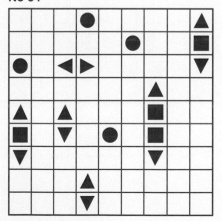

No 85

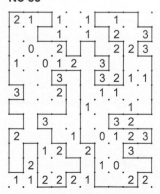

No 86

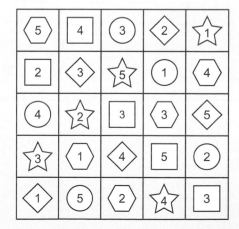

No 87

The value of the letter in the central square is double the sum total of the values of the letters in the other squares. Thus the missing value is 18, so the missing letter is R.

No 90

No 94

5	4	2	■	7	9	1	■	1	4	7	■	3
3	1	0	■	9	6	0	3	0	■	5	1	7
9	2	0	2	0	■	2	■	8	4	2	1	6
7	■	6	■	9	3	0	9	9	■	6	1	■
1	5	0	9	0	■	4	1	■	5	0	1	8
■	0	■	1	■	7	0	0	2	6	■	■	0
4	0	1	8	9	3	■	7	0	0	4	8	2
3	■	■	3	2	0	6	0	■	5	■	8	■
9	7	8	0	■	1	2	■	6	0	9	0	9
■	3	2	■	9	0	0	0	3	■	4	■	0
6	2	0	0	5	■	1	■	6	1	8	8	3
1	3	8	■	6	4	8	2	5	■	8	7	2
8	■	7	5	0	■	3	2	8	■	9	4	3

No 95

1S	2S	2W	2S	**2W**
1E	1N	2E	1N	1W
1S	2S	■	1E	2W
1E	2E	2N	1S	2W
2N	1E	2W	1E	1N

No 96

3	4	1	2	5
5	3	2	4	1
1	2	3	5	4
4	1	5	3	2
2	5	4	1	3

No 88

2	5	3	3	6	3	3
5	6	6	1	1	5	2

1	5	4	0	2	6	4
2	4	4	1	2	0	0

2	0	0	6	0	3	5
4	0	3	2	2	3	5

1	0	4	5	4	4	6
1	5	6	1	1	3	6

No 93

A=56, B=143, C=51, D=16, E=67, F=199, G=194, H=67, I=83, J=393, K=261, L=150, M=654, N=411, O=1065.

No 89

2	2	2	2	2	2
3	1	1	4	4	4
3	1	1	4	4	4
1	4	4	3	3	2
1	4	4	3	3	2
1	3	3	2	2	1

No 91

44 – The numbers on opposite points of the star total the number in the centre.

No 92

29	12	16	35	43	**11**
31	24	28	**9**	26	28
23	27	**24**	30	19	23
22	34	26	18	**18**	28
16	28	29	32	18	23
25	**21**	23	22	22	33

No 97

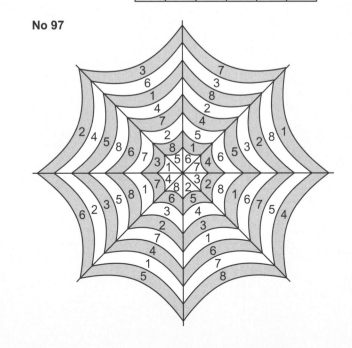

No 1

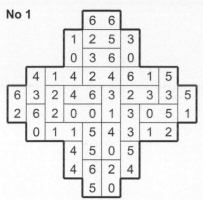

```
            6 6
          1 2 5 3
          0 3 6 0
      4 1 4 2 4 6 1 5
    6 3 2 4 6 3 2 3 3 5
    2 6 2 0 0 1 3 0 5 1
      0 1 1 5 4 3 1 2
            4 5 0 5
            4 6 2 4
            5 0
```

No 2

8: Replacing the 4 hearts value from scale A into scale B gives 2 spades + 1 diamond + 2 diamonds = 6 spades, thus 3 diamonds = 4 spades. Multiplying scale A by two gives 4 spades + 2 diamonds = 8 hearts and converting the 4 spades value to diamonds gives 3 diamonds + 2 diamonds = 8 hearts, so 5 diamonds = 8 hearts. Thus 4 spades + 8 hearts = 3 diamonds + 5 diamonds = 8 diamonds.

No 3

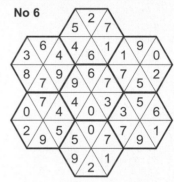

No 4

| 109 |

16	14	21	7	2	7	14	81
30	4	24	30	9	28	8	133
21	22	4	6	26	21	13	113
20	7	9	22	20	29	30	137
6	4	12	19	12	27	4	84
8	1	28	16	21	20	24	118
6	15	15	11	17	18	8	90
107	67	113	111	107	150	101	86

No 5

The hour hand moves forward by 2, 3, 4 and 5 hours and the minute hand moves forward 10 minutes each time.

No 6

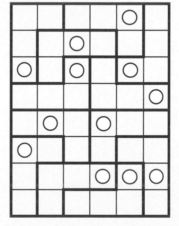

No 7

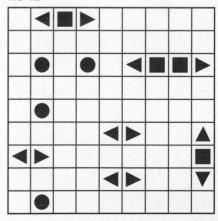

No 8

No 9

5	1	6	3	4	2
2	3	4	1	5	6
6	4	2	5	1	3
1	2	3	4	6	5
4	6	5	2	3	1
3	5	1	6	2	4

No 10

C	C	A	B	A	B
A	C	B	A	C	B
A	A	B	C	B	C
B	A	C	B	C	A
C	B	C	A	B	A
B	B	A	C	A	C

No 11

No 12

No 13

4401

No 16

The sum total of the values of the letters in the two top squares minus the sum total of the values of the letters in the bottom two squares equals the value of the letter in the central square. Thus the missing value is 13, so the missing letter is M.

No 14

```
    2        3 2    3
  2  0     1     3 1  0
     0
  3        1    0
  3   1 2        3
  3 2       2 3     0
    1      3        2
           1 0   3  1
                1 1
  1                1
   0             2  1
      1   2 2      0
  2 1   3 2     3 1
```

No 15

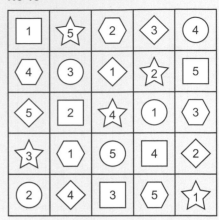

No 17

2	2	1	6	5	0	0
2	5	5	3	3	2	5

2	1	2	4	4	0	1
4	0	1	6	3	4	6

6	6	1	6	4	0	6
6	2	1	0	1	0	5

4	2	1	3	4	5	3
4	3	3	0	5	5	3

No 18

4	1	1	2	2	4
1	3	3	2	2	1
1	3	3	2	2	1
4	4	4	1	1	1
4	4	4	1	1	1
1	3	3	4	4	2

No 19

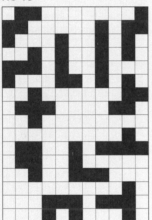

No 20

B – Assign a number to each letter according to its place in the alphabet, so E=5, L=12, P=16, S=19 and Z=26. Then take the lowest number from the highest in the point directly opposite to give the centre total, so the missing letter is B (=2).

No 21

58	15	19	26	**43**	12
29	**28**	28	25	33	30
14	35	28	**48**	19	29
36	39	33	8	24	33
21	32	34	30	19	**37**
15	24	**31**	36	35	32

No 22

A=95, B=127, C=27, D=83, E=12, F=222, G=154, H=110, I=95, J=376, K=264, L=205, M=640, N=469, O=1109.

No 23

```
4 2 6 5 ■ 7 6 3 8 ■ 6 3 6
6 ■ 7 ■ 5 0 0 ■ 6 ■ 5 3 ■
7 8 5 9 3 ■ 3 ■ 1 8 9 0 3
5 1 ■ 7 5 3 8 8 4 ■ 8 4 4
7 6 4 0 ■ 4 ■ 6 ■ 6 5 3 9
■ ■ 1 ■ 1 7 8 5 4 9 ■ ■ 1
7 5 9 3 1 ■ ■ 5 4 2 1 8
4 ■ 8 6 3 4 4 2 ■ 8 ■
8 9 3 4 ■ 0 ■ 0 ■ 1 9 6 3
8 4 9 ■ 6 3 4 9 5 5 ■ 5 0
3 2 1 5 4 ■ 5 ■ 8 6 3 8 9
■ 6 2 ■ 4 ■ 7 6 2 ■ 2 ■ 1
5 6 4 ■ 8 6 4 8 ■ 7 6 3 1
```

No 24

1S	1S	1W	1W	2S
2E	2S	1E	1E	1N
2N	1E	■	2N	2S
1S	1N	1S	1W	1W
2N	2E	1W	2N	1N

No 25

3	5	2	1	4
1	4	3 <	5	2
2	3	1	4	5
5	2	4	3	1
4	1 <	5	2 <	3

No 26

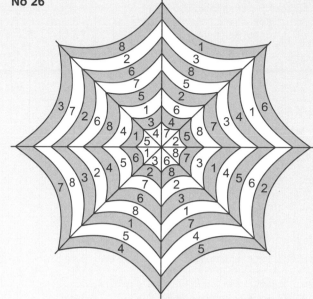

No 27

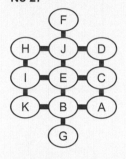

No 28

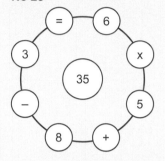

No 29

		4		3			
8							6
		2		6			
							2
5			7				
							3
7			9				

No 30

9	x	3	–	5	=	22
–	■	+	■	+		
2	x	7	+	1	=	15
x	■	x	■	–		
8	–	6	x	4	=	8
=		=		=		
56		60		2		

No 31

30 – The numbers in each horizontal row, each vertical column and each of the two diagonal lines of seven smaller squares total 175.

No 32

C

No 33

	●	●		2	3			1	●
	4	3		●	●	●	2		2
●	●			2	4	●	2	2	●
2		2						1	●
	0	1	●	1					
		2						1	
●	2	1		●	●	1	2	●	
	●				●	5	4		●
	1		1		●	●	●	4	●
				1	3	●	●	3	1

No 34

Circle = 7, cross = 3, pentagon = 4, square = 9, star = 6.

No 35

E	F	D	C	B	A
B	A	C	F	E	D
F	B	A	E	D	C
D	E	B	A	C	F
A	C	E	D	F	B
C	D	F	B	A	E

No 36

				6	6					
			5	0	0	5				
			3	1	3	2				
		4	4	5	5	0	3	6	3	
1	6	2	3	3	0	4	1	2	5	
1	4	0	1	1	3	4	5	6	1	
	2	3	1	2	0	6	2	6		
			0	2	4	5				
			4	5	2	0				
				4	6					

No 37

A	C	C	B	B	A
C	B	C	B	A	A
B	B	A	A	C	C
A	C	B	A	C	B
C	A	A	C	B	B
B	A	B	C	A	C

No 38

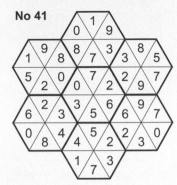

No 39

141

11	25	29	1	3	3	26	98
16	5	12	14	15	17	15	94
28	6	10	23	9	2	10	88
11	12	20	24	3	1	19	90
30	8	11	25	24	4	15	117
8	26	25	20	12	15	26	132
28	12	10	30	21	12	13	126

132	94	117	137	87	54	124	102

No 40

E

No 41

No 42

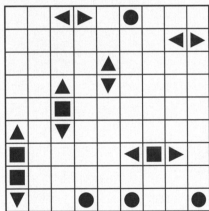

No 43

D - The numbers move one place
each time in the direction shown,
with the last number moving to
take the place of the first:

No 44

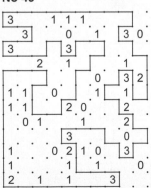

No 46

7111

No 45

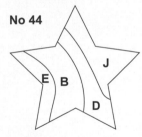

No 47

4	1	6	3	2	5
1	5	4	6	3	2
5	2	3	4	1	6
6	4	2	1	5	3
2	3	1	5	6	4
3	6	5	2	4	1

No 48

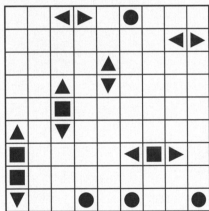

No 49

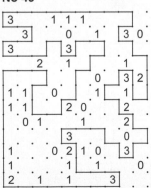

No 50

3 (square)	1 (circle)	4 (diamond)	2 (star)	5 (hexagon)
2 (circle)	4 (star)	3 (hexagon)	5 (diamond)	1 (square)
5 (star)	3 (diamond)	2 (square)	1 (hexagon)	4 (circle)
1 (diamond)	2 (hexagon)	5 (circle)	4 (square)	3 (star)
4 (hexagon)	5 (square)	1 (star)	3 (circle)	2 (diamond)

No 51

The value of the letter in the top left square is the sum total of the values of the letters in the other squares. Thus the missing value is 26, so the missing letter is Z.

No 52

C – Two of the colours of the five outer circles are repeated in the central rings.

No 53

36
84 24
66 36
50

No 54

4	4	4	1	1	3
1	1	1	4	4	3
1	1	1	4	4	3
3	4	4	2	2	4
3	4	4	2	2	4
1	2	2	1	1	3

No 56

6 – Multiply the two numbers in opposite petals to give the central number (6 x 12 = 72).

No 58

A=120, B=111, C=6, D=21, E=85, F=231, G=117, H=27, I=106, J=348, K=144, L=133, M=492, N=277, O=769.

No 55

No 57

26	**6**	48	24	73	14
37	31	**24**	32	36	31
40	49	31	**21**	20	30
24	39	36	41	**21**	30
27	47	21	52	10	34
37	19	31	21	31	**52**

No 59

9	4	5	3	6	4	■	5	2	8	4	6	0
■	8	5	■	1	5	4	0	6	■	2	2	■
4	3	5	2	0	■	0	■	1	9	6	5	3
3	■	6	■	9	■	4	1	7	■	7	■	0
6	7	0	■	3	9	2	0	■	2	7	3	0
■	1	6	8	■	1	2	2	5	9	■	9	9
5	■	1	3	8	■	4	2	0	■	8	■	
1	0	■	8	0	0	2	0	■	4	6	8	■
3	0	2	7	■	3	1	0	9	■	7	8	1
8	■	4	■	7	5	0	■	3	■	3	■	3
9	2	6	4	9	■	3	■	4	6	9	1	0
■	3	6	■	2	8	4	1	6	■	3	8	■
5	0	7	3	8	7	■	5	0	8	0	9	8

No 62

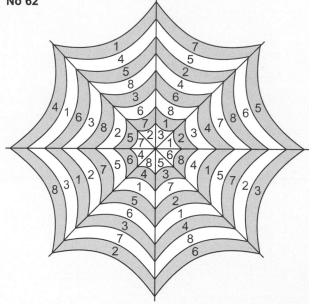

No 60

2S	1W	1E	1E	1S
2E	2E	1N	3W	2S
2S	1N	■	1W	3W
2E	**3N**	1S	1S	1W
1N	3E	1W	2N	2N

No 61

4	2	3	1	5
5	1	4	3	2
3	4	5	2	1
2	5	1	4	3
1	3	2	5	>4

No 63

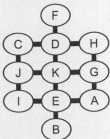

No 64

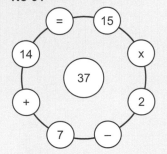

No 65

1					3
		6		9	
6					5
			4		
	1				3
			7		
4					1

No 66

9	x	3	+	6	=	33
x		+		−		
5	x	7	+	2	=	37
+		−		x		
1	+	4	x	8	=	40
=		=		=		
46		6		32		

No 67

49 – Reading along each row from left to right, the sequence of numbers is the first number plus 1 equals the second number minus 2 equals the third number plus 3 equals the fourth number minus 4 equals the fifth number plus 5 equals the sixth number minus 6 equals the seventh number.

No 68

D

No 69

●	●		1		3	●	●		0
●	3			●		●	3	2	
		3	4	●				1	●
1	●	●	●		1			2	1
1		●			0		●	3	
0	1	1				2	●	●	1
			1	1					
		●	3		●	●	2	●	
1	3	●	●	3		3		1	
	●	3		●	2	●			

No 70

E	D	F	C	B	A
A	E	D	B	F	C
F	B	C	D	A	E
B	C	A	E	D	F
D	A	E	F	C	B
C	F	B	A	E	D

No 71

Circle = 6, cross = 2, pentagon = 9, square = 3, star = 7.

No 72

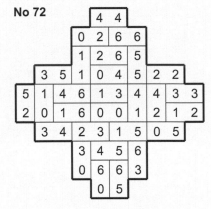

No 73

A	B	B	C	C	A
C	B	A	B	C	A
B	C	C	A	A	B
A	C	C	A	B	B
C	A	A	B	B	C
B	A	B	C	A	C

No 74

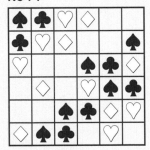

No 75

3	18	9	11	27	27	3	**98**
24	4	20	28	22	17	27	**142**
20	13	17	3	17	29	24	**123**
21	5	24	22	15	26	5	**118**
7	15	12	17	8	6	26	**91**
25	21	3	29	6	22	21	**127**
20	7	12	13	25	16	3	**96**

120	**83**	**97**	**123**	**120**	**143**	**109**	**79**

112

No 76

D

No 80

A - Reading from left to right, top to bottom, each number increases first by one, then by 2, 3, 4, 5, 6, 7 and 8.

No 78

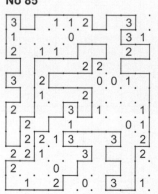

No 77

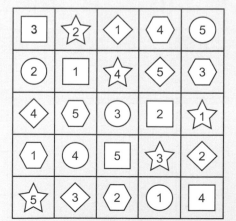

No 79

5: Multiplying scale B by five gives 5 spades + 5 hearts = 5 diamonds. Replacing this 5 diamonds value into scale A gives 1 spade + 5 spades + 5 hearts = 8 hearts, thus 6 spades + 5 hearts = 8 hearts, so 6 spades = 3 hearts, and 2 spades = 1 heart. Converting the hearts value to spades in scale B gives 1 spade + 2 spades = 1 diamond, thus 3 spades = 1 diamond. Thus 1 diamond + 1 heart = 3 spades + 2 spades = 5 spades.

No 81

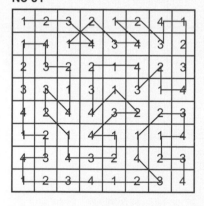

No 82

1	2	4	5	6	3
2	6	5	4	3	1
4	1	3	6	5	2
6	3	2	1	4	5
3	5	6	2	1	4
5	4	1	3	2	6

No 83

1617

No 84

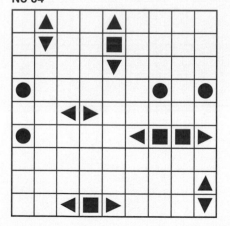

No 85

No 86

271

No 87

The value of the letter in the central square is the value of the letter in the bottom right square minus the sum total of the values of the letters in the other squares. Thus the missing value is 6, so the missing letter is F.

No 90

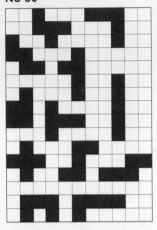

No 94

1	3	8	3		5	8	3	4		5	1	2
5		4		7	4	1		5	3	0		1
7	6	6	5	9	8		1	9		1	4	6
	3		9		3		7	6	8	8		
8	9	4	9		1	7	5	7	3	7		5
4			8	2	9	7	0			2	6	
1	1	9	0		3		7		4	2	1	9
2	8		8	7	4	3	3	3			7	
0		4	9	6	5	7	0		3	8	6	5
	5	3	2	9		1		1		0		
4	9	9		6	0		3	6	5	3	7	3
1		8	7	6		9	2	0		4		2
9	6	0		6	2	0	7		8	0	5	1

No 95

2E	1W	3S	2S	1S
3E	1S	1S	2W	2W
2S	2N		1E	2N
2N	1W	1E	3N	3W
1E	2E	2E	1W	1N

No 88

5	2	1	1	1	5	6
3	6	6	2	3	1	3

0	5	0	5	6	5	1
1	2	6	6	4	4	1

4	2	0	0	3	5	6
1	2	0	2	4	0	6

5	3	3	4	2	4	3
5	0	3	4	4	0	2

No 93

A=34, B=57, C=18, D=111, E=43, F=91, G=75, H=129, I=154, J=166, K=204, L=283, M=370, N=487, O=857.

No 96

1	3	2	5	4
4	1	5	3	2
3	2	4	1	5
2	5	1	4	3
5	4	3	2	1

No 89

1	1	1	3	3	3
2	4	4	3	3	3
2	4	4	3	3	3
1	3	3	2	2	1
1	3	3	2	2	1
4	1	1	2	2	1

No 91

P – Starting at the top and moving clockwise, first miss no letter, then one, then two, then three, then four, then five to arrive at V in the centre.

No 92

21	16	20	26	32	23
28	23	**18**	17	23	29
23	35	23	**11**	17	29
16	**25**	23	35	15	24
13	21	35	22	25	**22**
37	18	19	27	**26**	11

No 97

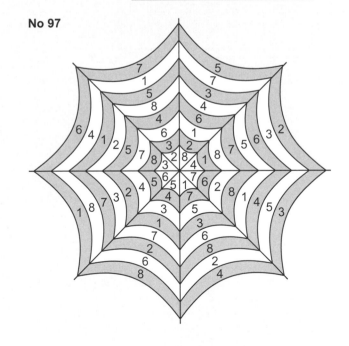

No 1

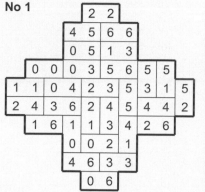

No 2

3: Adding together scale A and scale B gives 1 diamond + 1 heart + 1 spade + 2 diamonds = 7 spades + 1 heart, so 3 diamonds + 1 spade + 1 heart = 7 spades + 1 heart, thus 3 diamonds = 6 spades, and 1 diamond = 2 spades. Using this formula, convert diamonds value in scale A to spades, thus 2 spades + 1 heart = 7 spades, so 1 heart = 5 spades. Thus 1 spade + 1 heart = 1 spade + 5 spades = 6 spades which equals 3 diamonds.

No 3

No 4

11	13	21	13	29	28	18	133
20	20	4	19	5	18	23	109
3	19	4	12	20	18	6	82
9	1	4	22	8	20	27	91
23	12	10	23	24	15	27	134
5	6	17	21	29	19	2	99
21	27	5	4	11	14	24	106

92	98	65	114	126	132	127	124

(115)

No 5

The hour hand alternately gains 2 hours and loses 3 hours and the minute hand gains 12½ minutes each time.

No 6

No 7

No 8

No 9

3	2	5	4	1	6
2	5	4	6	3	1
6	1	3	2	5	4
5	4	1	3	6	2
4	3	6	1	2	5
1	6	2	5	4	3

No 10

C	A	C	B	A	B
C	B	B	A	C	A
A	A	B	C	B	C
A	C	A	B	C	B
B	C	A	C	B	A
B	B	C	A	A	C

No 11

No 12

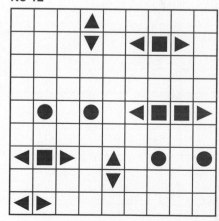

No 13

5275

No 16

The sum total of the values of the letters in the top two squares equals that of the central square, as does the sum total of the values of the letters in the bottom two squares. Thus the missing value is 23, so the missing letter is W.

No 14

```
      2 2 1 2
  2   2 2 1      0 2
        3
    1   3 2    0   0 2
  1              3
    1 0     3
  3 1       0   3
            2 3 2 1 2
                3 2
    2 2 2 2
            1 3     0 3
            2   0
  2 2     3   3 2 1   1
```

No 15

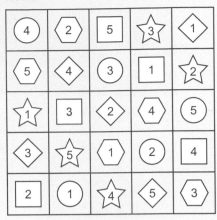

No 17

4	4	6	1	6	2	2
5	1	1	3	5	1	3

5	4	3	3	4	0	5
2	3	0	3	6	0	0

5	4	2	5	2	6	0
5	2	0	1	2	6	6

3	1	4	3	2	0	1
6	1	4	5	6	4	0

No 18

1	4	4	3	3	1
2	2	2	2	2	1
2	2	2	2	2	1
1	3	3	3	3	2
1	3	3	3	3	2
1	4	4	4	4	3

No 19

No 20

M – Assign a number to each letter according to its place in the alphabet, so A=1, B=2, C=3, E=5, H=8 and U=21. Start from the top and move clockwise, adding each number to the next in order to reach the following number, so H + M (13) = U.

No 21

25	16	20	24	**33**	29
22	**24**	24	25	27	25
28	38	24	**18**	12	27
18	36	27	30	13	**23**
22	14	26	24	31	30
32	19	**26**	26	31	13

No 22

A=131, B=63, C=18, D=46, E=96, F=194, G=81, H=64, I=142, J=275, K=145, L=206, M=420, N=351, O=771.

No 23

3	4	7	■	3	2	1	1	■	2	3	2	5
6	■	1	9	6	5	■	7	2	4	■	3	
7	4	0	4	■	1	5	0	■	7	1	4	5
6	5	■	8	2	0	3	8	■	7	6	2	6
■	2	6	■	7	5	0	■	9	■	4	■	
3	6	3	4	9	0	■	3	2	4	7	8	5
2	■	7	■	1	■	■	1	■	2	■	3	
8	1	8	1	7	5	■	4	5	4	6	1	7
■	3	■	2	■	6	1	2	■	8	4	■	
1	4	4	2	■	3	0	5	5	6	■	1	2
3	6	1	9	■	1	1	6	■	9	4	8	2
9	■	5	4	1	■	5	3	2	7	■	7	
8	9	2	6	■	7	4	5	2	■	8	1	9

No 24

1E	3S	1S	1W	1W
1N	3E	2W	1S	1N
1S	3E	■	1W	2S
1S	1N	1E	2N	2W
2E	3N	1E	2W	1N

No 25

2	1	4	>3	5
4	2	5	1	3
5	4	3	2	>1
1<	3	>2	5	4
3	5	1	4	2

No 26

No 27

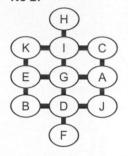

No 28

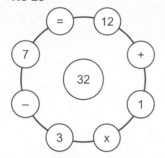

No 29

5					
	3		6		1
3					
					1
	7		9		
					4
1		1		5	

No 30

9	−	6	x	4	=	12
−	■	+	■	x		
1	x	5	+	8	=	13
x	■	x	■	−		
7	+	3	x	2	=	20
=		=		=		
56		33		30		

No 31

29 – Reading down each column, take 4 from each preceding number until the central number, after which add 5 to each preceding number.

No 32

E

No 34

Circle = 1, cross = 6, pentagon = 2, square = 8, star = 4.

No 35

D	E	F	C	B	A
C	A	B	E	D	F
A	D	C	F	E	B
B	F	D	A	C	E
F	B	E	D	A	C
E	C	A	B	F	D

No 33

1	●	●		1	●	3	2		●
	2				3	●	●		2
	0		●		●		2		●
0		1		●	3	1	0		
		0		●		1		1	0
1		0			2		●		1
●					●		3		
	●		2		●	4	●	●	3
2	2	4	●	●	●	●	3	2	●
	●		●	4				1	

No 36

			0	4				
		4	6	1	0			
		3	5	1	0			
2	2	6	2	4	6	5	4	
6	0	3	2	5	5	1	3	1	1
0	6	2	0	3	1	5	2	2	0
6	0	5	1	6	5	4	4	
		4	5	3	4			
		3	3	3	6			
			1	2				

No 37

A	B	C	B	A	C
B	C	C	A	B	A
C	B	B	A	A	C
C	A	A	B	C	B
A	A	B	C	C	B
B	C	A	C	B	A

No 38

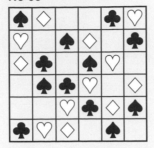

No 39

83

19	26	5	8	12	16	25	111
24	5	22	12	14	2	10	89
4	19	9	10	5	28	15	90
23	1	13	5	15	27	19	103
13	15	14	10	19	14	5	90
13	14	3	21	8	23	2	84
18	30	20	6	10	17	9	110

114	110	86	72	83	127	85	89

No 40

E

No 41

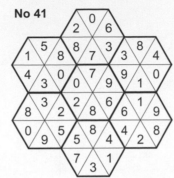

No 42

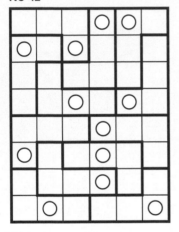

No 43

A - The numbers in all four corners total 77, as do the numbers in the remaining squares.

No 44

No 45

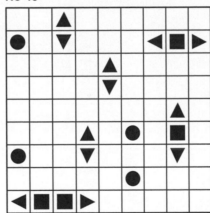

No 46

6214

No 47

5	2	4	1	3	6
3	6	5	2	1	4
2	1	3	4	6	5
4	5	1	6	2	3
1	4	6	3	5	2
6	3	2	5	4	1

No 48

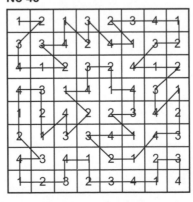

No 49

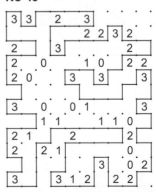

No 50

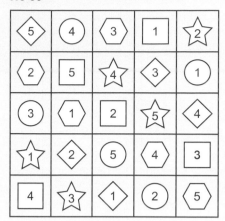

No 51

The value of the letter in the central square is half the sum total of the values of the letters in the other squares. Thus the missing value is 24, so the missing letter is X.

No 52

H – It has 3 touching squares of the same colour.

No 53

32

No 54

3	2	2	3	3	4
3	2	2	1	1	3
3	2	2	1	1	3
1	1	1	2	2	1
1	1	1	2	2	1
1	4	4	3	3	3

No 56

10 – The number in the centre is double the sum of the numbers in opposite petals.

No 58

A=111, B=39, C=32, D=137, E=137, F=150, G=71, H=169, I=274, J=221, K=240, L=443, M=461, N=683, O=1144.

No 55

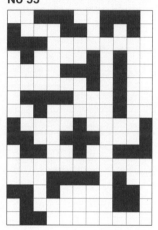

No 57

16	**9**	28	29	48	26
25	26	30	24	26	**25**
22	54	**26**	14	14	26
28	23	26	38	**13**	28
25	24	26	**24**	28	29
40	20	20	27	27	22

No 59

2	5	3	3	6		1	5	3	7	3	3
6		3		7	4	8		9	6	2		7
9	5	2	7	0		7	6	0		2	9	8
	7			2	9	0		5			6	3
7	1	8	4		5		2	0	4	1	7	0
2	1	3		3	6	5	0		1	7	
5	0	4	6	2	8		9	4	2	4	7	8
	6	1		1	1	2	5		4	3	1
5	9	0	7	9	0		2		5	6	5	1
1	4		3		2	8	3		2	
8	2	5		8	6	1		9	2	3	4	5
3		9	7	6		8	1	0		1		1
6	4	0	1	7	3		4	4	8	2	2

No 60

3S	3S	2E	3W	3W
1S	1W	1E	3S	2W
3E	**3E**		1W	1S
1S	2N	3N	3N	2N
1E	3E	1N	1N	2W

No 61

4	2	5	3	1
1	5	2	4	3
5	1	3	2	4
3	4	1	5	2
2	3	4	1	5

No 62

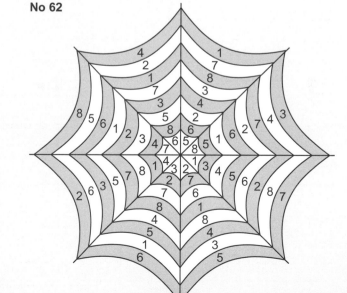

No 63
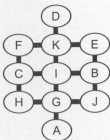

No 64
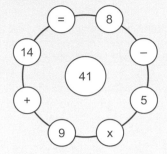

No 65

	9			1		7
		1		9		1
6						
		2			2	
2						
			9		5	

No 66

4	+	9	−	2	=	11
x		−		x		
1	x	7	−	6	=	1
+		x		+		
5	−	3	x	8	=	16
=		=		=		
9		6		20		

No 67
31 – Reading down each column, add each number to the preceding number.

No 68
B

No 69
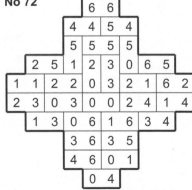

No 70

E	D	F	C	B	A
B	C	A	E	F	D
A	E	B	F	D	C
D	F	E	A	C	B
F	B	C	D	A	E
C	A	D	B	E	F

No 71
Circle = 6, cross = 1, pentagon = 8,
square = 7, star = 9.

No 72
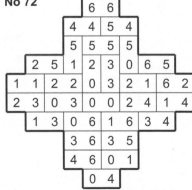

No 73

C	A	B	B	C	A
C	A	A	C	B	B
A	C	B	B	C	A
B	B	C	A	A	C
B	C	C	A	A	B
A	B	A	C	B	C

No 74
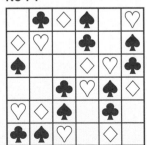

No 75

							136

14	20	3	21	6	22	11	97
20	8	21	30	3	6	14	102
5	6	17	5	22	26	4	85
13	7	17	29	29	15	28	138
19	28	22	15	7	23	6	120
25	23	28	3	3	27	15	124
23	30	17	26	14	11	20	141

119	122	125	129	84	130	98	122

No 76

F

No 78

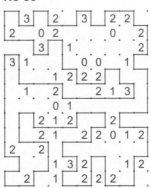

No 80

C - The numbers in the three columns of each square total 27, 28 and 29.

No 81

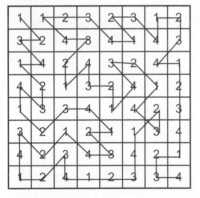

No 82

2	4	3	1	5	6
1	6	5	3	2	4
6	3	1	2	4	5
4	5	2	6	3	1
3	1	4	5	6	2
5	2	6	4	1	3

No 83

1105

No 77

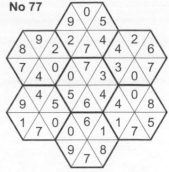

No 79

9: Replacing the value of 4 diamonds from scale B into scale A gives 1 spade + 3 hearts + 2 hearts = 11 spades, so 5 hearts = 10 spades, thus 1 heart = 2 spades. Multiplying scale B by two gives 6 hearts + 2 spades = 8 diamonds. Converting this spades value to hearts gives 6 hearts + 1 heart = 8 diamonds, thus 7 hearts = 8 diamonds. So 4 spades + 8 diamonds = 9 hearts.

No 84

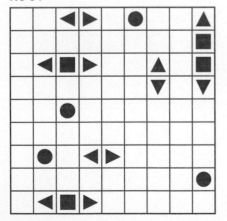

No 85

No 86

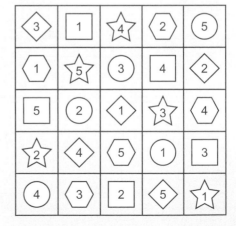

No 87

The sum total of the values of the letters in the top left and bottom right squares is equal to the sum total of the values in the other squares. Thus the missing value is 14, so the missing letter is N.

No 90

No 88

| 1 | 2 | 6 | 5 | 6 | 5 | 2 |
| 1 | 3 | 4 | 2 | 3 | 0 | 2 |

| 1 | 0 | 1 | 6 | 0 | 4 | 6 |
| 5 | 3 | 6 | 5 | 4 | 4 | 2 |

| 5 | 1 | 6 | 0 | 1 | 4 | 5 |
| 5 | 3 | 6 | 0 | 2 | 1 | 3 |

| 6 | 3 | 1 | 5 | 3 | 2 | 2 |
| 0 | 3 | 0 | 4 | 4 | 4 | 0 |

No 89

2	3	3	3	3	2
1	1	1	1	1	3
1	1	1	1	1	3
2	4	4	3	3	4
2	4	4	3	3	4
2	1	1	4	4	2

No 91

N – Start from the top and move clockwise, first 2 places forwards, then 3 back, 4 forwards, 5 back, 6 forwards (N), then 7 back, to G.

No 93

A=15, B=122, C=17, D=120, E=140, F=137, G=139, H=137, I=260, J=276, K=276, L=397, M=552, N=673, O=1225.

No 92

36	23	26	36	**43**	24
43	31	26	16	33	**39**
25	42	31	49	21	20
40	43	33	**13**	20	39
22	**27**	38	46	33	22
22	22	**34**	28	38	44

No 94

4	8	2	3	7		1	6	1		3	9	2
9	3	4		6	4	0		7	1	5	2	
7	1	1	5	6		8		3	0	6	4	2
		5		1	9	0	2	9		8		5
1	3	3	3	0		2	9		3	4	7	7
1	4		6		1	0	5	4	9		3	
4	6	5	7	6	0		4	1	0	4	4	5
	7		8	3	7	6	0		5		9	1
3	4	9	0		2	0		1	0	8	0	0
7		1		8	6	0	2	2		0		
8	5	1	6	3		0		7	3	0	4	5
	2	1	4	5		7	1	5		9	1	2
9	9	9		4	2	2		8	3	0	7	6

No 97

No 95

2S	2S	1S	1W	3W
1E	3S	3S	1S	1W
2S	1E		2N	2N
3N	1W	**1W**	1E	2N
3N	2E	2E	1N	2N

No 96

4	5	2	3	1
3	2	1	5	4
2	1	5	4	3
5	3	4	1	2
1	4	3	2	5

No 1

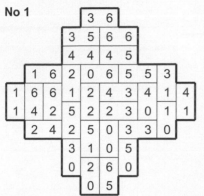

```
        3 6
      3 5 6 6
      4 4 4 5
  1 6 2 0 6 5 5 3
1 6 6 1 2 4 3 4 1 4
1 4 2 5 2 2 3 0 1 1
  2 4 2 5 0 3 3 0
      3 1 0 5
      0 2 6 0
        0 5
```

No 2

3: Replacing the value of spades from scale A into scale B gives 1 diamond + 2 hearts + 1 diamond = 5 hearts, thus 2 diamonds + 2 hearts = 5 hearts, so 2 diamonds = 3 hearts*. Multiplying scale B by three gives 3 spades + 3 diamonds = 15 hearts. Using the * values gives 3 spades + 3 diamonds = 10 diamonds, so 3 spades = 7 diamonds. So 3 spades + 3 hearts = 7 diamonds + 2 diamonds, thus 9 diamonds, so 1 spade + 1 heart = 3 diamonds.

No 3

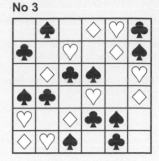

No 4

| | | | | | | | 90 |

16	17	27	6	10	18	4	98
7	23	8	24	17	27	24	130
23	6	1	21	10	22	21	104
12	9	23	4	20	23	15	106
26	22	6	27	29	28	8	146
23	15	25	30	14	27	16	150
24	16	14	12	15	26	10	117

131	108	104	124	115	171	98	110

No 5

Clocks gain 3¾ hours each time.

No 6

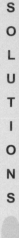

No 7

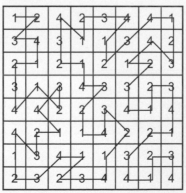

No 8

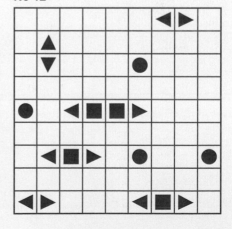

No 9

6	2	4	3	1	5
5	1	2	6	3	4
4	5	3	1	6	2
2	3	6	5	4	1
3	4	1	2	5	6
1	6	5	4	2	3

No 10

C	B	B	A	C	A
A	A	C	B	B	C
B	C	A	B	A	C
B	C	C	A	A	B
C	B	A	C	B	A
A	A	B	C	C	B

No 11

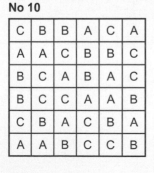

No 12

No 13

7626

No 16

Successively, each group of letters have values divisible by 2, 3, 4 and 5. Thus in the final group, the missing value is 20, so the missing letter is T.

No 19

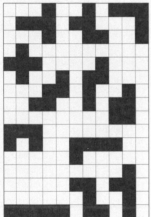

No 14

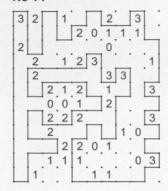

No 17

4	0	3	0	3	2	1
0	1	6	0	3	5	1

0	0	2	2	6	5	6
6	3	1	2	6	3	2

0	5	2	5	2	4	4
5	1	3	5	0	4	1

5	2	1	5	6	4	1
6	4	6	4	4	3	3

No 15

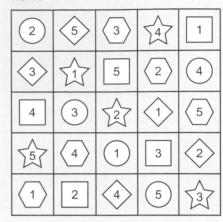

No 18

2	2	2	1	1	1
1	3	3	1	1	3
1	3	3	1	1	3
4	3	3	3	3	1
4	3	3	3	3	1
4	4	4	4	4	4

No 20

J – Start from the top and move clockwise, going back three letters in the alphabet each time, finally moving from M to J, then from J to G.

No 21

17	14	18	**34**	44	25
36	25	22	15	**27**	27
32	**44**	25	15	8	28
15	37	27	35	13	25
13	19	**28**	37	29	26
39	13	32	16	31	**21**

No 22

A=53, B=03, C=15, D=85, E=139, F=56, G=18, H=100, I=224, J=74, K=118, L=324, M=192, N=442, O=634.

No 23

1	3	7	5	6		2	1	2	1	3		5
0		1	4	0		9		3	6	0	1	4
4	6	7		1	2	0		3	7	4	5	5
0		4	5	0		4	1	2		5		
	7	5	8		8	5	6		3	9	1	5
2	5		7	1	9		5	7	4			5
1	6	4	7		5		4		8	1	7	5
1			7	2	8		6	5	8		2	7
7	1	2	5		5	6	7		8	2	3	
	2		9	5	4		9	0	6		3	
3	8	6	4	0		4	2	4		4	1	3
3	1	1	1	5		3		3	2	5		2
2		9	5	0	2	0		7	8	6	1	6

No 24

1S	2S	2S	2W	3S
1S	3E	1N	1W	1W
3E	1N	■	2S	2N
3E	1W	1S	3N	2W
1E	1N	2W	1E	2N

No 25

5	3	1	2	4
1	4	3	5	>2
2	1	5	4	3
3	2	4	1	5
4	5	2	3	1

No 26

No 27

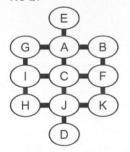

No 28

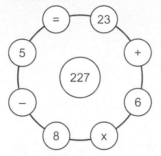

= , 23, 5, +, 227, −, 6, 8, x

No 29

5							
		1		8		1	
3							
						1	
	7		9				
						4	
1		3		3			

No 30

7	+	9	−	2	=	14
−	■	+	■	x		
4	−	3	x	6	=	6
+	■	x	■	+		
8	x	5	+	1	=	41
=		=		=		
11		60		13		

No 31

145 and 148 – From the top left corner, follow a path around and spiral towards the centre, adding 3 to each number every time.

No 32

E

No 33

●	3		2	●		1	●		●
●	4	●		2			2	4	2
●	3		2	●	2		●		●
2		1		3	●				●
●			●	2	1		0	2	●
2	●	3					0		1
	●				1				
0				1		●		●	2
		0	1	●		●	●		3	●
●	1			2	●	2	2		●

No 34

Circle = 1, cross = 3, pentagon = 4, square = 2, star = 7.

No 35

F	D	E	C	B	A
B	A	D	E	C	F
E	B	F	D	A	C
A	F	C	B	D	E
D	C	A	F	E	B
C	E	B	A	F	D

No 36

				5	5				
			3	3	0	0			
			3	4	1	1			
	0	3	1	1	2	5	4	4	
2	2	3	0	6	1	4	2	2	5
6	6	2	1	4	6	0	0	6	2
	3	5	0	1	6	1	5	3	
			4	4	5	4			
			5	6	0	3			
				2	6				

No 37

C	B	A	C	A	B
C	B	C	A	A	B
B	A	A	B	C	C
B	C	C	A	B	A
A	C	B	C	B	A
A	A	B	B	C	C

No 38

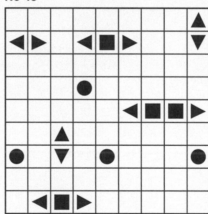

No 39

							120

13	27	12	10	1	18	14	95
18	13	5	30	23	30	17	136
28	11	10	3	7	9	29	97
15	28	30	29	1	23	6	132
17	8	18	15	18	14	6	96
22	20	5	10	18	13	10	98
2	30	19	18	18	3	6	96
115	137	99	115	86	110	88	102

No 40
F

No 41

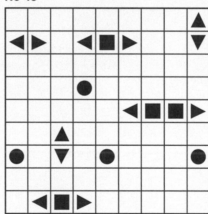

No 42

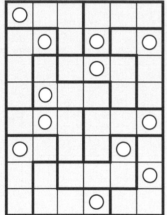

No 43
B - The letters in the four corners move forward one place in the alphabet each time, while those remaining move back one place.

No 44

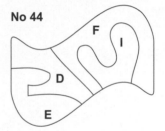

No 45

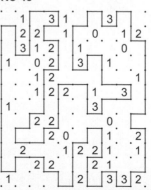

No 46
2101

No 47

4	2	5	1	3	6
1	3	4	2	6	5
2	6	1	5	4	3
3	5	2	6	1	4
5	4	6	3	2	1
6	1	3	4	5	2

No 48

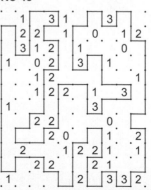

No 49

No 50

(2)	5	4	3	1
3	1	2	5	4
1	2	5	4	3
5	4	3	1	2
4	3	1	2	5

No 51

The value of the central letter is the sum total of the letters in the top left and bottom right squares divided by the sum total of the letters in the top right and bottom left squares. Thus the missing value is 9, so the missing letter is I.

No 52

A – It spirals outwards in a clockwise direction.

No 53

C – From the top, the alphabet is continued individually in each colour.

No 54

1	2	2	4	4	1
2	2	2	2	2	4
2	2	2	2	2	4
3	3	3	2	2	3
3	3	3	2	2	3
1	4	4	4	4	1

No 56

12 – Start from the top, then add 3, minus 7, add 4, minus 8, add 5, minus 9, add 6, then minus 10, to reach the centre total of 2.

No 55

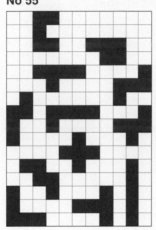

No 57

19	15	19	**48**	57	21
30	29	38	23	34	25
41	44	29	27	**9**	29
24	45	**34**	31	23	22
33	**31**	25	35	22	33
32	15	34	15	34	**49**

No 58

A=59, B=55, C=106, D=104, E=63, F=114, G=161, H=210, I=167, J=275, K=371, L=377, M=646, N=748, O=1394.

No 59

4		6	7	8		5	2	2	8		2
6	3	5		6	2	4	1	8		3	4	6
4	2	0	7	1	9		6	7	1	3	1
7		6		9	6	7	8		3		1
1	9	4	2	3		3	1		9	5	6	1
1	6			1	5	7	4	6	0		2	0
	2	9	4	4		3	5	1	3	0	
4	0		7	6	8	8	6	0		8	2
7	7	1	9		1	3		3	7	6	5	7
5		8		4	4	2	9		0		2
1	8	8	2	6			6	2	5	2	5	0
9	4	4		7	1	2	8	7		9	7	8
5		7	5	9	2			1	5	8		0

No 60

1S	2S	1E	2S	**2W**
2S	1N	1S	3S	2W
2N	1S	■	1S	2S
2E	3E	1S	2N	1N
2N	3N	1W	3W	3N

No 61

1	2	3	4	5
5	1	4	2	3
2	5	1	3	4
4	3	2	5	1
3	4	5	1	2

No 62

No 63

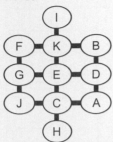

No 64

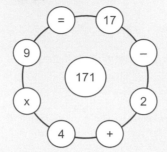

No 65

3					1
		6		9	
4					7
			4		
	1				3
			7		
4				1	

No 66

8	–	1	x	5	=	35
–		+		+		
3	x	9	+	6	=	33
+		–		x		
7	+	4	–	2	=	9
=		=		=		
12		6		22		

No 67

4320 – Reading across each row, multiply the first number by 6, then multiply the number which results by 5, then multiply the number which results by 4, then multiply the number which results by 3, then multiply the number which results by 2.

No 68

C

No 69

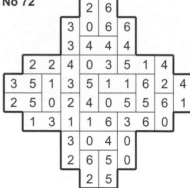

No 70

D	E	C	F	B	A
E	F	A	B	D	C
A	B	F	C	E	D
F	A	E	D	C	B
B	C	D	A	F	E
C	D	B	E	A	F

No 71

Circle = 1, cross = 5, pentagon = 6, square = 2, star = 3.

No 72

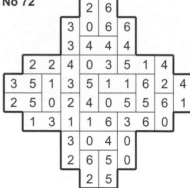

No 73

A	A	B	C	B	C
B	B	A	C	C	A
C	B	A	B	C	A
C	A	C	A	B	B
B	C	C	A	A	B
A	C	B	B	A	C

No 74

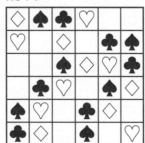

No 75

							97
9	3	14	3	12	2	18	61
28	3	19	27	3	15	11	106
7	14	19	3	3	3	20	69
11	11	2	10	11	21	29	95
20	6	16	26	10	5	22	105
19	27	9	23	5	24	21	128
8	5	5	5	23	22	19	87
102	69	84	97	67	92	140	94

No 76

D

No 80

D - Even numbers increase by 5 each time, while odd numbers decrease by 3.

No 78

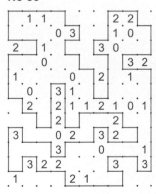

No 77

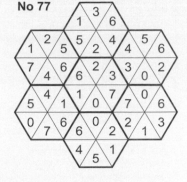

No 79

10: Replacing the value of 3 diamonds from scale B into scale A gives 1 spade + 1 heart + 2 hearts = 2 spades, thus 1 spade + 3 hearts = 2 spades, so 3 hearts = 1 spade. Multiplying scale B by three gives 3 spades + 3 hearts = 9 diamonds and converting the spades values to hearts gives 9 hearts + 3 hearts = 9 diamonds, thus 12 hearts = 9 diamonds, so 4 hearts = 3 diamonds. Thus 3 diamonds + 2 spades = 4 hearts + 6 hearts = 10 hearts.

No 81

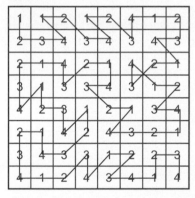

No 82

3	5	4	6	1	2
1	3	2	5	6	4
5	1	3	2	4	6
2	6	1	4	3	5
6	4	5	1	2	3
4	2	6	3	5	1

No 83

4450

No 84

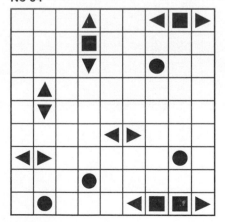

No 85

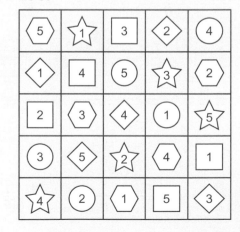

No 86

(grid of shapes with numbers)

5	1	3	2	4
1	4	5	3	2
2	3	4	1	5
3	5	2	4	1
4	2	1	5	3

No 87

Working from the value of the letter in the top left square, add one to give the value in the top right, then add 2 to this to give the value in the centre, then add 3 to this to give the value in the bottom left, then add 4 to this to give the value in the bottom right. Thus the missing value is 18, so the missing letters is R.

No 90

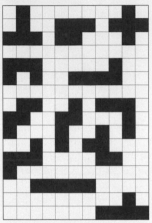

No 88

| 2 | 5 | 1 | 0 | 6 | 1 | 0 |
| 3 | 5 | 5 | 0 | 3 | 2 | 6 |

| 3 | 6 | 0 | 1 | 1 | 2 | 6 |
| 4 | 6 | 1 | 1 | 4 | 2 | 2 |

| 4 | 2 | 3 | 0 | 1 | 1 | 0 |
| 2 | 5 | 5 | 2 | 3 | 6 | 5 |

| 0 | 4 | 5 | 3 | 4 | 3 | 4 |
| 4 | 6 | 6 | 3 | 4 | 0 | 5 |

No 93

A=59, B=127, C=82, D=08, E=16, F=186, G=209, H=90, I=24, J=395, K=299, L=114, M=694, N=413, O=1107.

No 89

3	2	2	4	4	2
2	3	3	3	3	1
2	3	3	3	3	1
3	4	4	1	1	4
3	4	4	1	1	4
4	3	3	1	1	1

No 91

P – Assign a number to each letter according to its place in the alphabet. Each letter is divisible by 4 and the missing letter is thus P (16).

No 92

18	**16**	25	17	24	33
13	26	28	36	**17**	13
28	24	**23**	12	16	30
16	31	22	32	18	**14**
31	22	15	10	23	32
27	14	20	**26**	35	11

No 94

2	4	9	■	8	1	1	2	6	■	3	2	4
2	■	1	5	3	■	7	6	■	5	1	■	8
4	3	6	■	9	■	3	■	4	2	8	9	5
0	■	5	■	8	9	8	■	1	4	■	■	1
■	6	2	7	■	6	■	6	7	7	9	4	9
2	8	6	■	9	8	7	2	2	■	4	■	0
6	1	■	3	1	2	■	1	6	6	■	6	2
5	■	5	■	2	2	5	4	8	■	7	9	5
9	8	7	5	4	5	■	4	■	4	5	0	
■	2	■	3	1	■	7	7	7	■	1	■	6
9	6	4	4	8	■	5	■	2	■	8	3	5
3	■	1	2	■	6	0	■	8	3	7	■	1
5	7	0	■	2	3	0	8	8	■	5	0	3

No 95

1E	3S	2S	1W	2S
1N	3E	**1W**	3S	1W
1S	2S	■	2N	1W
2N	1N	1E	1E	3N
2N	3E	1N	3W	2W

No 96

3	5	1 <	4	2
2	3	4	5	1
1 <	4	3 >	2	5
4	2	5 >	1	3
5	1	2	3	4

No 97

No 1

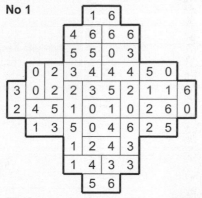

No 2

6: Replacing the 1 heart value from scale B into scale A gives 1 diamond + 1 spade + 1 diamond = 9 spades, thus 2 diamonds = 8 spades and 1 diamond = 4 spades. Multiplying scale B by four gives 4 spades + 4 diamonds = 4 hearts and converting the spades values to diamonds gives 1 diamond + 4 diamonds = 4 hearts, so 5 diamonds = 4 hearts. Thus 4 spades + 4 hearts = 1 diamond + 5 diamonds, so 6 diamonds.

No 3

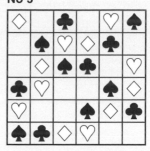

No 4

61

14	4	13	19	16	21	1	88
14	7	11	10	25	10	17	94
7	9	16	30	6	11	16	95
22	1	24	2	15	11	21	96
8	2	23	10	25	7	26	101
9	15	17	28	19	12	21	121
4	11	15	7	25	10	18	90

78	49	119	106	131	82	120	94

No 5

Clocks lose 3 hours 7 minutes, 4 hours 7 minutes, 5 hours 7 minutes and 6 hours 7 minutes.

No 6

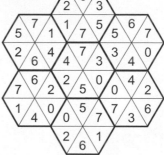

No 7

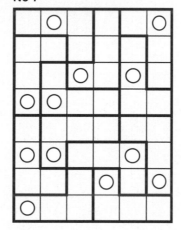

No 8

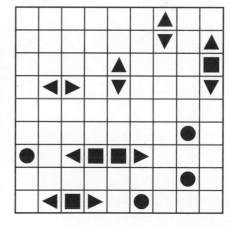

No 9

5	6	2	1	3	4
6	3	4	2	1	5
3	1	5	4	2	6
2	5	1	6	4	3
1	4	3	5	6	2
4	2	6	3	5	1

No 10

C	A	B	A	C	B
B	A	C	B	A	C
A	C	A	B	C	B
C	B	A	C	B	A
A	B	C	C	B	A
B	C	B	A	A	C

No 11

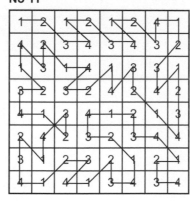

No 12

No 13

5010

No 16

The value of the letter in the top right square is the value of the letter in the central square divided by the sum total of the values of the letters in the top left, bottom left and bottom right squares. Thus the missing value is 2, so the missing letter is B.

No 14

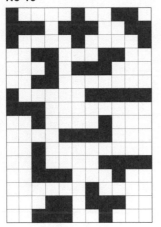

No 15

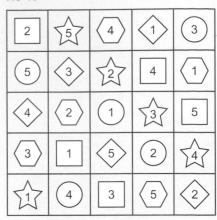

No 17

1	2	2	6	4	2	0
5	2	0	3	4	3	4

1	1	0	6	4	2	1
2	6	0	6	5	6	4

4	2	2	3	1	3	5
3	5	4	1	1	3	0

0	6	5	5	0	6	0
3	4	5	3	6	5	1

No 18

4	4	4	1	1	4
3	4	4	2	2	2
3	4	4	2	2	2
1	1	1	3	3	1
1	1	1	3	3	1
2	4	4	3	3	2

No 19

No 20

T – Start at the top and move forwards in the alphabet first 2 places, then 3, then 2, then 3, then 2 (to T), then 3 to W.

No 21

35	33	27	**30**	28	31
33	20	17	17	34	63
31	50	**46**	14	14	29
32	22	34	30	38	**28**
18	**36**	41	49	30	10
35	23	19	44	**40**	23

No 22

A=75, B=17, C=50, D=136, E=64, F=92, G=67, H=186, I=200, J=159, K=253, L=386, M=412, N=639, O=1051.

No 23

1	2	6	9		7	1	2		4	7	0	5
6		3	8		4		2	1	1	5		0
9	6	2		1	6	4	3		2	0		2
	4	7	8	6	8		9	5	3	1	1	6
6	2		3		2	7	8			6		
1	9	8	0	9	0		3	3	5	7	7	8
3		4	4	5			6	1	9		2	
7	7	7	1	8	6		1	7	8	4	9	9
	1			9	6	0		5		3	2	
5	0	6	7	2	9		7	2	8	8	7	
1		2	3		8	1	9	5		2	8	8
8		8	1	7	0		7		4	1		8
8	4	8	8		2	6	0		2	6	0	0

No 24

2S	4S	2W	2W	1W
3E	1S	2W	1S	1N
2S	3E	■	1W	1S
2E	**2E**	2N	1S	4W
4E	3N	4N	1W	3N

No 25

3<	5	2	4	1
1	4	3	2	5
4	2	1	5	3
5	1	4	3	2
2	3	5	1	4

No 26

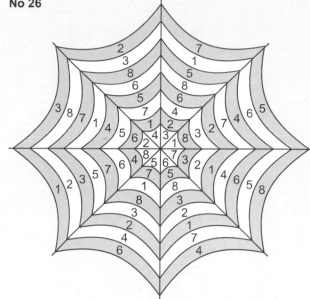

No 27

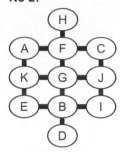

No 28

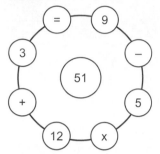

No 29

		4		3		
8						6
		2		6		
						2
5			7			
						3
7			9			

No 30

1	+	7	−	6	=	2
x	■	+	■	−		
4	x	9	+	3	=	39
+	■	−	■	x		
8	−	2	x	5	=	30
=		=		=		
12		14		15		

No 31

41 – In the first row, add 5 to the first number, subtract 8 from the second, add 5 to the third, etc; in the second row, add 8 to the first number, subtract 5 from the second, etc; then repeat this process for the remaining rows, adding and subtracting 5 and/or 8 alternately.

No 32

D

No 33

No 34

Circle = 6, cross = 7, pentagon = 2, square = 8, star = 9.

No 35

D	F	C	E	B	A
E	B	D	F	A	C
A	D	B	C	F	E
C	E	A	B	D	F
F	A	E	D	C	B
B	C	F	A	E	D

No 36

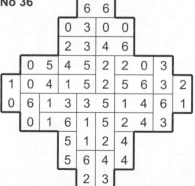

No 37

A	C	A	B	C	B
B	A	C	B	C	A
C	A	B	A	B	C
C	B	A	C	A	B
B	B	C	C	A	A
A	C	B	A	B	C

No 38

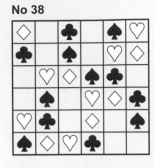

No 40

D

No 41

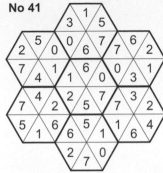

No 39

106

27	5	26	29	4	14	7	112
10	23	24	29	2	2	22	112
30	29	10	25	5	5	10	114
30	1	2	23	1	24	19	100
3	18	22	23	5	29	2	102
27	18	2	6	4	7	19	83
29	3	5	14	21	21	18	111

156	97	91	149	42	102	97	113

No 43

C - The numbers in the three horizontal rows of each square total 31, 16 and 47.

No 42

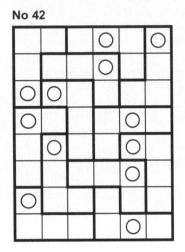

No 44

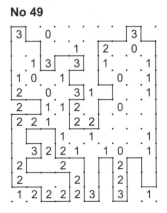

No 46

2546

No 45

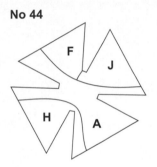

No 47

1	4	2	5	6	3
3	5	6	4	1	2
4	2	5	6	3	1
5	1	4	3	2	6
2	6	3	1	5	4
6	3	1	2	4	5

No 48

1	2	4	3	4	2	3	1
1	4	3	1	2	1	4	2
2	3	2	1	4	2	4	3
3	2	3	4	3	1	2	3
4	1	4	1	2	4	1	4
1	3	2	4	1	3	2	1
3	2	3	3	2	3	2	3
4	1	2	4	1	4	1	4

No 49

No 50

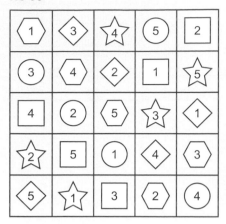

No 51

The sum total of the values of the letters in the top left and central squares is equal to the sum total of the values of the letters in the other squares. Thus the missing value is 20, so the missing letter is T.

No 52

2 – The other red pointers move two places on in the alphabet each time (other colours move two places back).

No 53

D – it is a 180° rotation of No 2 (other rotations are: 1 and 6, 3 and 7, 4 and 5).

No 54

4	3	3	1	1	2
2	1	1	2	2	4
2	1	1	2	2	4
2	4	4	2	2	3
2	4	4	2	2	3
2	4	4	3	3	1

No 56

9 – Divide the highest of the numbers in opposite petals by the lowest to give the central number (63 = 7 x 9).

No 58

A=106, B=46, C=85, D=102, E=95, F=152, G=131, H=187, I=197, J=283, K=318, L=384, M=601, N=702, O=1303.

No 55

No 57

34	**3**	12	30	48	14
27	23	21	10	**26**	34
21	43	23	19	15	20
23	25	26	**27**	12	28
13	33	30	34	10	**21**
23	14	**29**	21	30	24

No 59

3	7	8	■	5	1	5	■	8	8	9	1	3
8	■	5	1	8	9	1	■	1	8	9	■	0
9	0	1	■	1	3	3	3	1	■	8	9	1
9	■	2	■	2	■	2	2	2	■	■	2	2
7	8	9	1	■	2	8	■	3	8	9	1	4
■	4	■	4	3	0	4	4	8	■	3	■	6
■	6	6	6	■	3	■	3	■	5	6	2	■
2	■	4	■	6	6	8	3	5	7	■	0	■
2	2	5	7	4	■	7	3	■	4	2	7	3
4	2	■	■	7	6	3	■	6	■	8	■	4
8	4	4	■	9	4	8	4	2	■	4	9	0
4	■	8	3	2	■	7	0	4	5	5	■	5
4	6	7	8	5	■	6	7	2	■	5	9	1

No 60

2S	2S	1E	4S	3S
1N	3E	1W	3W	1N
2S	1S	■	1W	1W
2E	1W	3N	2N	1W
1E	4N	**3N**	1E	2N

No 61

1	3	4	5	2
3	5	2	4	1
2	4	5	1	3
4	1	3	2	5
5	2	1	3	4

No 62

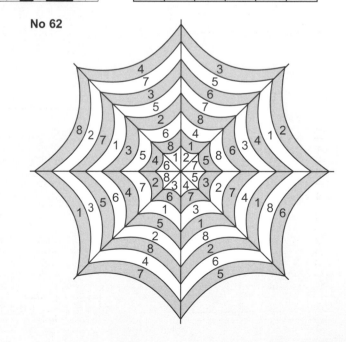

No 63

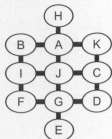

No 64

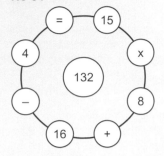

No 65

	9			1		7
		1		9		1
6						
		2			2	
2						
			9		5	

No 66

7	+	9	x	4	=	64
–		–		x		
1	x	3	+	6	=	9
+		x		–		
5	–	2	x	8	=	24
=		=		=		
11		12		16		

No 67

7 – In the first column, deduct 16 then 17 from each successive number; in the second column, deduct 14 then 15; in the third, deduct 12 then 13; in the fourth, deduct 10 then 11; in the fifth, deduct 8 then 9; in the sixth, deduct 6 then 7; and in the seventh, deduct 4 then 5. Thus 70 – 10 = 60 – 11 = 49 – 10 = 39 – 11 = 28 – 10 = 18 – 11 = 7.

No 68

A

No 69

2	●			●	2		●	2	1
●	3		2		●	2	2	●	2
2	●	4	●	3					●
		●	●	4		●			●
2	●		●	●	1	1	1	2	
●	3	●	●		1				0
			3				0		
			2	●	3	●			
1	3	●			●				0
1	●	●	2	1			0		

No 70

D	F	E	C	B	A
F	A	B	D	C	E
A	D	F	B	E	C
E	C	A	F	D	B
B	E	C	A	F	D
C	B	D	E	A	F

No 71

Circle = 2, cross = 5, pentagon = 1, square = 4, star = 7.

No 72

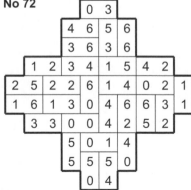

No 73

A	C	A	B	C	B
C	A	B	C	A	B
B	C	C	A	B	A
A	B	A	C	B	C
C	B	C	B	A	A
B	A	B	A	C	C

No 74

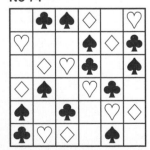

No 75

								97
17	21	29	15	27	6	2		117
24	27	23	8	11	16	28		137
13	11	14	29	25	24	8		124
19	20	26	10	6	6	6		93
9	1	7	13	4	16	21		71
11	13	16	11	24	12	12		99
24	6	22	1	11	26	4		94
117	99	137	87	108	106	81		88

No 76

E

No 78

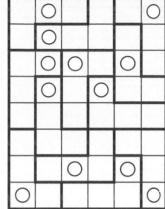

No 77

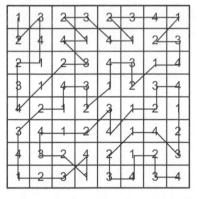

No 79

9: Replacing the 1 spade value from scale B into scale A gives 2 diamonds + 1 heart + 1 heart = 5 diamonds, thus 2 hearts = 3 diamonds. Multiplying scale B by three gives 3 hearts + 6 diamonds = 3 spades and converting the diamonds value to hearts gives 3 hearts + 4 hearts = 3 spades, so 7 hearts = 3 spades. Thus 3 spades + 3 diamonds = 7 hearts + 2 hearts = 9 hearts.

No 80

A - Even numbers decrease by 5 each time, while odd numbers increase by 3.

No 81

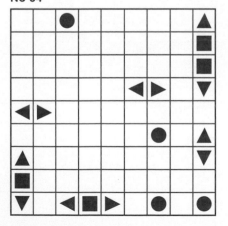

No 82

1	2	5	6	3	4
4	5	6	3	1	2
2	4	3	5	6	1
5	6	1	4	2	3
6	3	2	1	4	5
3	1	4	2	5	6

No 83

1077

No 84

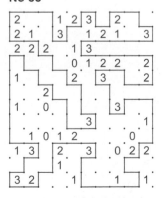

No 85

No 86

295

5

No 87

The value of the letter in the central square is the sum total of the value of the letters in the top left and bottom left square divided by the sum total of the values of the letters in the top right and bottom right squares. Thus the missing value is 9, so the missing letters is I.

No 90

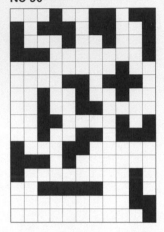

No 88

| 2 | 3 | 5 | 4 | 1 | 0 | 2 |
| 2 | 2 | 6 | 5 | 1 | 0 | 0 |

| 6 | 3 | 3 | 6 | 1 | 0 | 6 |
| 1 | 6 | 4 | 4 | 4 | 1 | 0 |

| 4 | 5 | 3 | 0 | 4 | 4 | 5 |
| 4 | 2 | 3 | 5 | 0 | 2 | 5 |

| 2 | 3 | 2 | 1 | 6 | 3 | 3 |
| 1 | 5 | 6 | 5 | 6 | 0 | 1 |

No 93

A=54, B=62, C=14, D=115, E=75, F=116, G=76, H=129, I=190, J=192, K=205, L=319, M=397, N=524, O=921.

No 89

4	1	1	1	1	3
2	4	4	1	1	1
2	4	4	1	1	1
2	1	1	3	3	3
2	1	1	3	3	3
4	2	2	1	1	2

No 91

J – Assign a number to each letter according to its place in the alphabet (J=10), then divide the highest number by the lowest in opposite points to give the central number.

No 92

26	36	9	**56**	27	26
44	56	26	33	10	**11**
51	11	**12**	52	42	12
17	16	58	6	35	48
16	**8**	23	22	54	57
26	53	52	11	**12**	26

No 94

7	8	9		8	5	9		7	5	9		5
5	2	7		7	5	3	8	6		7	5	0
1	7	8	9	3		5		3	1	3	5	1
3		0		4	7	0	4	2		3	4	
4	3	5	8	9		4	3		7	8	9	1
	6		3		6	5	3	2	1			6
8	9	0	7	5	1		8	5	9	3	4	9
0			1	2	3	4	5		7		0	
6	2	5	7		4	2		6	4	1	8	4
	6	2		6	2	8	8	9		3		0
4	2	7	8	9		5		8	5	4	2	3
7	7	7		5	4	2	7	8		2	3	8
0		8	3	5		6	2	7		5	2	2

No 95

4E	1E	4S	2S	2S
2E	1W	2S	2W	1W
2N	2S		2W	1N
3E	3N	2W	1E	1S
3E	1N	2N	4N	4W

No 96

2	1	3	5	4
1	4	5	3	2
4	3	1	2	5
5	2	4	1	3
3	5	2	4	1

No 97

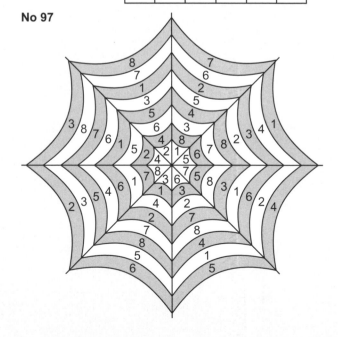

No 1

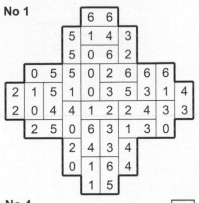

No 2

7: One spade = 1 heart + 1 diamond in scale B, so 1 spade = 3 diamonds in scale A. Thus in scale B, 1 heart = 2 diamonds. In scale C there are 2 diamonds and 4 spades, thus 4 spades = 12 diamonds, so 12 diamonds + 2 diamonds = 14 diamonds = 7 hearts.

No 3

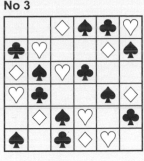

No 4

							111
15	26	30	21	8	5	9	114
29	5	8	12	13	20	23	110
3	7	5	10	7	5	8	45
8	2	30	26	28	22	19	135
21	17	24	25	1	1	28	117
6	18	24	5	25	11	2	91
7	14	4	24	5	12	2	68
89	89	125	123	87	76	91	65

No 5

The hour hand moves forward 2 hours and the minute hand backwards first 3, then 5, then 7, then 9 minutes each time.

No 6

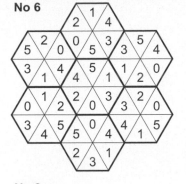

No 7

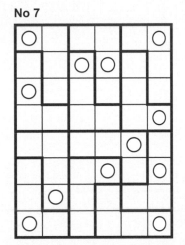

No 8

●	3		●				0	
●	●		3	3	1			
	4	4	●	●	1	2	●	0
●		●	●	4		●		
●	5	●	6	●	1			
	●	●					1	●
1				●	2			1
0		●	2	2	●	1	1	
	2			3			1	●
●	2	●		1	●	●	1	

No 9

4	1	6	2	3	5
1	3	2	5	4	6
6	2	5	4	1	3
2	4	3	6	5	1
5	6	1	3	2	4
3	5	4	1	6	2

No 10

C	A	A	B	B	C
C	B	A	B	C	A
B	A	C	C	A	B
B	C	B	C	A	A
A	C	B	A	B	C
A	B	C	A	C	B

No 11

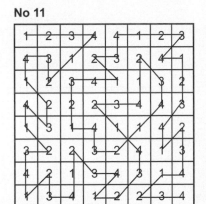

No 12

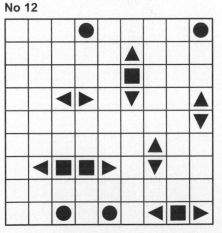

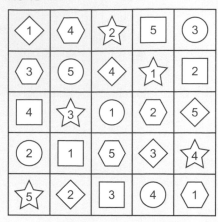

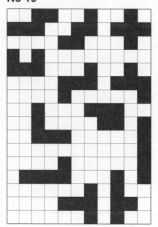

SOLUTIONS

No 13
5655

No 16
Working from the value of the letter in the top left square, add 3 to give the value of the letter in the top right, then take 5 from this to give the value of the letter in the centre, then add 8 to this to give the value of the letter in the bottom left, then take 4 from this to give the value of the letter in the bottom right square. Thus the missing value is 5, so the missing letter is E.

No 19

No 14

No 15

No 17

3	2	2	1	6	2	6
5	4	5	0	4	1	5

5	0	2	4	0	2	0
5	4	2	3	3	0	0

6	3	5	3	6	6	1
0	2	0	3	2	6	1

6	3	6	5	4	5	4
3	1	1	4	4	1	1

No 18

1	4	4	1	1	3
1	3	3	4	4	2
1	3	3	4	4	2
3	4	4	2	2	4
3	4	4	2	2	4
3	3	3	2	2	1

No 20
H – Assign a number to each letter according to its place in the alphabet, then multiply the numbers in opposite points to give the central number.

No 21

16	24	22	29	28	50
34	28	**33**	20	29	25
35	43	28	22	**16**	25
27	37	29	34	17	**25**
30	**12**	32	28	43	24
27	25	25	**36**	36	20

No 22
A=14, B=01, C=65, D=32, E=119, F=15, G=66, H=97, I=151, J=81, K=163, L=248, M=244, N=411, O=655.

No 23

6	8	3	8	■	4	2	7	9	■	9	7	0
4	■	7	■	6	1	5	■	7	■	7	5	■
8	9	1	7	5	■	7	■	5	0	1	8	1
9	2	■	7	5	9	2	6	6	■	9	0	4
7	8	4	9	■	3	■	7	■	8	8	9	0
■	1	■	1	3	1	8	3	5	■	■	■	0
4	2	6	9	5	■	■	4	2	7	8	9	■
4	■	■	6	2	8	3	2	1	■	1	■	■
3	1	6	7	■	0	■	0	■	4	5	2	9
7	8	9	■	7	8	9	1	2	6	■	5	8
7	5	8	9	1	■	3	■	7	8	9	5	5
■	3	3	■	5	■	8	9	0	■	4	■	0
6	9	9	■	8	5	9	0	■	8	5	9	1

No 24

2S	2S	1W	1W	1W
2S	1W	2S	1W	1S
3E	1N	■	1N	2W
4E	**2E**	1S	1S	2N
4N	1W	2E	2W	4N

No 25

3	5	1	4	2
1	2	3	5	4
2	4	5	1	3
5	3	4	2	1
4	1	2	3	5

No 26

No 27

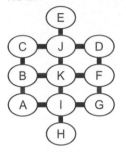

No 28

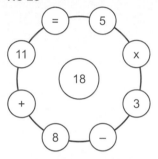

No 30

4	+	7	−	1	=	10
x	■	−	■	+		
8	−	5	x	3	=	9
−	■	+	■	x		
2	x	6	+	9	=	21
=		=		=		
30		8		36		

No 31

5 – Any 2x2 block of four squares contains numbers which total 40, thus:

12	5
18	**5**

or (put another way):

5	22
9	4

No 32

D

No 34

Circle = 2, cross = 4, pentagon = 6, square = 1, star = 8.

No 35

C	D	E	B	A	F
D	F	B	C	E	A
F	C	A	E	D	B
A	B	D	F	C	E
E	A	F	D	B	C
B	E	C	A	F	D

No 29

	9			1		7
		1		9		1
6						
		2			2	
2						
			9		5	

No 33

●	2				0		●	●	1
3	●	2		0				●	3	1
●		●		1	1		3		
2	5	●	3		●		●	●	1
●	4	●			●	3		
		●	●		2			
0		4	●	3		●	1	0	
				●				0	
	0			●	5	●			1
		0		●	●	●	3	●	

No 36

		1	5				
	2	2	6	6			
	3	6	5	5			
4	6	6	2	2	4	1	0
4	0	0	1	0	5	6	2	5	1
3	3	0	3	0	4	1	3	4	1
2	0	6	0	5	2	6	1
	3	3	5	5			
	3	2	4	4			
		1	4				

6

299

No 37

A	A	B	C	B	C
B	A	C	B	C	A
C	C	B	B	A	A
B	C	A	A	B	C
C	B	A	C	A	B
A	B	C	A	C	B

No 38

No 39

119

12	30	1	5	30	20	13	111
27	2	13	27	15	24	26	134
13	10	15	3	30	15	2	88
2	14	13	28	1	8	29	95
11	17	11	30	2	25	28	124
27	7	23	9	19	11	11	107
6	10	22	11	2	6	23	80

98	90	98	113	99	109	132	93

No 40

F

No 41

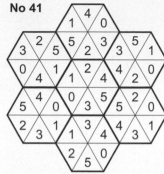

No 42

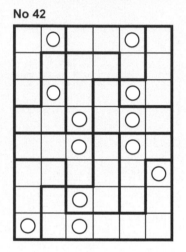

No 43

B - The numbers in all four corners total that in the central square, as do the numbers in the remaining four squares.

No 44

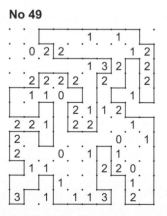

No 45

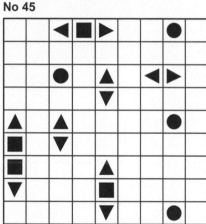

No 46

6777

No 47

4	6	1	2	3	5
6	3	4	5	1	2
3	2	6	1	5	4
2	5	3	4	6	1
5	1	2	3	4	6
1	4	5	6	2	3

No 48

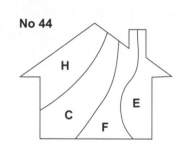

No 49

No 50

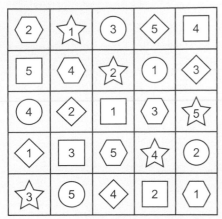

No 51

Per group, the difference in values of letters is either 4, 8, 12 and/or 16. Thus the missing value is 14, so the missing letter is N.

No 52

C – All four balls of one colour total an even number.

No 53

A – All rows move down one, with the bottom row becoming the top row.

No 54

2	2	2	1	1	4
2	4	4	4	4	3
2	4	4	4	4	3
3	2	2	2	2	4
3	2	2	2	2	4
2	3	3	1	1	4

No 56

16 – Start from the top and move anticlockwise, deducting first 7, then 9 each time, to reach 16, which minus 9 equals 7.

No 55

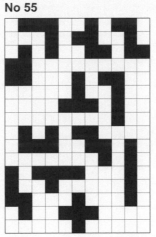

No 57

29	**46**	38	20	16	27
34	31	13	23	29	46
29	16	25	29	**60**	17
33	14	**33**	31	28	37
24	31	44	**38**	25	14
27	38	23	35	18	**35**

No 58

A=82, B=30, C=39, D=26, E=86,
F=112, G=69, H=65, I=112, J=181,
K=134, L=177, M=315, N=311, O=626.

No 59

4	6	4	1	8	4		5	4	1	7	6	0
	3	2		6	2	5	9	4		7	1	
4	4	1	7	6		0		3	0	0	0	3
4		8		7		8	9	2		3		1
3	3	4		6	5	2	8		7	2	1	2
	4	1	6		8	3	8	5	0		5	5
	6		8	4	0		4	2	4		7	
1	5		7	3	5	2	4		5	1	6	
7	3	8	9		9	8	7	6		4	2	7
0		3		7	4	1		1		1		4
2	2	7	2	9		9		4	7	6	9	0
	6	2		8	6	4	2	5		7	3	
8	3	5	0	0		4	2	0	0	4	2	

No 62

No 60

2E	1W	4S	1S	3W
1S	2S	2E	3W	2S
4E	2S		1W	3W
2E	2E	2N	1N	3N
1N	3N	1E	4N	**4W**

No 61

5	2	>1	4	3
2	3	5	1	4
1	4	3	5	2
4	1	2	3	5
3	5	>4	2	>1

No 63

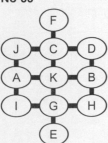

No 64

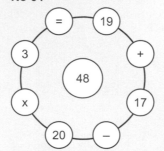

No 65

	9			7	1
		1		3	7
6					
		2			2
2					
			9		5

No 66

8	–	4	x	6	=	24
+	■	x	■	–		
1	+	9	x	2	=	20
x	■	–	■	+		
5	–	3	+	7	=	9
=		=		=		
45		33		11		

No 67

9 – Reading from left to right across each row, every number decreases by the same amount as the preceding number. In the bottom row, the numbers decrease by 8.

No 68

E

No 69

1			1	●		●	4	3	●
●		0		3	●	●	●	●	
●			2	●	6	●	6	●	2
1	2	3	●	4	●	●			
1		●	●	3		2		1	●
●									1
		1			0		0		
	0		●			1	2	2	1
	1			2	2		●	●	
1	●			1	●	●		2	

No 70

B	E	A	D	F	C
E	F	C	A	D	B
D	C	B	F	A	E
A	B	F	C	E	D
F	D	E	B	C	A
C	A	D	E	B	F

No 71

Circle = 6, cross = 5, pentagon = 9, square = 2, star = 8.

No 72

		1	1						
	2	5	6	6					
	4	5	5	5					
2	4	1	4	6	1	6	1		
3	4	4	4	1	2	0	0	1	2
0	2	0	6	0	4	0	5	3	2
	2	6	3	5	1	3	0	2	
		3	6	0	3				
		5	6	4	5				
		3	3						

No 73

C	C	A	A	B	B
A	B	B	C	C	A
C	A	B	C	A	B
A	B	A	B	C	C
B	A	C	B	A	C
B	C	C	A	B	A

No 74

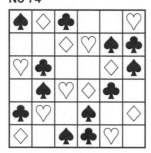

No 75

19	13	23	12	16	17	5	105
14	5	17	5	11	9	18	79
2	24	27	17	30	18	30	148
13	15	19	28	2	11	24	112
15	3	15	4	21	15	15	88
18	28	8	26	11	17	12	120
17	15	14	28	29	22	11	136

98	103	123	120	120	109	115	128

No 80

D - The numbers in all four corners increase by 2, while those in the remaining squares decrease by 4.

No 81

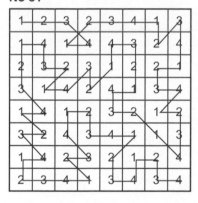

No 76

D

No 78

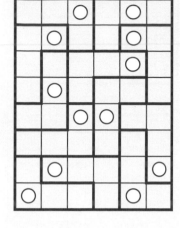

No 82

2	1	3	5	4	6
4	3	2	1	6	5
1	6	4	2	5	3
3	4	5	6	1	2
5	2	6	4	3	1
6	5	1	3	2	4

No 83

0202

No 77

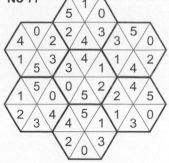

No 79

7: In scale A, 8 diamonds = 1 heart + 2 spades, so in scale B, 2 diamonds = 1 heart. Replacing the 8 diamonds in scale A with 4 hearts gives 1 heart + 2 spades = 4 hearts, 2 spades = 3 hearts, so 2 spades = 6 diamonds, thus 1 spade = 3 diamonds. Converting the diamonds value to spades in scale C gives 3 spades; and converting the hearts value to spades in scale C gives 4 spades. Thus 3 spades + 4 spades = 7 spades.

No 84

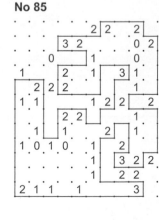

No 85

No 86

3	1	2	4	5
5	2	4	3	1
4	5	1	2	3
1	4	3	5	2
2	3	5	1	4

No 87

The sum total of the values of letters in the top left and bottom left squares equals that of the values of the letters in the other squares. Thus the missing value is 23, so the missing letter is W.

No 90

50 – Think of the star as being made of two superimposed triangles, the numbers in the three angles of each totalling the number in the centre.

No 88

2	4	4	4	4	3
3	1	1	3	3	2
3	1	1	3	3	2
4	1	1	2	2	1
4	1	1	2	2	1
3	4	4	1	1	2

No 89

No 91

41	17	23	30	37	47
44	32	31	17	35	36
55	34	32	22	15	37
8	60	35	42	22	28
19	28	40	43	33	32
28	24	34	41	53	15

No 92

A=137, B=19, C=52, D=102, E=45, F=156, G=71, H=154, I=147, J=227, K=225, L=301, M=452, N=526, O=978.

No 93

1	3	5	3	■	1	7	2	9	■	6	3	8
7	■	2	■	4	8	6	■	2	6	7	■	7
9	6	0	7	1	0	■	5	8	■	3	4	9
■	1	■	0	■	5	■	6	7	9	5	■	■
2	9	7	4	■	2	8	2	0	1	4	■	5
0	■	■	2	4	0	8	0	9	■	■	3	4
3	8	7	3	■	7	■	4	■	1	2	6	1
6	8	■	■	3	9	1	0	9	5	■	■	8
5	■	3	2	9	4	9	5	■	2	6	1	0
■	4	5	1	9	■	8	■	1	■	■	4	■
6	3	5	■	7	2	■	2	5	3	8	7	4
1	■	1	6	3	■	2	6	5	■	2	■	4
7	4	4	■	9	6	7	0	■	9	0	0	8

No 94

2S	1E	3S	1E	4W
4E	3S	1E	3S	3W
1N	3E	■	1W	2S
1E	1N	2E	3N	4W
2E	4N	3N	2N	4W

No 95

2	4	5	1	3
5	3	1	4	2
3	2	4	5	1
4	1	2	3	5
1	5	3	2	4

No 96

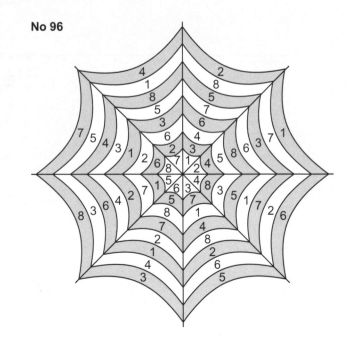